AF474001

Reading
Design

Reading Design

The Visual Language of Common Objects

CRAIG HODGETTS
WITH HSINMING FUNG

UNICORN PUBLISHING GROUP

Contents

7 Foreword
Paola Antonelli

15 Preface
Sir Peter Cook

19 Introduction
Craig Hodgetts

27 Chapter 1 Discipline
55 Chapter 2 Glut
81 Chapter 3 Veil
103 Chapter 4 Guts
125 Chapter 5 Elan
149 Chapter 6 Streamline
181 Chapter 7 Utility
209 Chapter 8 Funk
233 Chapter 9 Jazz
259 Chapter 10 Remix
285 Chapter 11 Whimsy

313 Biographies, Acknowledgements and Reproduction Credits

Foreword

Paola Antonelli

Adventure! That's what every object, building, road trip, meal, and conversation represents to Craig Hodgetts. In all the years I've known him, I can hardly recall a moment when he was bored. Every detail – no matter how mundane – is, for him, a gateway into a universe of creative pathways, past and future, endlessly linked and always open to new connections. Rabbit holes, each one. This book offers a rare glimpse into his mesmerizing thought process and with it, a series of precious lessons in design, seen from the angle of an omnivorous creator.

If boundless curiosity is his nature, then nurture played its part too. Craig came of age in places, times, and practices bursting with new ideas and grounded in solid technology. He studied automotive engineering at the General Motors Institute in Flint, Michigan; scenic design at Oberlin College, the famous liberal arts school in Ohio; and architecture at UC Berkeley and Yale. After stints in London with revered architect James Stirling and New York with Lester Walker, he landed in Los Angeles in the late 1960s. There, he became a central figure in a wild and collaborative ecosystem of makers and thinkers fearlessly testing original, uninhibited ideas between fact and fiction – helped, of course, by the gravitational pull of Hollywood's imagination and fabrication engine. His collaborators span from Robert Mangurian, with whom he co-founded Studio Works in 1969, to Hsinming Fung, cofounder of Hodgetts + Fung and Craig's creative and life partner for the past 40+ years.

This diverse background is why Craig's laser focus ignores the traditional jolts between scales of creative production. He is equally analytical and passionate about a chair as he is about a city block. Whether it's architecture, art, furniture, cars, worlds, or movie productions, the objects he "reads" in this book are grouped not by typology, material, or technique but rather by attitude. Reading Design means finding the attitude in every single object – whether discipline, jazz, utility, guts, or else – to connect it with others of different ilk and distill the essence of the design process. The goal is to uncover, as the book's subtitle puts it, the "Visual Language of Common Objects," by weighing an object's presence against the original idea behind it, and by considering the designer's chemistry of materials, technology, process, and narrative.

This idiosyncratic take on the design universe also requires a unique attitude, which Craig has tempered in the course of his long career as an architect, designer, and educator. For decades, he has been a singular voice in the architectural landscape, a connector and visionary whose works are born not only from a fertile imagination but also from a love for technology and a healthy dose of irreverence. He has expanded the scope of architecture. Always projected towards the future, he has promoted a non-denominational design culture that has nurtured his contemporaries and influenced the recent generations of Los Angeles architects. True to form, this book is not a retrospective. It's not a victory lap. It's a provocation, an invitation to think differently about what it means to design in a changing world.

Craig doesn't spotlight much of his own work in these pages – but you should seek it out. His career is the key to understanding what's inside this book. From his early inflatables to the reimagining of the Hollywood Bowl; from a foldable cardboard chair to a neighborhood library in Los Angeles Hyde Park; from a building development with integrated digital billboards on Sunset Boulevard to an unforgettable exhibition design for the Case Study Houses show at MoCA's Temporary

Contemporary (now Geffen Contemporary) you will be able to trace that same shared rhetoric he is seeking in these pages.

He's been wrestling with important questions for decades: the necessity of prototyping, the ethics of design in a tech-heavy era, the demands of sustainability, accessibility, and yes – the search for beauty. And he has consistently embraced experimentation. He sees design as an inherently creative act – sometimes absurd, often joyful – that is always rooted in engineering, material logic, and an acute awareness of cultural and social contexts.

This book is an invitation to engage in a critical dialogue about the role of design in shaping our world, our perceptions, our behavior, and ultimately in transforming our lives. It is a valuable contribution to the ongoing conversation about the meaning of design in the 21st century and a reminder that design, at its best, is not just about creating beautiful objects or functional spaces, but about creating a better world. And it's a journey into the restless, radiant mind of a unique design kitsune. If only we could bottle it.

Preface

Sir Peter Cook

I have had so many wonderful conversations with Craig, as have my students and other friends from London. He's chirpy. Insightful, gentle, chatty and gives newcomers a clear view of Los Angeles that they will never get from anyone else. He is genuinely supportive of his immediate circle of friends – including that coterie of immensely talented architects the 'Ten' who have in parallel, inflamed the Los Angeles scene over the last forty years.

Meanwhile he and his wife Ming Fung have made some insightful and witty architecture in that city, such as the temporary library for UCLA and the Wild Beast Pavilion for CalArts. Yet Craig's background goes back to vehicle design before the architecture, which is intriguing and certainly gives his observations an extra dimension. Perhaps it was this mix that had caught the eye of that great British critic and L.A. fan Reyner Banham, who had himself trained as an aircraft engineer and introduced us at a Friday soiree in the late 1960s. Many years later, happening to be passing through Yale to see a retrospective show of James Stirling's students (clever enough stuff) it was a display of Craig's student work that stood out beyond the rest. It was inventive, fulsome and above all: very, very clear.

It is this same directness – open without being blandly innocent – that distinguishes any conversation with him, and I think this *is* the man. "Why did you switch from automobile design to architecture?" I once asked him, "because there were more girls there," he answered, and in his case, it was not just a cute response – I'm sure this *was* the real reason.

His open-eyed approach to people, places and things is compulsive – and surely must blend with the clarity of his drawings to lead to an irresistible compendium. The book will go some way towards projecting his totally infectious enthusiasm that is at the same time quite sensitive. Hence it is no surprise that the Hodgetts+Fung manipulation of the Hollywood Bowl goes just far enough: it's Hollywood but not coarse and a reflection of that same sensitivity.

There has to be a reason why such Midwesterners gravitated to L.A. and found themselves, why Craig and Ming live in the house of a prop-man inventor with quirky fittings and details – symbolically sitting on the top of a Hollywood ridge from which you can see both Downtown *and* the Valley, theirs is an open-eyed world which is also why they have been great pedagogues.

What a delight then, to chat along with Craig and carry his conversations in your hand.

Introduction

Craig Hodgetts

Design is always telling us something. Perhaps suggesting how we must behave or giving us permission to stretch the limits. Perhaps it is magnifying our self-image or bending us to its will. Or helping to give flight to our imagination. It may be overt, utilizing symbols that appeal to the psyche, or the subconscious, couching its agenda in abstract form, yet inevitably, whether acknowledged or not, every design broadcasts a message, ready to play a part in our behavior.

This is intended to be an easy-going compendium that highlights the terms of different design postures rather than a strait-laced visual encyclopedia based simply on good taste. Today, with lifestyles and opinions jostling for status, every product must try to speak the language of its likely user, for the nature of aesthetic choice is that it leaps across socio-political boundaries, scientific and professional differences, national and religious quarrels to form bonds with distinct, even opposing philosophies. That is the essential power of design – to convey subliminal messages that transcend conscious categories to connect on an intuitive plane. It's a language apparent to all but understood by only a few.

The relationships between things illustrated here are to some degree irrefutable, even though they may reach far into irreconcilable cultures, such as Tom Wolf reveals in *Mau-Mauing the Flak-Catchers*. One might say that the rough and ready appearance of Funk had its roots in the anti-establishment ranks of the hip-hop generation, but nothing could explain the vast political and social differences among adherents. If anything, many share a disdain for convention and value unrestricted individuality. But is that true? Doesn't each individual lay claim to a group identity that shares, in fact, adheres to a certain code of dress, craftsmanship, personal style and attitude? And wouldn't they be surprised to find the different things they value on the same page with their opposite number – an example that would, together, typify the tenuous bonds between objects that share design characteristics beyond function and applications?

I was bolstered in this quest by my wife and design partner Hsinming Fung, whose outsize role in shaping this book caps forty years of collaboration and teaching. In that time, our practice ricocheted from architecture to design for motion pictures, entertainment companies and major museum exhibitions. Those exercises offered innumerable opportunities for learning and observation, as well as to experience firsthand the sensibility of our peers, critics, and the general public.

From this wellspring of experience, it became increasingly clear that there were few design guideposts with this kind of overview.

Some were narrowed by institutional might. Others by cult like aficionados. Others still by powerful social circles. And still others by simple visual charm. In all, the aesthetic triumphs came to dominate the rest of the field.

This is not a book about connoisseurs and collecting, nor is it an academic treatise on the recent history of design, with an emphasis on questions of provenance, value or practicability. It is rather to encourage diverse visions, to expand the conversation, and to prompt consideration of design as an agent with attitude and character, capable of continuity or disruption.

Notations

DISCIPLINE

MESSAGE:

"Order is imperative. There is no place for sentimentality, empathy, or nostalgia."

ATTRIBUTES:

Absolute control, authentic materials, precision, honesty, consistency of thought, convey uncompromised value when geometry and logic govern design.

Introduction

For centuries, prior to the Industrial Revolution, the informal practice of visualizing objects (or even buildings) before their fabrication was most likely in the hands of artists, laborers, and artisans. With skills in crafting, as well as conceiving and fashioning the finished product, members of Medieval guilds — often working directly from raw materials without the benefit of documentation or established processes — were the arbiters of what we now call "design."

Skills such as carving and drawing were often combined. Volumes by Vitruvius and Palladio, among others – short on specifics and long on illustrative material – served as rough guides for the sculptors and craftspeople who would shape and assemble the parts.

The transition to a design process founded on precise documentation that could act as a reliable manual for construction likely began during the Industrial Revolution, sometime before the preparation of drawings for Joseph Paxton's Crystal Palace. Forty years later, it had matured enough to describe the extremely complex components for the Eiffel Tower with a level of detail that enabled the prefabrication of thousands of parts and, remarkably, their assembly, one by one, into one of the marvels of the 19th century. Though never codified in that period, methods for showing front, side, and top views of each part were rapidly adopted – and with that came a bias toward designs favoring flat planes and 90-degree angles. This would become the bedrock of modern, disciplined design documentation, eventually combining measurements in exhaustive detail, notes on materials, and specifications for required strength.

Implicit rules still govern those documents and simmer in the background as the functional agenda is met and often surpassed. Testing aesthetic boundaries while respecting those rules was first explored in the Bauhaus with the design and fabrication of idealized chairs, teapots, and fabrics, which operated within strict functional and material limits. Coined the "International Style" in 1932 by historian Henry Russell Hitchcock and architect Phillip Johnson in their influential catalog for the exhibition by that name at the Museum of Modern Art, it was a rigorous aesthetic derived from Bauhaus principles and championed by Arthur Drexler, the museum's director. The style demanded adherence to a highly disciplined geometric code, whether for a clock, skyscraper, or electric shaver, giving it a fundamental, *scalable* nature that led to its profound impact on virtually the entire environment and most everyday objects.

The goal, in extreme cases, was to achieve legacy status by erasing any trace of personal expression – creating objects without debt to precedent or overt references to the era in which they were born, the region of their manufacture, or the clientele. These principles were adopted wholeheartedly, beginning in the mid-1950s, by designer Dieter Rams in his products for Braun, embodying his dictum "less, but better."

The poster child for this genre is Mies van der Rohe's Seagram building, in New York City. As architectural critic Lewis Mumford wrote: "It has the aesthetic impact that only a unified work of art carried through without paltry compromises can have." Adhering to an overriding aesthetic discipline, with few exceptions for functional attributes, the Seagram injected much-needed sobriety into the post-WWII era, when demands for housing and manufactured goods spawned an aesthetic free-for-all. This new discipline ushered in a period in which a relaxed design vocabulary became tantamount to mutiny. This design doctrine – favored mostly by men in suits and ties, exchanging ritual handshakes as fastidious assistants served refreshments in pared down, strictly hierarchical offices – influenced the ways Madison Avenue blanketed the airwaves, couture houses drew on geometric forms, and even the design of snack foods, such as Pringles potato chips (introduced in 1968), followed Euclidian principles.

An undisputed virtue of such discipline was its capacity to facilitate and increase production since every component would be rectilinear and readily replicable many times, whether for a skyscraper façade or a bookcase. By jettisoning the prior centuries' decorative embellishments, exaggerated profiles, and autonomous swagger, the constraints of uniformity predictably lowered costs and streamlined production.

The masters of this idiom – Mies van der Rohe, Henry Dreyfus, Charles Basset of SOM, and Massimo and Lella Vignelli – demanded fanatical attention to detail. From the Seagram Building to Braun's impeccably executed household devices, the designs have become classics, without question. Nonetheless, today's marketplace of ideas has challenged such a singular approach – as a far more diverse contemporary culture veers sharply away from a regimented way of life.

Discipline Observations

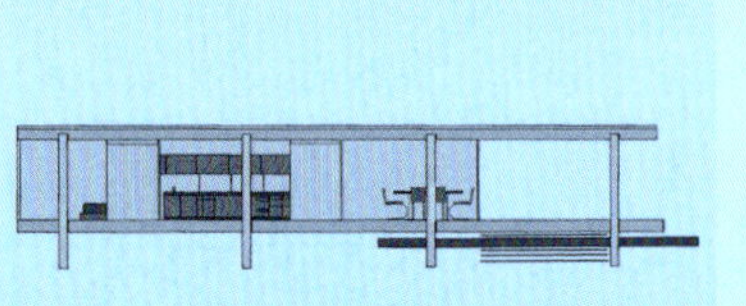

Fig. 1A FARNSWORTH HOUSE (p. 46)

YEAR 1951
DESIGNER
Ludwig Mies van der Rohe
LOCATION
Plano, Illinois, USA

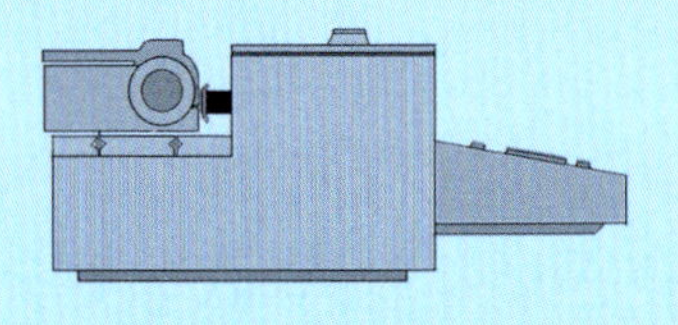

Fig. 1B PRAXIS 48 ELECTRIC TYPEWRITER (p. 46)

YEAR 1964
DESIGNER
Ettore Sottsass
MANUFACTURER
Ing. C. Olivetti & C.S.p.A, Italy

Both the simplicity and the immaculate execution of this paean to Bauhaus principles elevate it to cult status. Raised slightly above the ground plane on slender extensions of its eight columns and cantilevered slightly beyond the constraints of its structural grid, and painted a brilliant white, it "floats," over an uninterrupted landscape.

Although the owner/occupant of this house must conform to the demands that transparency and internal rigor impose upon everyday life, that discipline is rewarded by the beauty and order conferred by its rarified presence.

By separating the functions of the typewriter into two distinct elements, designer Ettore Sottsass recognized the conceptual difference between "input" from a keyboard, and "manifestation" in the form of a box containing the mechanical mechanism.

With sharp corners, rectangular forms, and an architectural sensibility, the design magnifies its visual presence, setting it apart from a family of softly contoured office equipment. A visually disengaged keyboard, with a polished plastic surface, is cantilevered from the heavy, ribbed mass of the mechanism, reaching out to the operator in a gesture recognizing the human-machine interface.

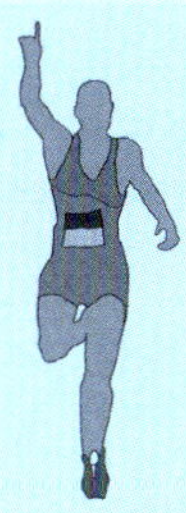

Fig. 1C RUNNING GEAR
(p. 47)

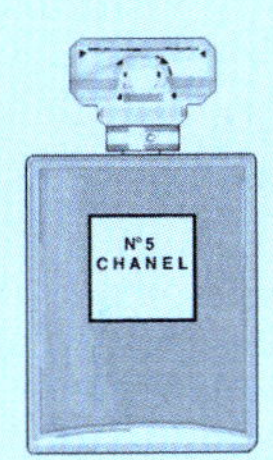

Fig. 1D CHANEL NO.5
(p. 47)

YEAR 1921
DESIGNER
Coco Chanel
MANUFACTURER
Parfums Chanel,
France

Competitive running-wear is one of the more significant items of athletic garb, along with biking and swimming. Important attributes such as the ability of fabrics to wick perspiration, non-bunching design, and lightweight, pliable footwear are the goals of rigorous research and testing of multiple prototypes. The unique conjunction of human metrics and performance-based design peaks with the development of specialized fabrics, and designs calibrated to enhance each aspect of a particular sport.

In the universe of ornate vessels dedicated to containing precious scents, the disciplined profile of the classic Chanel vial has endured for decades without compromise.

For the 1921 introduction of the perfume that would carry her name, Coco Chanel envisioned a pure, flawless vial that would set the scent apart by avoiding the ostentatious and ornate perfume containers of the period. The prismatic effect of its polished glass stopper acts as a timeless luxury attribute in contrast to the simple, even clinical bottle.

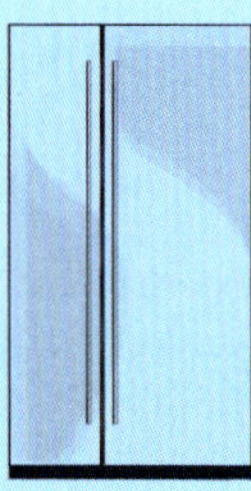

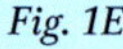

Fig. 1E JENNAIR NOIR™ SIDE-BY-SIDE REFRIGERATOR (p. 48)

YEAR 2025
MANUFACTURER
JennAir, a Subsidiary of Whirlpool Corporation, USA

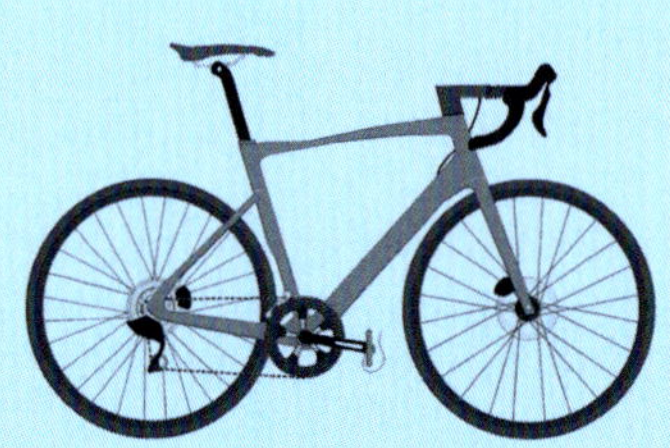

Fig. 1F BIANCHI SPECIALISSIMA RC (p. 48)

YEAR 2025
MANUFACTURER
Ducati, Italy

Recognition of the “background” role of large appliances in the kitchen environment rather than the “foreground” role of design in the showroom helps to explain a minimalist design language meant to reduce the visual impact on the surrounding kitchen cabinetwork. For those who remember the curving surfaces of traditional free-standing refrigerators as designed by Raymond Loewy, the crisp lines and rectilinear profile worn today by nearly every brand represent a turning point in which modern design principles govern the form of appliances whose destiny is to be integrated into a contemporary kitchen-scape.

In order to achieve the lightest weight possible while creating a stiff frame capable of absorbing the grueling stress of racing has led to extensive use of carbon fiber and the elimination of any and all excess. Special attention to details such as the cross-section of various members in response to a rigorous structural analysis of the twisting stresses imposed by vigorous pedaling is made possible by molding the frame as a singular unit rather than welding together an assortment of tubes, resulting in a balance between design discipline and structural capacity.

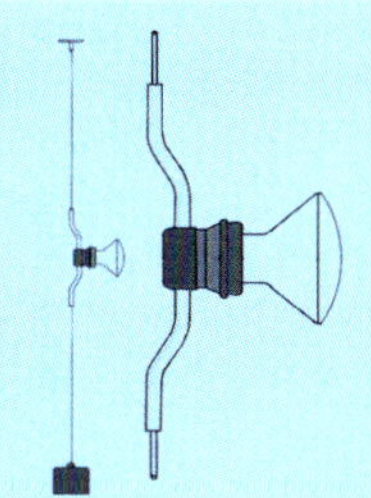

Fig. 1G

PARENTESI
(p. 49)

YEAR 1971
DESIGNERS
Achille Castiglioni and Pio Manzu
MANUFACTURER
Flos, Italy

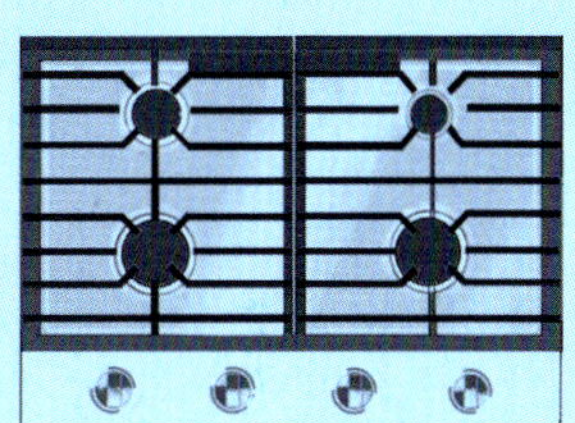

Fig. 1H

30" STAINLESS STEEL GAS COOKTOP
(p. 49)

YEAR 2025
MANUFACTURER
Samsung Electronics Co., Ltd., South Korea

A slender cable threaded through a crooked tube and stretched between a floor-bound weight and the ceiling provides structural stability for a clever, ultra-minimalist lamp which can be raised or lowered without the need for additional components. With an aesthetic inspired by the Italian "Art Povera" movement that favors the visual effect of commonplace things such as the dangling electric cord and an ordinary floodlight, the lamp represents a pitch perfect integration of structural principles with convenient operation.

Elimination of semantic gestures rooted in traditional technology, such as cast-iron grates, elaborate burners, and cumbersome regulators, has yielded a generation of cooktops that are efficient and easy to clean, with compact, ergonomic controls carefully placed to maximize cooking area. The arrangement of grillage elements stresses simplicity while featuring deviations from the grid to identify cooking areas.

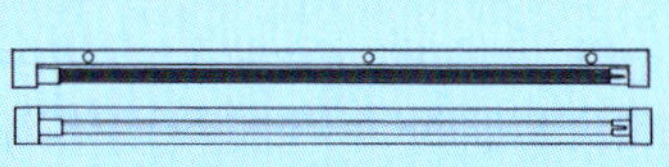

Fig. 1I

FLUORESCENT LIGHT DIFFUSER COVERS
(p. 49)

MANUFACTURER
Kastlite, USA

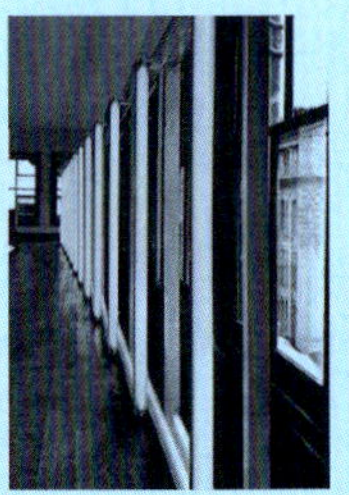

Fig. 1J

UNTITLED
(p. 49)

YEAR 1970
ARTIST
Dan Flavin
LOCATION
New York,
New York, USA

Used by artist Dan Flavin as the light-source for his installations, the common shop light, consisting of an enameled metal box housing an electrical ballast which energizes an off-the-shelf fluorescent tube by means of contact pins at either end, can be altered to emit colored light by means of a thin, tinted transparent cover slipped over the tube.

The recognition that light, by itself, is a creative medium, led artist Dan Flavin to the use of a generic, inexpensive fluorescent fixture. By creating installations focused on subtle interactions of light with its surrounding environment using such fixtures as a source, the bare, unadorned white boxes are arranged in such a way as to create striking effects with minimal means. The resulting luminous flux, anchored by the regulating silhouettes of stacked white cases creates unpredictable and somewhat uncanny effects as complementary colors mix and dissipate in thin air. Using a similar minimalist vocabulary he has created notable installations at major museums around the world.

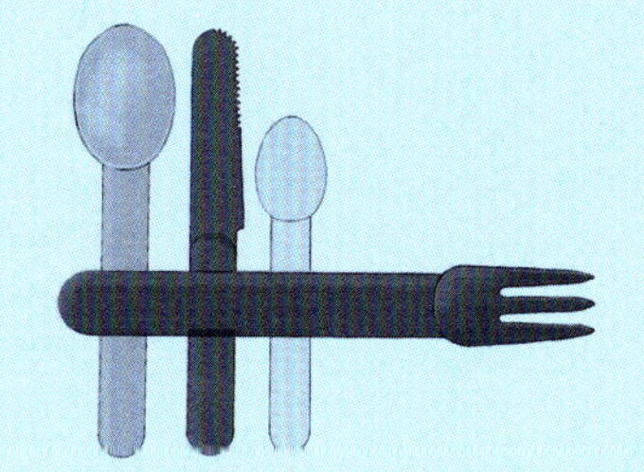

Fig. 1K PLASTIC FLATWARE (p. 50)

DESIGNER
Carsten Jorgensen
MANUFACTURER
Bodum Inc., Switzerland

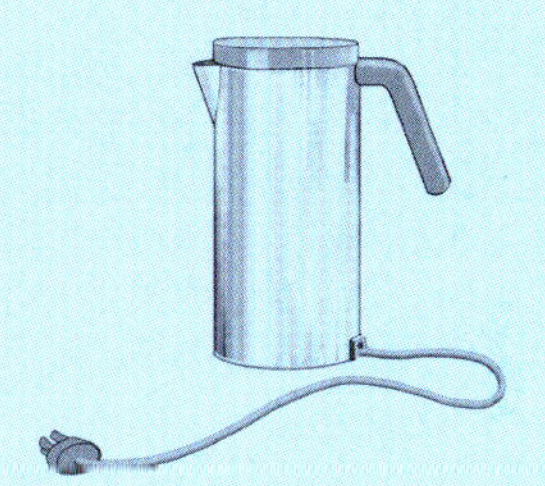

Fig. 1L HOT.IT WA09 ELECTRIC KETTLE (p. 50)

YEAR 2009
DESIGNER
Wiel Arets
MANUFACTURER
Centro Studio Alessi S.p.A., Italy

Designed to endure the rigors of daily use, the stubby proportions and primitive contours of this flatware directly reflect the constraints imposed by molded plastic construction. By avoiding the frivolous designs often employed to "upscale" inexpensive, disposable plastic flatware, and emphasizing its muscular proportions, the design conveys a message of durability and utility in spite of a playful array of integral colors.

Devoid of expressive elements, this kettle has sublimated all but the spout and the power cord to a rigorous expression of "pure" form, consisting exclusively of geometric solids. Attention to balance while pouring is achieved by the angle of the cantilevered handle.

Fig. 1M STACKING DINNERWARE (p. 51)

YEAR 1964
DESIGNERS
Massimo and Lella Vignelli
MANUFACTURER
Articoli Plastici Elettrici, Italy

The Heller line of dishware, designed by Massimo and Lella Vignelli in 1964, discarded the baggage of traditional ceramics in favor of melamine plastic and a machine aesthetic. This allowed the utilization of precision molds as well as the introduction of vivid color and severe, purist contours. Characterized by a vertical edge band around a flat, slightly mortised plate that enables secure stacking of more than a dozen plates, the lightweight and impact resistant design freed up much of the shelf space needed to store comparable numbers of plates made of traditional china.

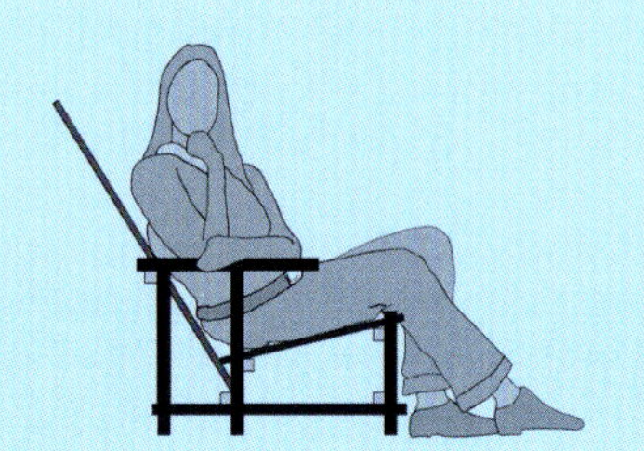

Fig. 1N RED BLUE CHAIR (p. 51)

YEAR 1918-1923
DESIGNER
Gerrit Rietveld
MADE IN
The Netherlands

By adhering strictly to "De Stijl" (The Style) principles of commercially available, standard pieces of lumber assembled in abstract space, Gerrit Rietveld envisioned a chair that could be easily mass-produced. The purity of that vision, and the discipline required to realize it prioritized those principles over comfort and ergonomics, which doomed its commercial success as furniture, but heralded its enduring reputation as an avant-garde pioneer.

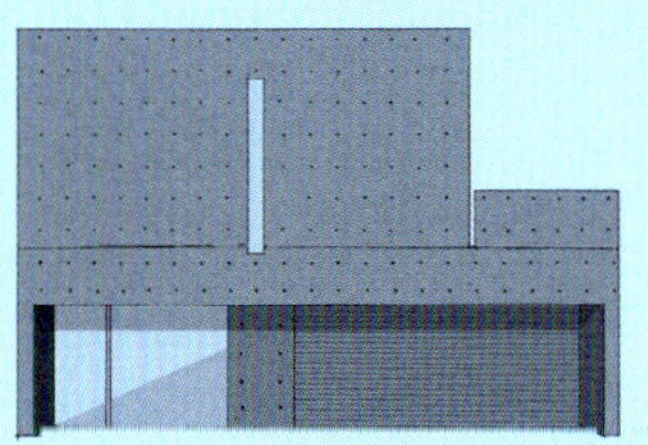

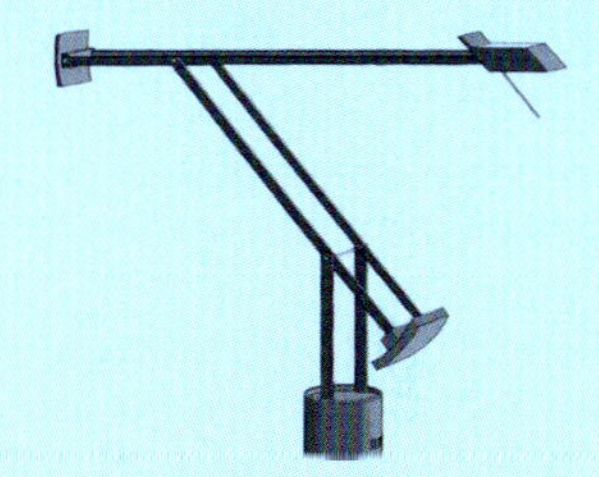

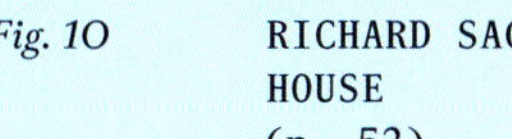

Fig. 1O RICHARD SACHS HOUSE (p. 52)

YEAR 2013
ARCHITECT
Tadao Ando
LOCATION
Malibu,
California, USA

Fig. 1P TIZIO TABLE LAMP (p. 53)

YEAR 1971
DESIGNER
Richard Sapper
MANUFACTURER
Artemide
S.p.A., Italy

By the disciplined exposure of the basic elements of concrete formwork, and by abandoning additional surface treatments, Tadao Ando is able to create minimalist environments in which space and light are the principal design elements. Although this house has a formidable street presence, it shelters generous spaces and grand views toward the Pacific that belie its fortress-like design.

By balancing the triple disciplines of gravity loads, electrical requirements, and affable ergonomics, this lamp displays an effortless resolution of often clashing components. Insulated pivots separate thin metal arms which not only support an adjustable high intensity lamp-house but also conduct low voltage electrical current. The resulting forms pivot together, counterbalanced by a shaped metal weight. The whole assembly, reminiscent of an Alexander Calder "mobile," pirouettes enticingly from its desktop perch.

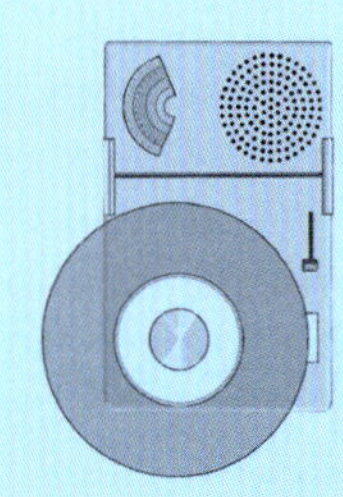

Fig. 1Q PORTABLE TRANSISTOR RADIO PHONOGRAPH, MODEL TP1
(p. 53)

YEAR 1959
DESIGNER
Dieter Rams
MANUFACTURER
Braun AG, Germany

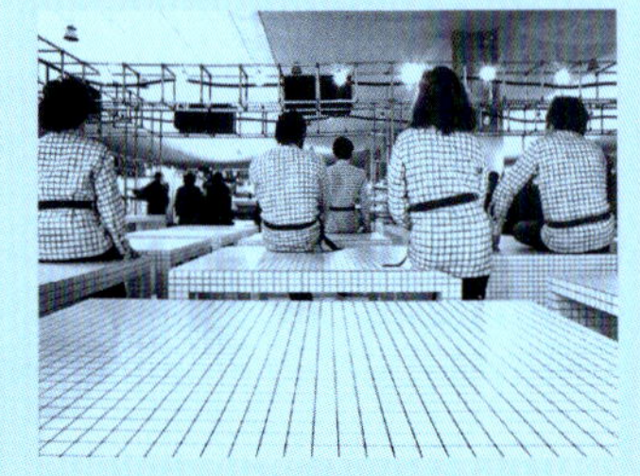

Fig. 1R QUADERNA TABLE 2600
(p. 53)

YEAR 1969-1972
DESIGNER
Superstudio
MANUFACTURER
Zanotta S.p.A., Italy

With indisputable logic, Dieter Rams' design has stripped away what might be considered superfluous to produce this compact phonograph. Of particular note is the insightful elimination of 270 degrees of redundant surface area beneath the now cantilevered disc itself. Rams' other work for Braun is driven by his conviction that:

> Good design is innovative.
> Good design makes a product useful.
> Good design is Aesthetic.
> Good design makes a product understandable.
> Good design is unobtrusive.
> Good design is honest.
> Good design is long-lasting.
> Good design is thorough, down to the last detail.
> Good design is environmentally friendly.
> Good design is as little design as possible.

At once a parody and a celebration of the restrictions imposed by a regulating grid, Superstudio's conceptual project lampoons the implicit dictatorship of an over-reliance on modularity.

Discipline Illustrations

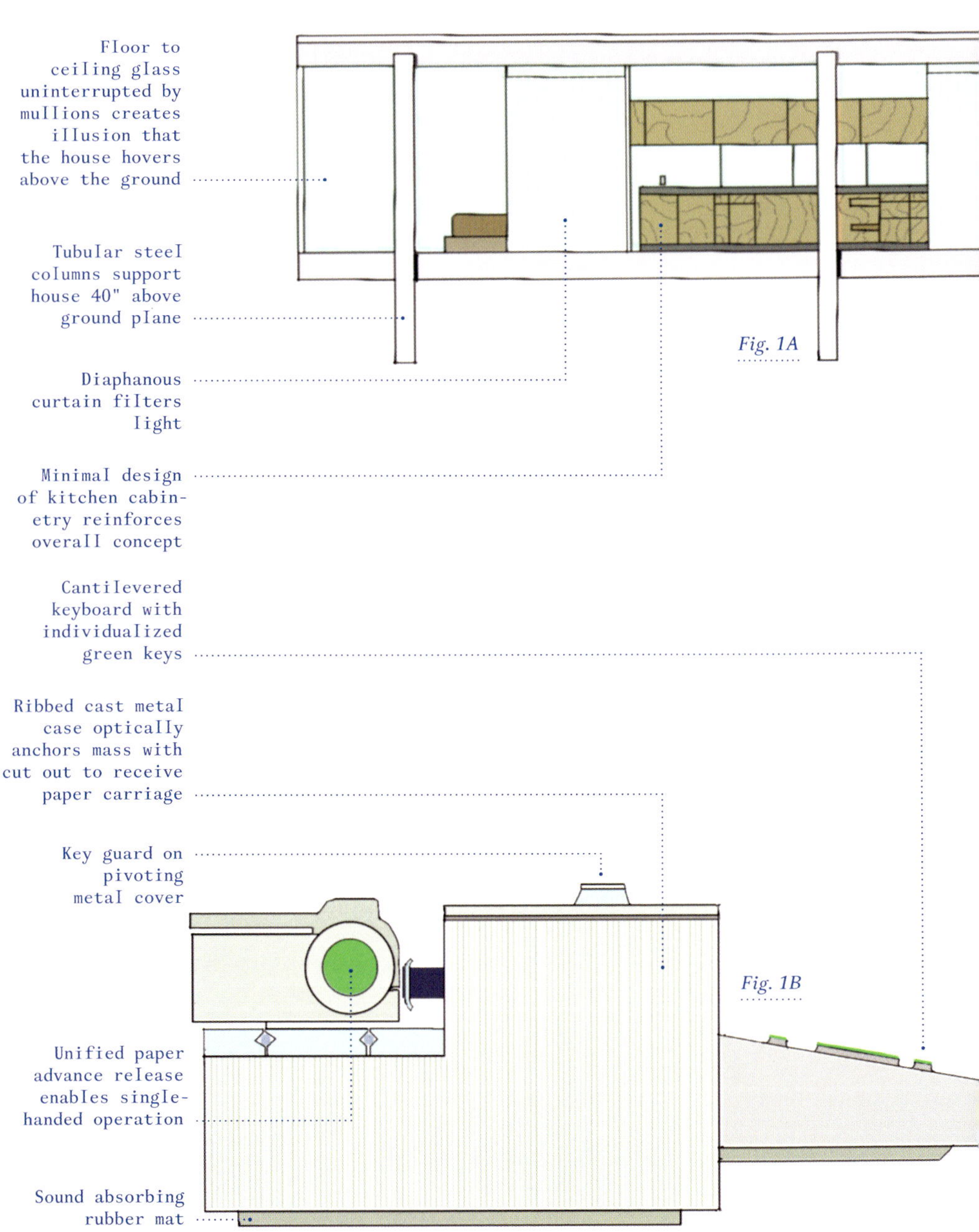

FARNSWORTH HOUSE (*Fig. 1A*),
PRAXIS 48 ELECTRIC TYPEWRITER (*Fig. 1B*)

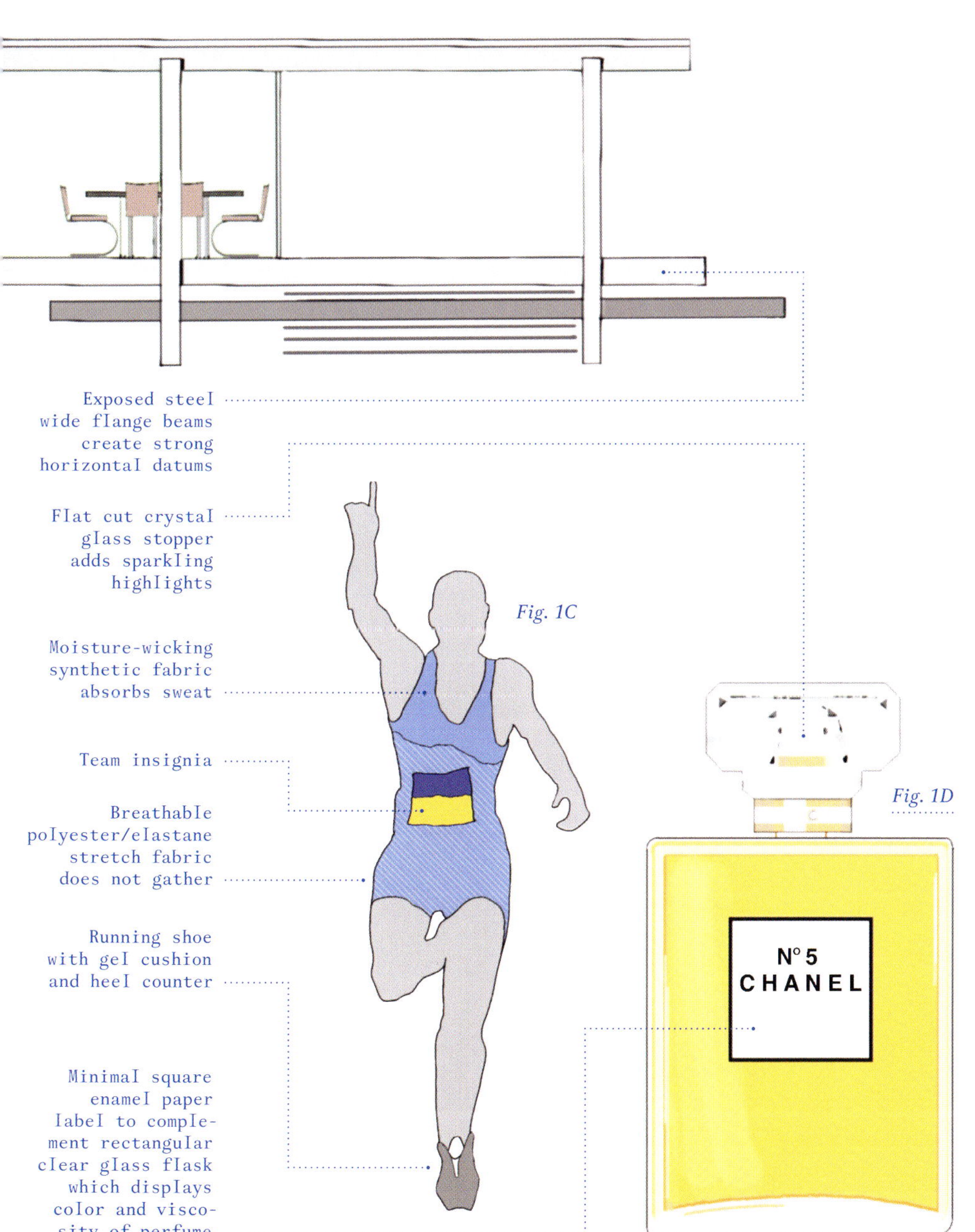

RUNNING GEAR (*Fig. 1C*), CHANEL NO.5 (*Fig. 1D*)

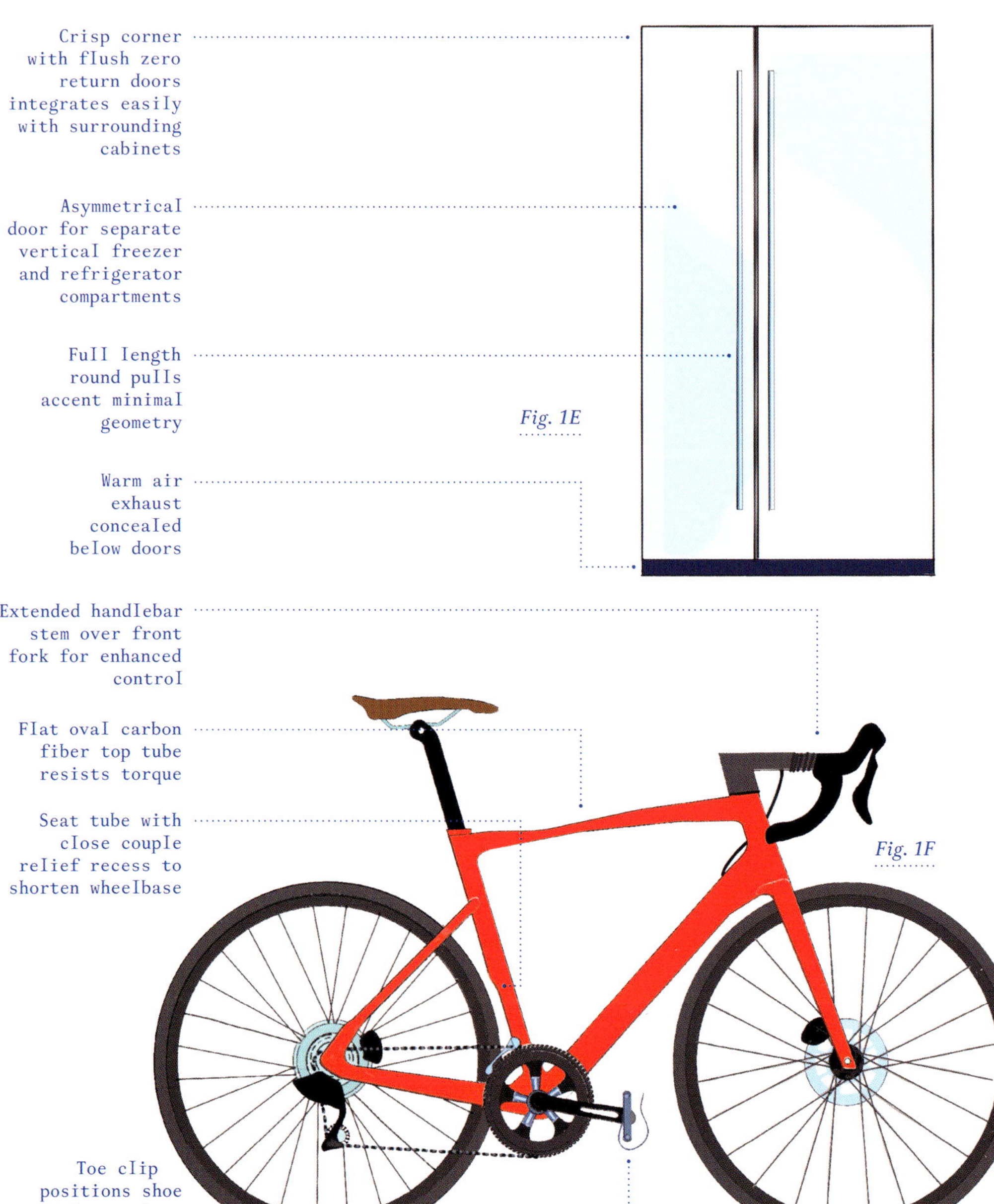

JENNAIR NOIR™ SIDE-BY-SIDE REFRIGERATOR (*Fig. 1E*), BIANCHI SPECIALISSIMA RC (*Fig. 1F*)

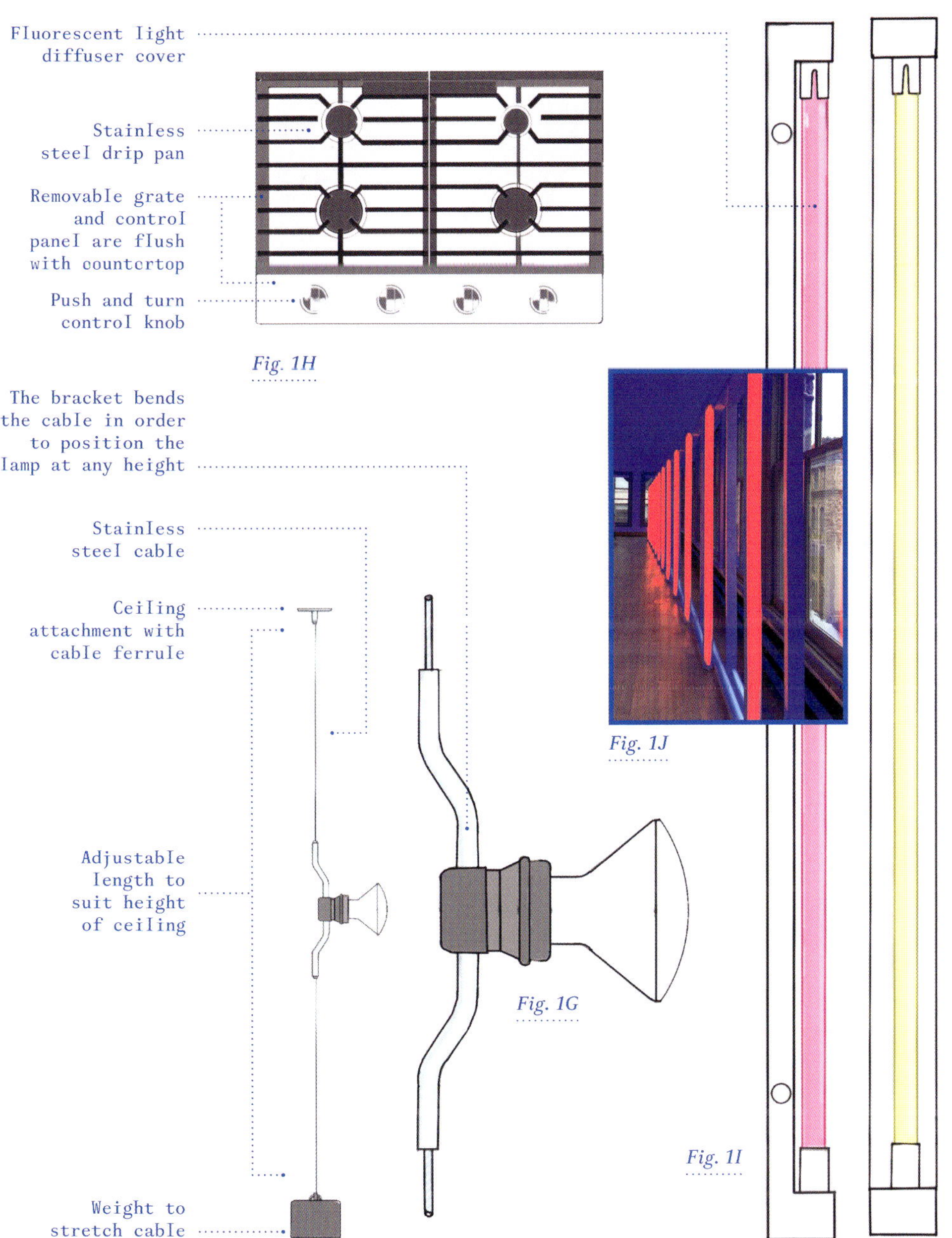

PARENTESI (*Fig. 1G*), 30" STAINLESS STEEL GAS COOKTOP (*Fig. 1H*), FLUORESCENT LIGHT DIFFUSER COVERS (*Fig. 1I*), UNTITLED (*Fig. 1J*)

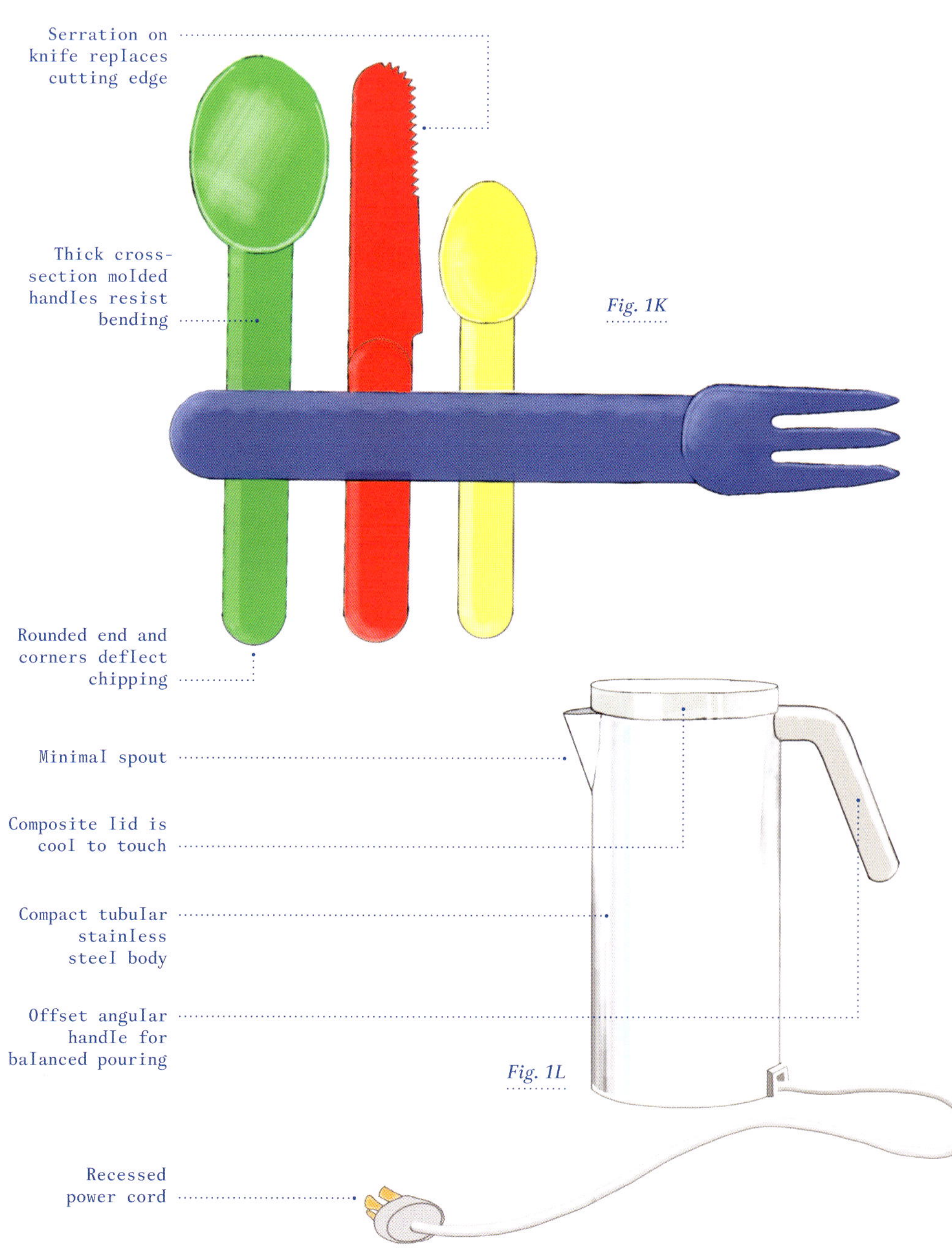

PLASTIC FLATWARE (*Fig. 1K*), HOT.IT WA09 ELECTRIC KETTLE (*Fig. 1L*)

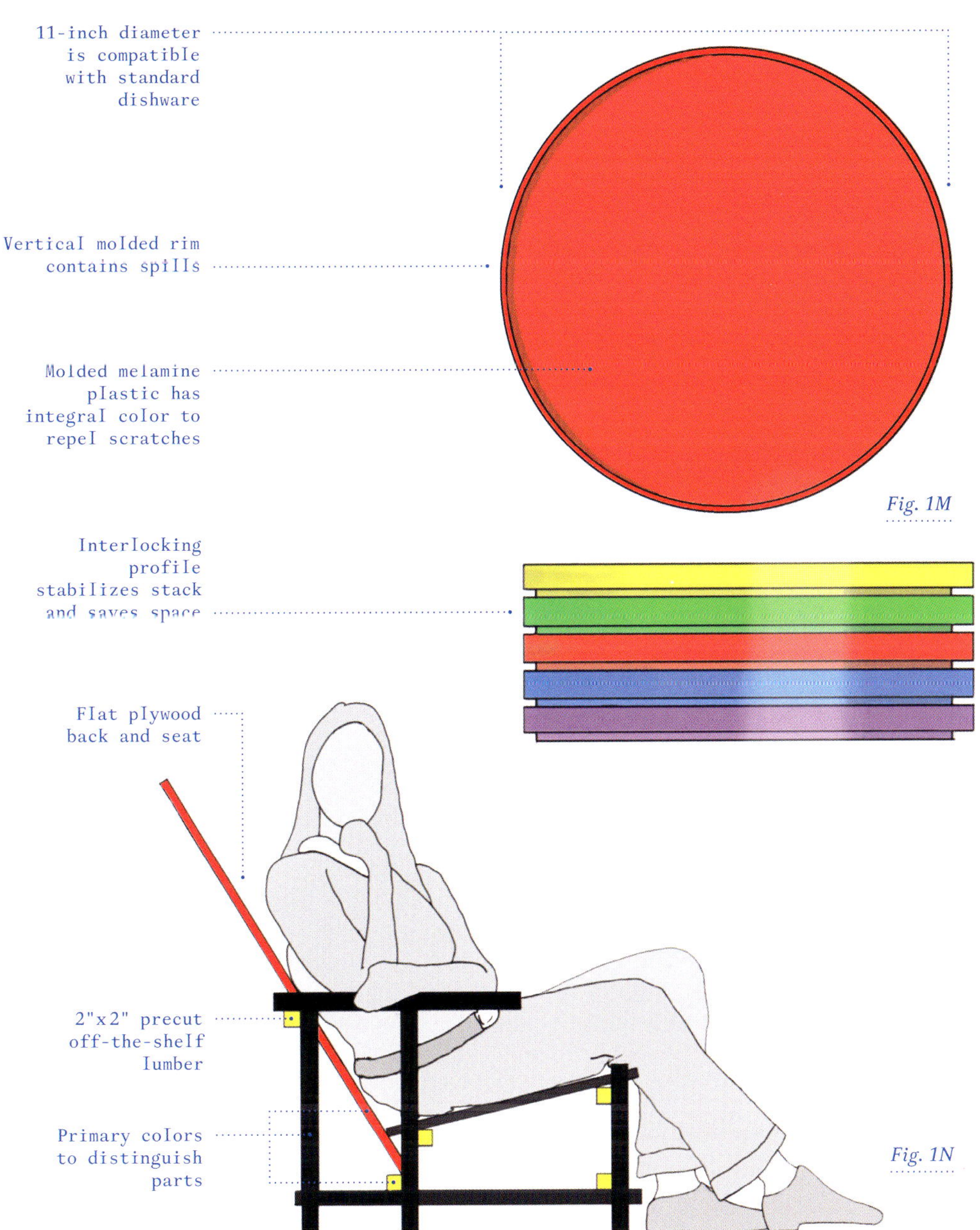

STACKING DINNERWARE (*Fig. 1M*), RED BLUE CHAIR (*Fig. 1N*)

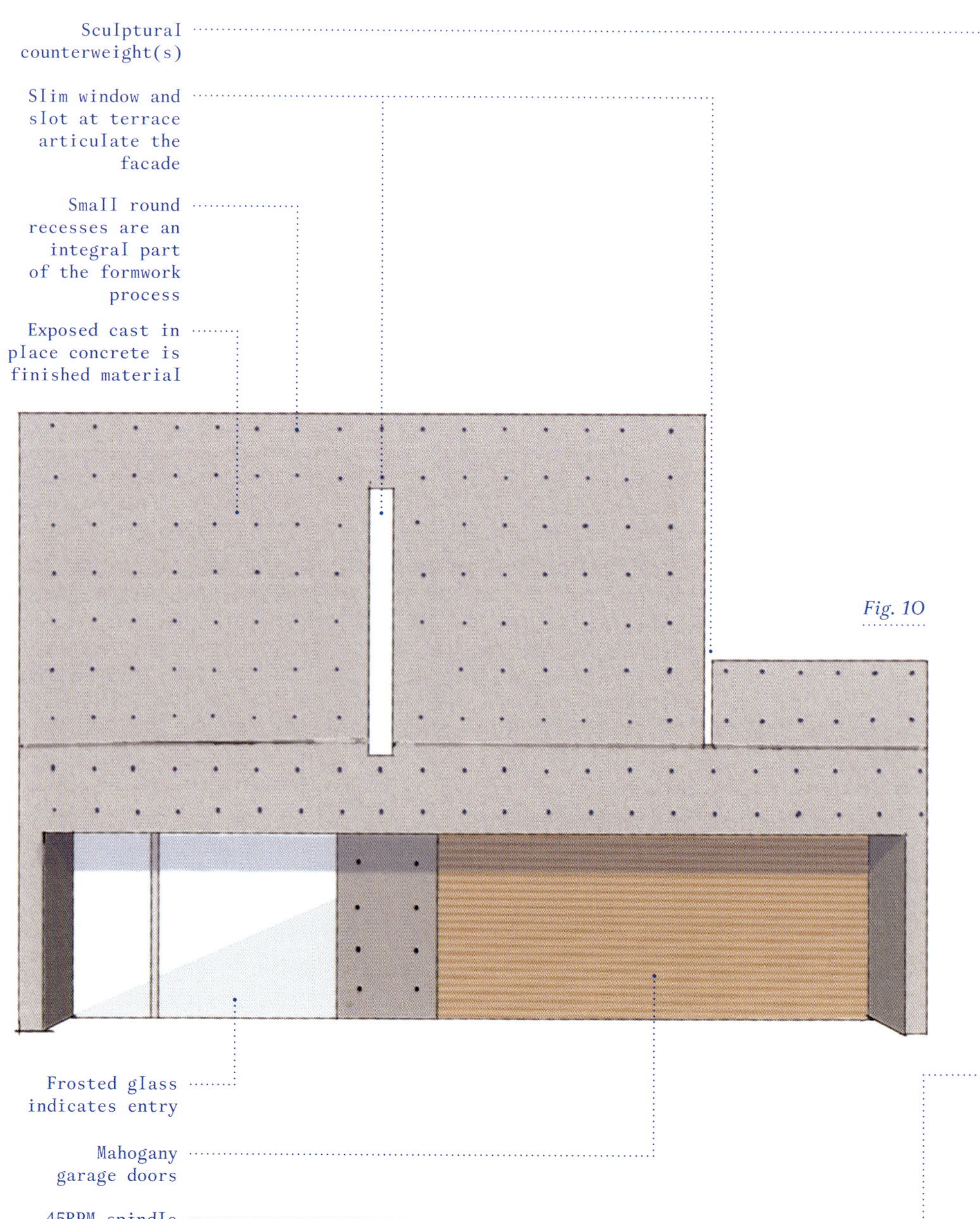

RICHARD SACHS HOUSE (*Fig. 10*)

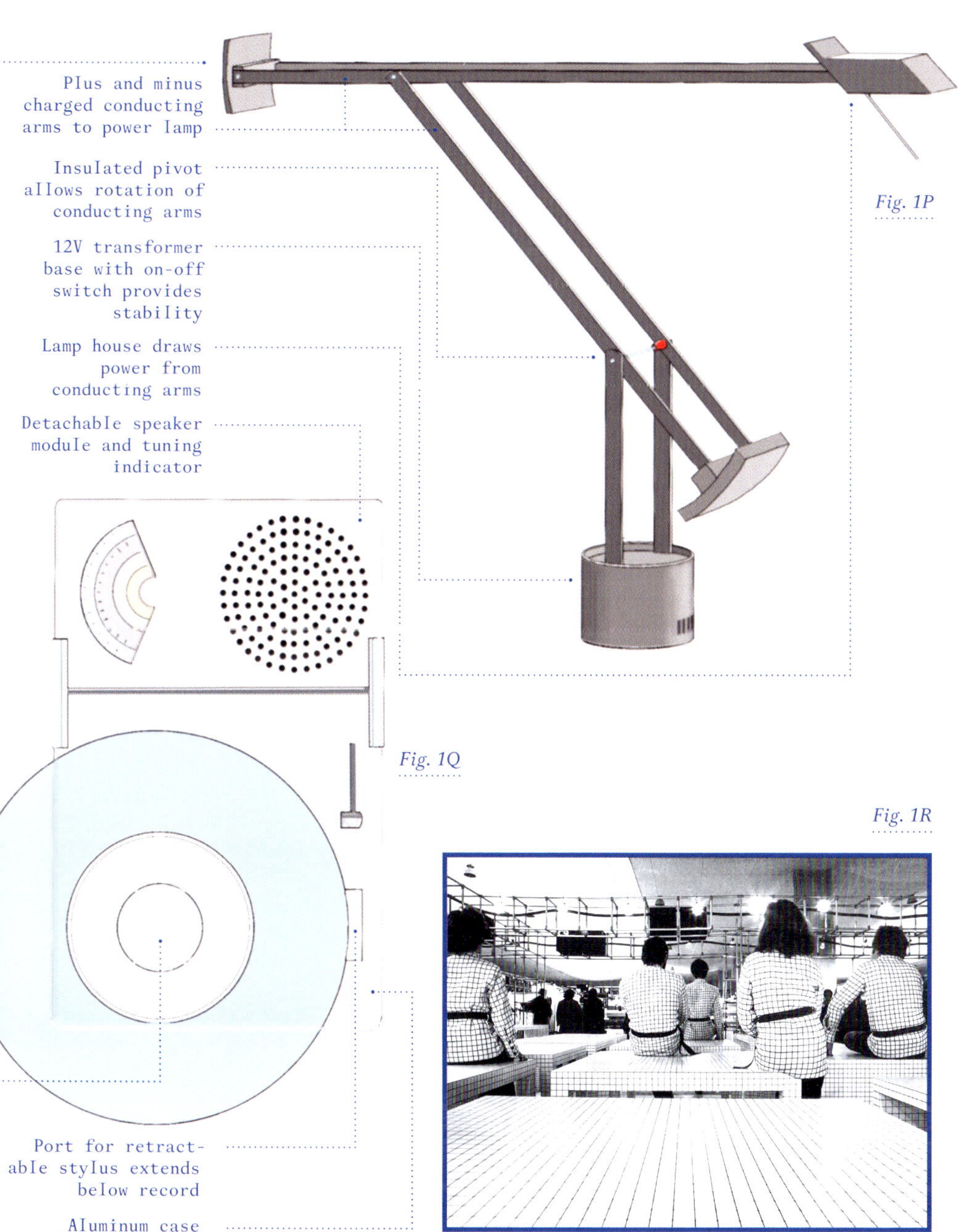

TIZIO TABLE LAMP (*Fig. 1P*),
PORTABLE TRANSISTOR RADIO PHONOGRAPH, MODEL TP1 (*Fig. 1Q*),
QUADERNA TABLE 2600 (*Fig. 1R*)

GLUT

Message: "There is no substitute for luxury. High rollers and deep pockets want to be pampered."
Attributes: Extravagant materials, exclusive design, numbered editions, bespoke features and ornament complement a prodigal lifestyle.

Introduction

If one were to assume the world, its buildings, costumes, and environments are here for our enjoyment, each object in the visual realm might be expected to flaunt its character by means of luxurious materials, intriguing patterns, and sensual forms. Extravagant objects are designed to engulf our senses, overwhelming us with opulent surfaces, materials, and colors, abandoning constraints, and, in so doing, igniting a voracious appetite for sensuous experience

The practice of rampant decoration was much in vogue throughout the 18th and 19th Centuries, especially in the Court of Louis XIV, and continued to be pursued throughout the 20th Century for special occasions, royalty, and the ultra-wealthy, which helped define today's social hierarchies. For more than two centuries, the exorbitant cost of creating and producing exquisitely crafted goods, and the elaborate liaisons necessary to acquire them, guaranteed the exclusivity of such items. In the current age, however, the ability to replicate elaborate designs at low-cost – due to automated processes, 3D printing, digital scanning, metal deposition, and robotics – has made look-alike "aristocratic" goods affordable and widely available to nearly everyone.

With that, the social currency of elaborate handmade goods has all but evaporated, reincarnated mostly as style branding which – despite such items' now widespread availability and the reduction of their status to logos – still triggers unfulfilled longings.

In the world of automobiles, power and luxury are co-mingled, with so-called supercars pampering owners with an intoxicating mix of high-tech instrument clusters and controls, with hand-crafted materials covering nearly every inch of the interiors and often engine compartments, as well, awash in polished metal and gleaming hex nuts. Such luxury is contrary to the *bonafides* of race-ready sports cars of the past century, whose frugal, utilitarian cockpits cut weight to increase speed and were far less concerned with projecting the luxurious feel usually reserved for town cars. Today's high-end vehicles deliver such excessive power that a few pounds of additional weight have only negligible effect on performance, but huge impact on sales, machismo, and pride of ownership.

That pride, epitomized by Uma Thurman's rendition of "If You've Got it,

Flaunt It" in the movie *The Producers* (2005), became a pervasive lifestyle trait toward the end of the last century. It surfaced in unleashed inhibitions at Studio 54, in the proliferation of ultra-luxury customized "pimp-mobiles," Aaron Spelling's famously palatial residence, and author Bret Easton Ellis's portrayal of decadence in *Less than Zero*. Fashion was quick to catch up, with flamboyant fabrics, most notably, in Dolce & Gabbana collections, and opulent shoes and handbags from established, formerly conservative makers, enticing customers with rare leathers and fittings. Soon, beginning in the late 1990s, exclusive shops with bespoke facades and plush interiors, many designed by architects at the top of their game, began appearing in upscale urban centers around the world, including, for example, OMA's Prada shop in Beverly Hills, whose facade disappears beneath the sidewalk, and SANAA's luminous Omotesandō flagship store for Dior in Tokyo.

Much the way their polished surfaces and voluptuous shapes sway our attention toward high-end retail, the intricate cast-aluminum sidewalk fence, translucent emerald facade, and other sumptuous materials of Herzog & de Meuron's 40 Bond Street condominium (2007) in New York City make clear that indulgence is job number one – the building often portrayed with an exotic supercar parked out front.

Meanwhile, the French, of course, dominate luxury in not only fashion, but also gastronomy. So, when it comes to spectacular cooking accoutrements, the Gallic equivalent of an exotic automobile is the grand kitchen range, notably by La Cornue. Its opulence abounds, from quatrefoil control knobs with crystal finials to enamel-inlaid doors with bastion-style hinges and reeded ferrules. The experience of standing over such a stove, manipulating its controls, must, in some sense, affirm one's status in the world. So too, with traditional patrician silverware.

Fondling a utensil so encrusted with imagery, at once visual and tactile, and feeling its balance enhance the luxurious experience of impaling, cutting, and savoring gourmet cuisine.

These days, as internet influencers, podcasts, and reality shows commandeer the airways, it's unclear whether the storied legacy of aristocratic lifestyles will endure – or whether even its relatively recent relics will get stored away in museums and collections, maybe awaiting a new dawn.

Glut Observations

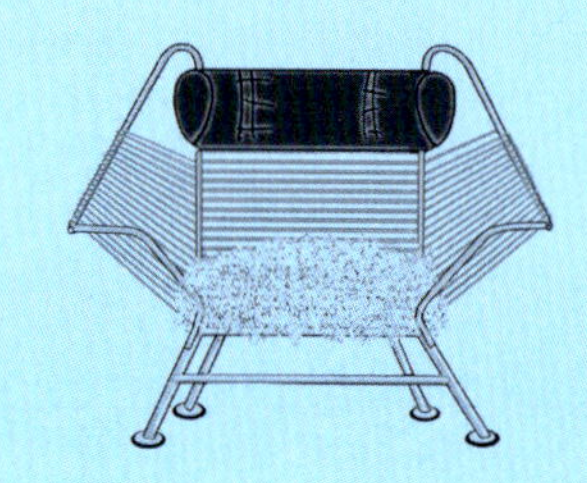

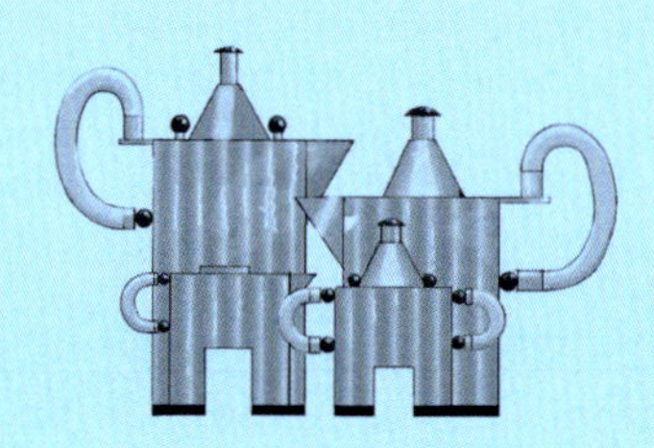

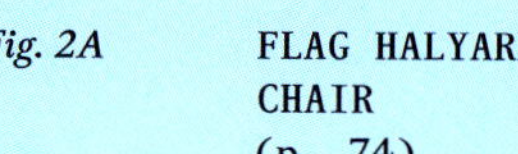

Fig. 2A FLAG HALYARD CHAIR (p. 74)

YEAR 1950
DESIGNER
Hans J. Wegner
MANUFACTURER
PP Møbler, Denmark

Fig. 2B TEA AND COFFEE SERVICE (p. 75)

YEAR 1985
DESIGNER
Michael Graves
MANUFACTURER
Alessi S.p.A., Italy

A well-chosen palette, a confident yet radical structure, and an intriguing presence establish this Danish lounge chair as a conspicuous presence in any environment. With an impeccable balance of unusual luxury materials, and commodious, yet compact dimensions, this chair declares its owner to be an adventurous but good-natured upper-class iconoclast daring to step outside conventional metrics of good taste.

Immaculate craftsmanship and a historically aware sensibility rescue this teapot from irrelevance because of evolving trends. By deriving its design from well-established Palladian architectural principles and avoiding embellishments which might threaten its integrity, this polished, well-groomed set has become a classic.

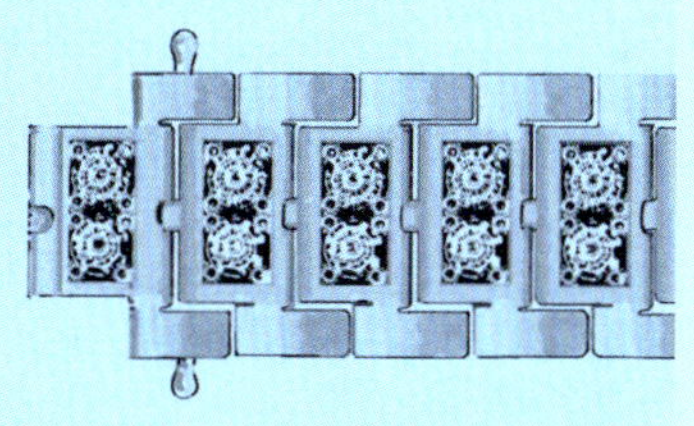

Fig. 2C

28 CARAT DIAMOND IN 18 KARAT GOLD LINK BRACELET (p. 75)

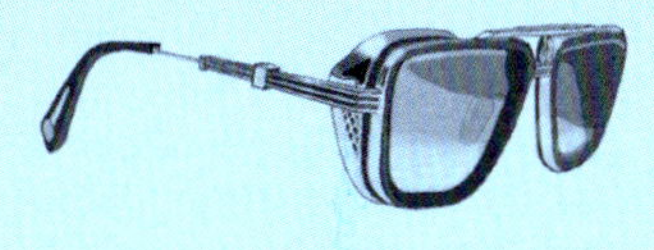

Fig. 2D

GTO-OBSIDIAN (p. 76)

MANUFACTURER
T Henri, Japan

To purveyors of heritage jewelry, the scarcity, workmanship, and weight in carats is reflected in the stratospheric cost. Established houses maintain a bevy of artists and craftspeople able to create one-off pieces showcasing diamond-studded links as well as to craft bespoke designs to enliven otherwise ordinary precious stones.

Glamour, wealth, and sunglasses, like Huey, Dewey, and Louie, seem to be inseparable from Monaco, yachts, and racing cars. Endless variations in scale, style (from futuristic Paco Rabanne to traditional jewel encrusted, ornate gold frames) are available to echo individual taste and aspirational status, invoking a true, wannabe, meritocratic spirit available to anyone.

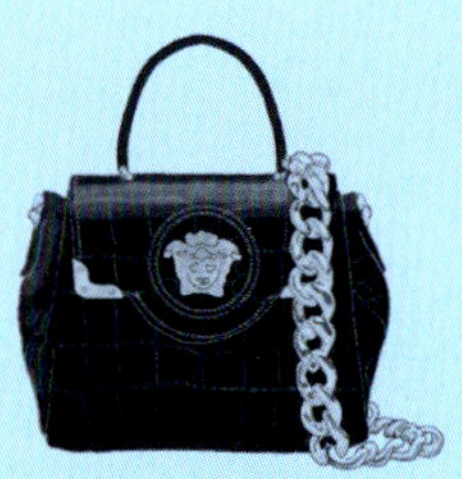

Fig. 2E LA MEDUSA HANDBAG (p. 76)

YEAR c.2022
DESIGNER
Gianni Versace
COMPANY
Gianni Versace U.R.L., Italy

The luxury handbag, crafted from exotic leathers, and assembled with immaculate craftsmanship by dedicated technicians, has become the *sine qua non* of upmarket aspirants, endowed matrons, and household names, a rare achievement for a common accessory with no purpose other than the transport of daily necessities. Featuring bespoke hardware, exotic skins, unique shapes and cultivated provenance, this signature handbag and its cousins are perhaps the world's most conspicuous accessory for upwardly mobile *fashionistas*. While God is indeed in the details, He can also be found in the brand itself, without which the more mundane functional attributes add little value.

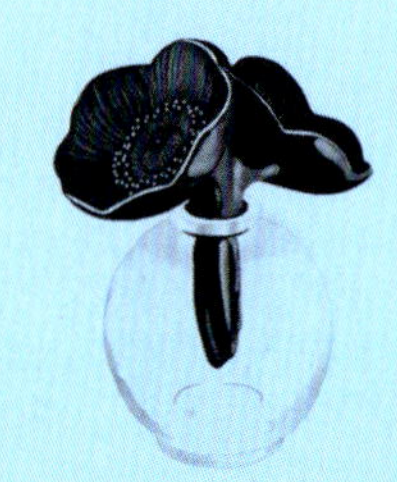

Fig. 2F DEUX ANÉMONES PERFUME BOTTLE (p. 76)

YEAR 1929-1935
DESIGNER
René Lalique
MANUFACTURER
Verrerie d'Alsace, France

With a lineage of more than two millennia, the perfume bottle has arguably been at the forefront of handcraft experimentation as well as artistic expression. Now far removed from the 1930s, this extraordinary vial showcases the craftsmanship employed in its creation and continues to inspire creative designs by the world's foremost designers and architects.

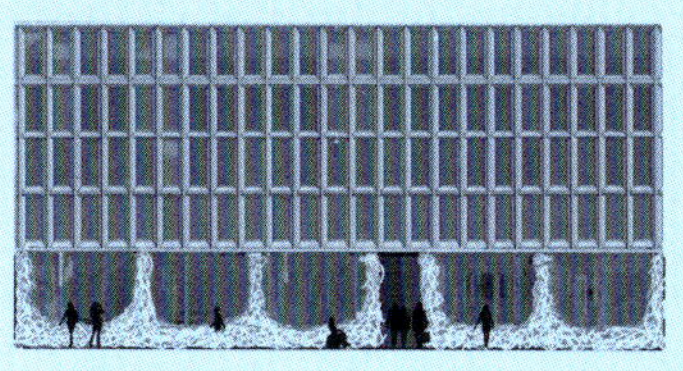

Fig. 2G 40 BOND APARTMENT BUILDING (p. 77)

YEAR 2007
ARCHITECTS
Herzog & de Meuron
LOCATION
New York, New York, USA

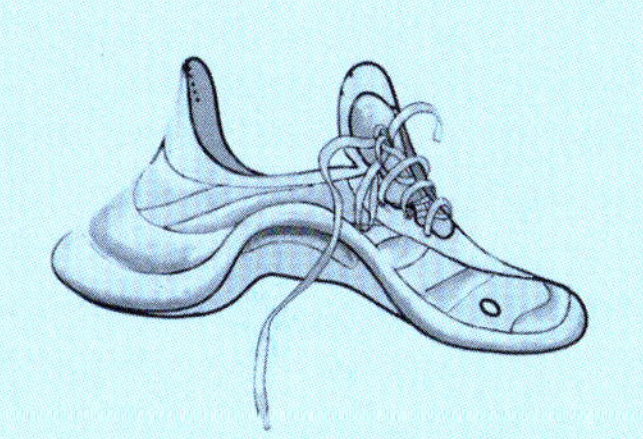

Fig. 2H LV ARCHLIGHT SNEAKER (p. 78)

YEAR 2018
DESIGNER
Nicolas Ghesquière
COMPANY
Louis Vuitton, France

The Herzog & de Meuron designed New York townhouse complex defies its sober neighbors with a luxurious display of exotic materials and an intricate sculptural "hedge" rendered in cast aluminum. The elegantly proportioned grid of polished green glass hovering over and beyond asserts a jewel-like presence – assuring passers-by that this is no ordinary residence, while providing a suitable background for the exotic automobiles generally stationed out front.

The reign of the stiletto heel has been upended by designs drawn from architecture and furnishings that display structural and material logic that recalibrate gender stereotypes while establishing new creative boundaries. Luxury footwear redefined by sculptural forms and brazen materials that often challenge anatomical realities has come to be the *de facto* display of forward-looking heiresses and fashion leaders.

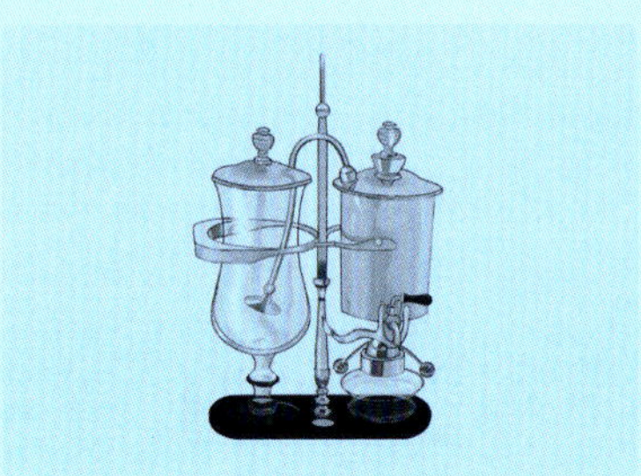

Fig. 2I AVANT GARDE ROYAL COFFEE MAKER (p. 78)

DESIGNERS
Jean-Luc Rieutort
MANUFACTURER
Royal Paris, France

If objects were people, appliances such as this would find themselves overdressed, and out of their element, and yet, this Rube-Goldberg-esque creation can be found in many rarified homes. Useful at ceremonies and entertaining at parties and events, it offers the owner a theatrical respite from the mundane rituals of hosting and tending bar.

Fig. 2J (top left) EXCALIBUR FLYING MONOTOURBILLON TITANIUM WATCH (p. 78)

MANUFACTURER
Roger Dubuis, Switzerland

Fig. 2K (bottom left) LUMINOR CHRONO GOLDTECH WATCH (p. 78)

MANUFACTURER
Panerai, Switzerland

Fig. 2L (top right) CALIBRE DE CARTIER (p. 78)

YEAR 2013
MANUFACTURER
Cartier, France

Fig. 2M (middle right) DB25 MOON PHASE STARRY SKY (p. 78)

MANUFACTURER
De Bethune, Switzerland

Fig. 2N (bottom right) KING GOLD, SPIRIT OF BIG BANG (p. 78)

MANUFACTURER
Hublot, Switzerland

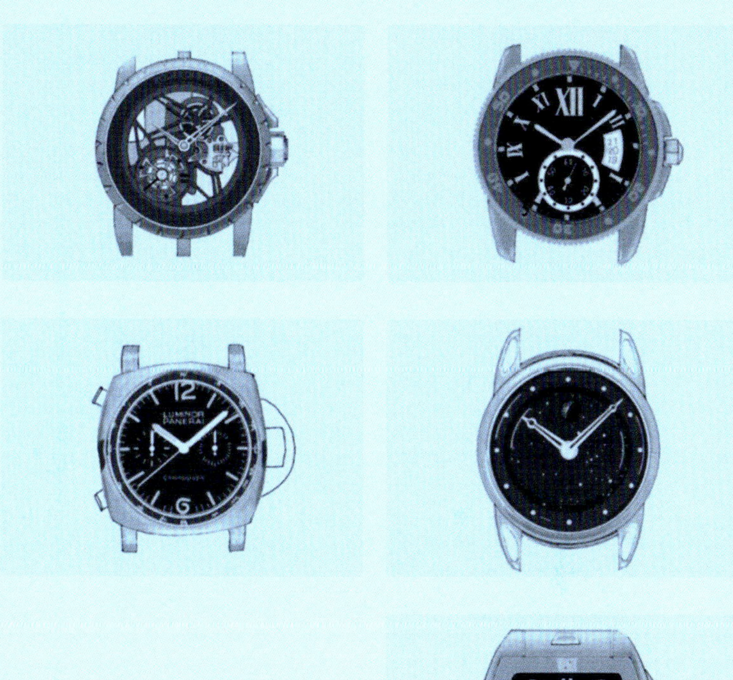

There are few spots more conspicuous on which to display symbols of personal wealth and power than the owner's wrist. With location, size, and shape confined to ordained principles, exposing the mysteries of signature movements, such as mainsprings, regulators, and escapements has become the ultimate declaration of status in the world of brokers, executives, and entertainers. Audacious, one-off craftsmanship animated by near-microscopic gears and levers impresses even those who question the utility of such timekeepers in an era of digital smartphones and internet devices.

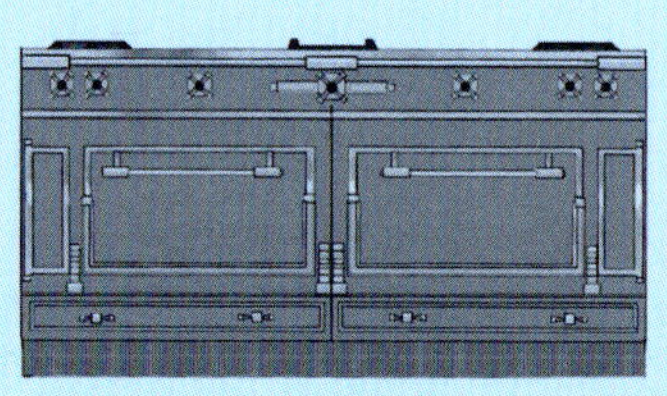

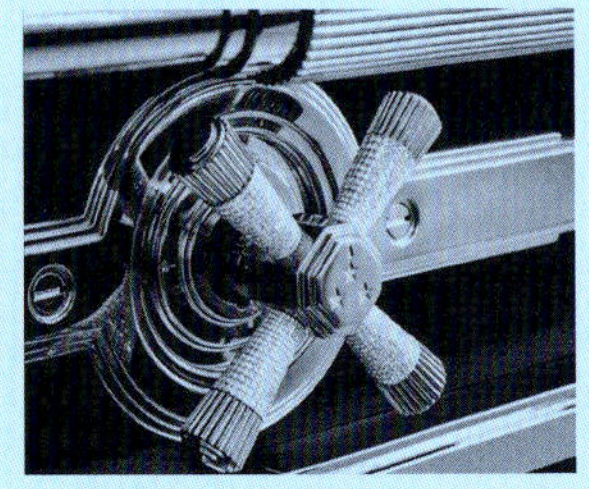

Fig. 2O CHÂTEAU SUPRÊME GRAND PALAIS 180 RANGE (p. 79)

MANUFACTURER
La Cornue,
France

Fig. 2P CONTROL KNOB (p. 79)

MANUFACTURER
La Cornue,
France

Majestic, even regal, the range of La Cornue stoves are designed to dominate the kitchen environment. Able to command homage simply by their aristocratic provenance, these benighted appliances employ traditional design features such as riveted porcelain panels, crystal encrusted, indexed regulators, and impressive cast iron grates that reference palatial residences from the Napoleonic era while opting for analogue features long discarded by contemporary makers despite available digital technology, yet offering the visceral experience of helming a culinary masterpiece while preparing a modern meal.

Machined from solid brass with integral click stops and crystal finials, these control knobs evoke the haptic sensation of a scientific instrument, lending an air of precision to the day's culinary activities.

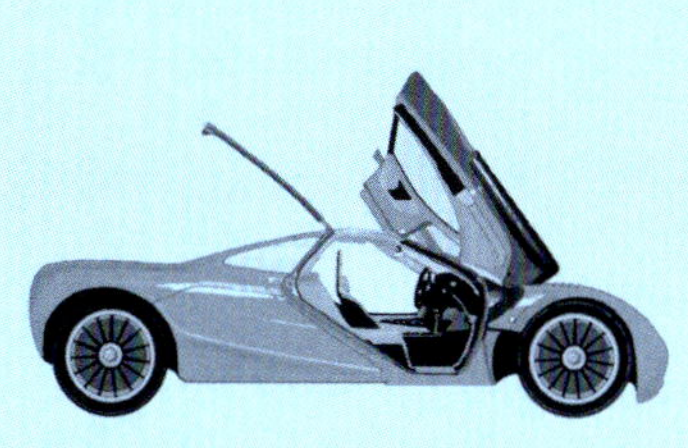

Fig. 2Q MCLAREN CAR
F1 LM
(p. 79)

YEAR 1998
CONCEPT
Gordon Murray
DESIGN
Peter Stevens
MANUFACTURER
McLaren Cars,
UK

The production spec follow-ups to McLaren's indomitable Formula One racers, much admired for their engineering brilliance and formidable handling, have successfully made the transition to a coveted street-worthy version without compromising performance. Gussied up with ultra luxurious materials, lavish instrumentation and a fashionable design well-suited to premier sightings, it has lost none of the verve, charisma, and capability that racing driver Bruce McLaren envisioned in 1963 when his hand-built M1 sports car won 43 races in the Can-Am series.

Glut Illustrations

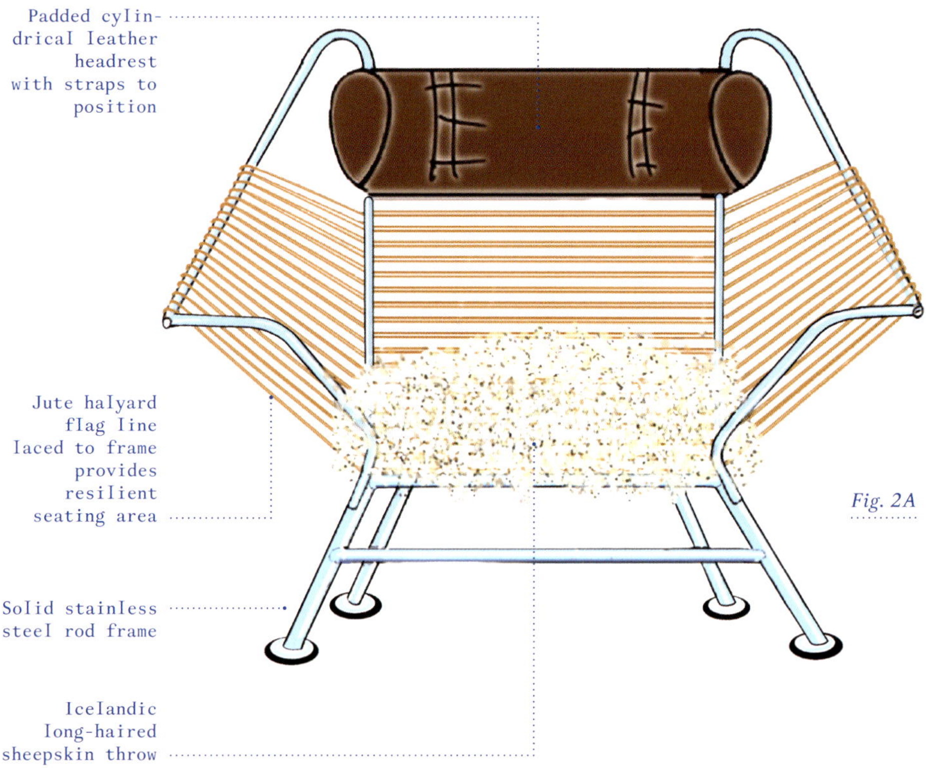

Padded cylindrical leather headrest with straps to position

Jute halyard flag line laced to frame provides resilient seating area

Fig. 2A

Solid stainless steel rod frame

Icelandic long-haired sheepskin throw

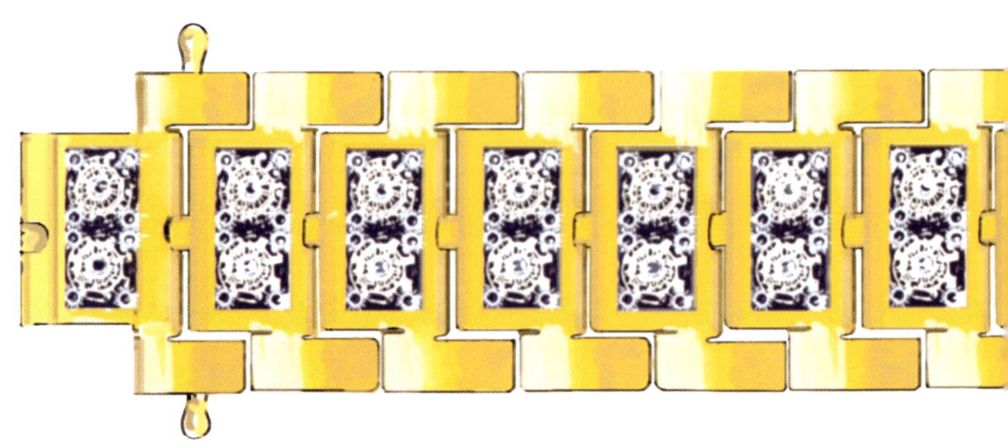

FLAG HALYARD CHAIR (*Fig. 2A*)

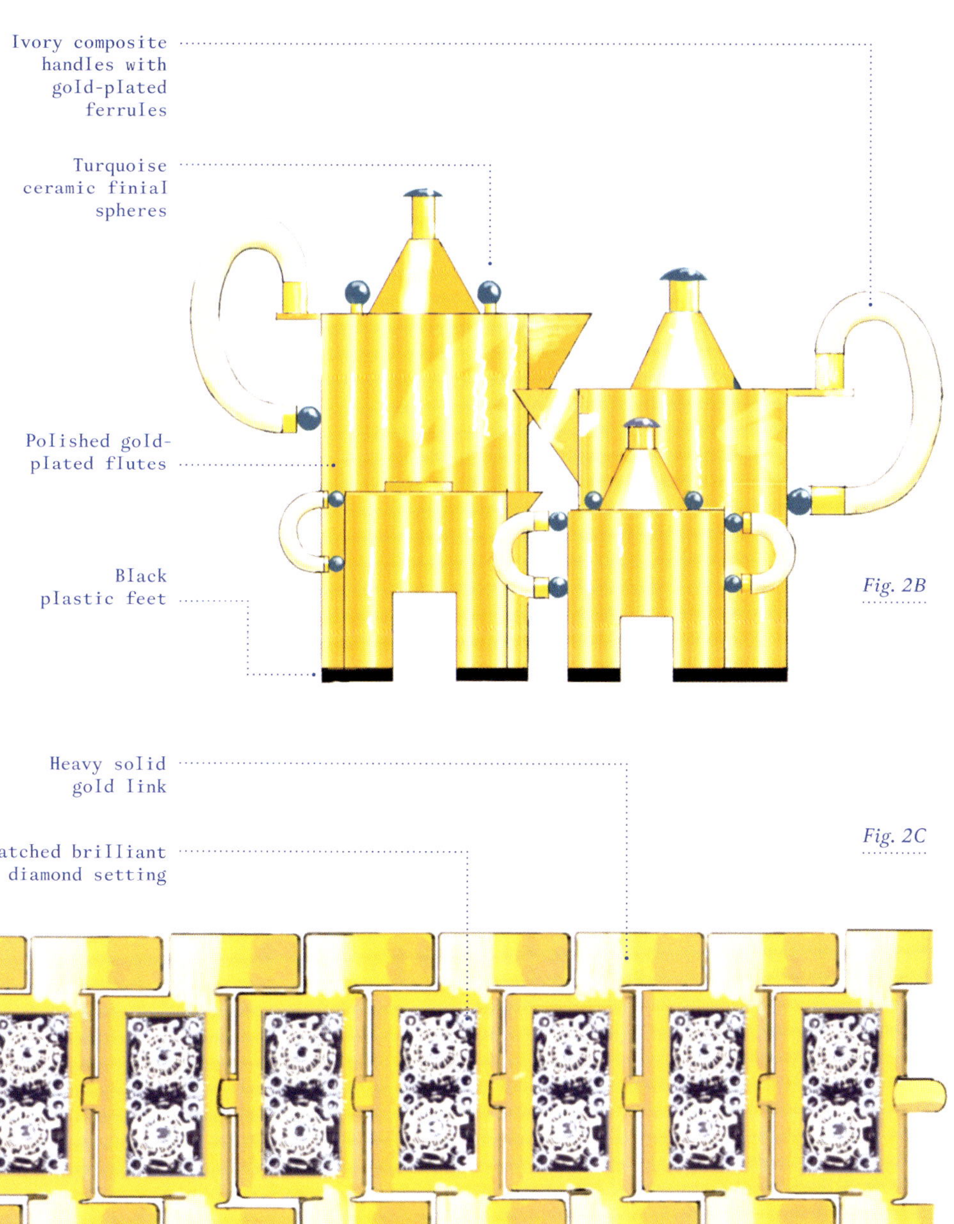

TEA AND COFFEE SERVICE (*Fig. 2B*),
28 CARAT DIAMOND IN 18 KARAT GOLD LINK BRACELET (*Fig. 2C*)

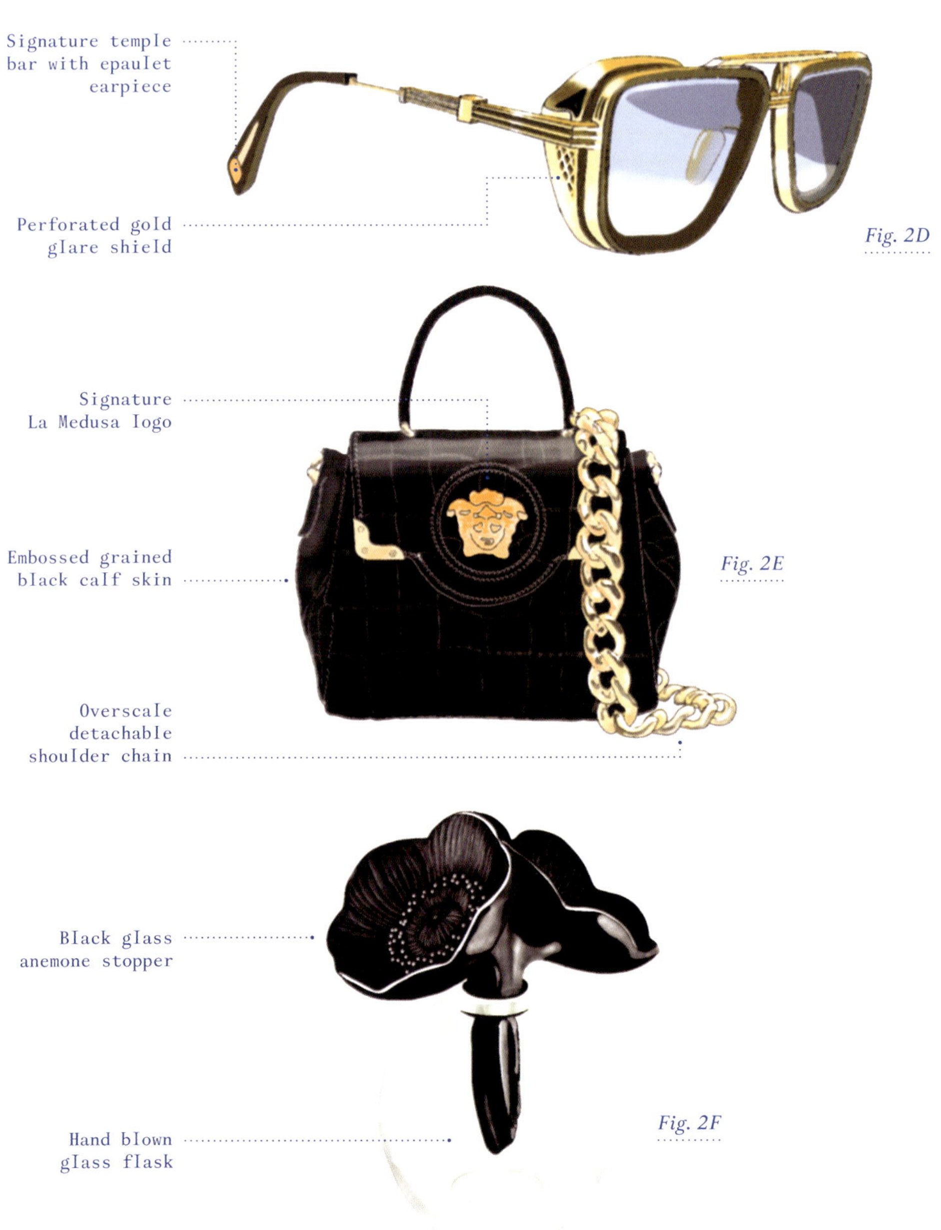

GTO-OBSIDIAN (*Fig. 2D*), LA MEDUSA HANDBAG (*Fig. 2E*), DEUX ANÉMONES PERFUME BOTTLE (*Fig. 2F*)

Laminated glass column cover with mirror finish stainless steel interior reflector creates optical effect of emerald cut precious stone

Fig. 2G

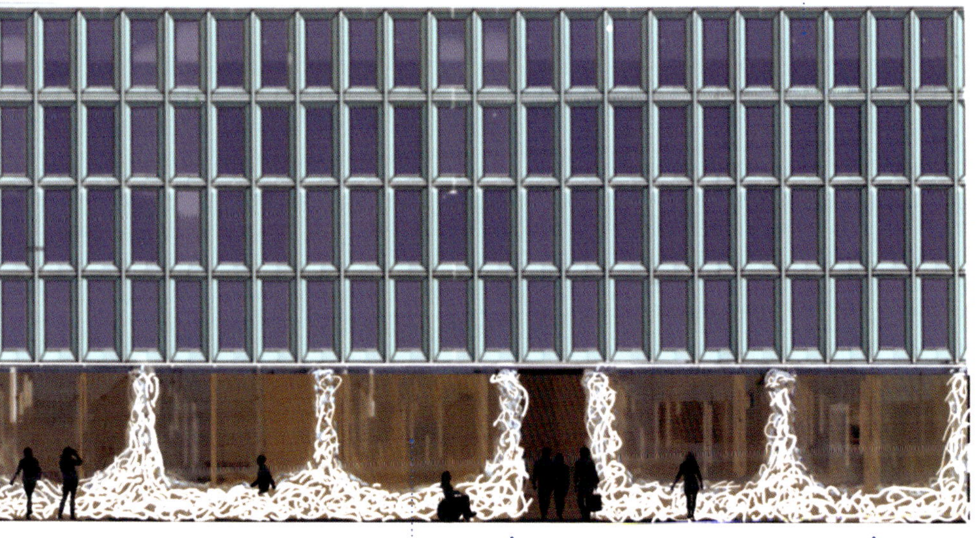

Copper column covers (behind fence)

Cast Aluminum "Graffiti" fence

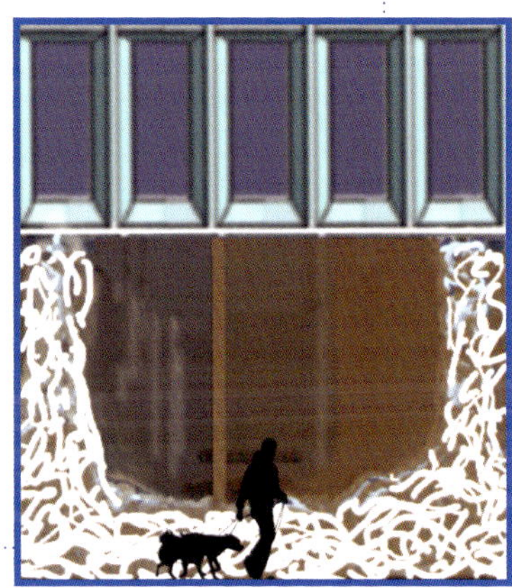

Fig. 2G.1
127 feet long and up to 27 feet high and fabricated by EXYD with engineering by DeSimone, the design of this cast aluminum fence was derived from NYC graffiti which was first modeled with computer software before prototyping in polystyrene foam. Installed in 2006, it has no immediate forbears.

40 BOND APARTMENT BUILDING (*Fig. 2G*)

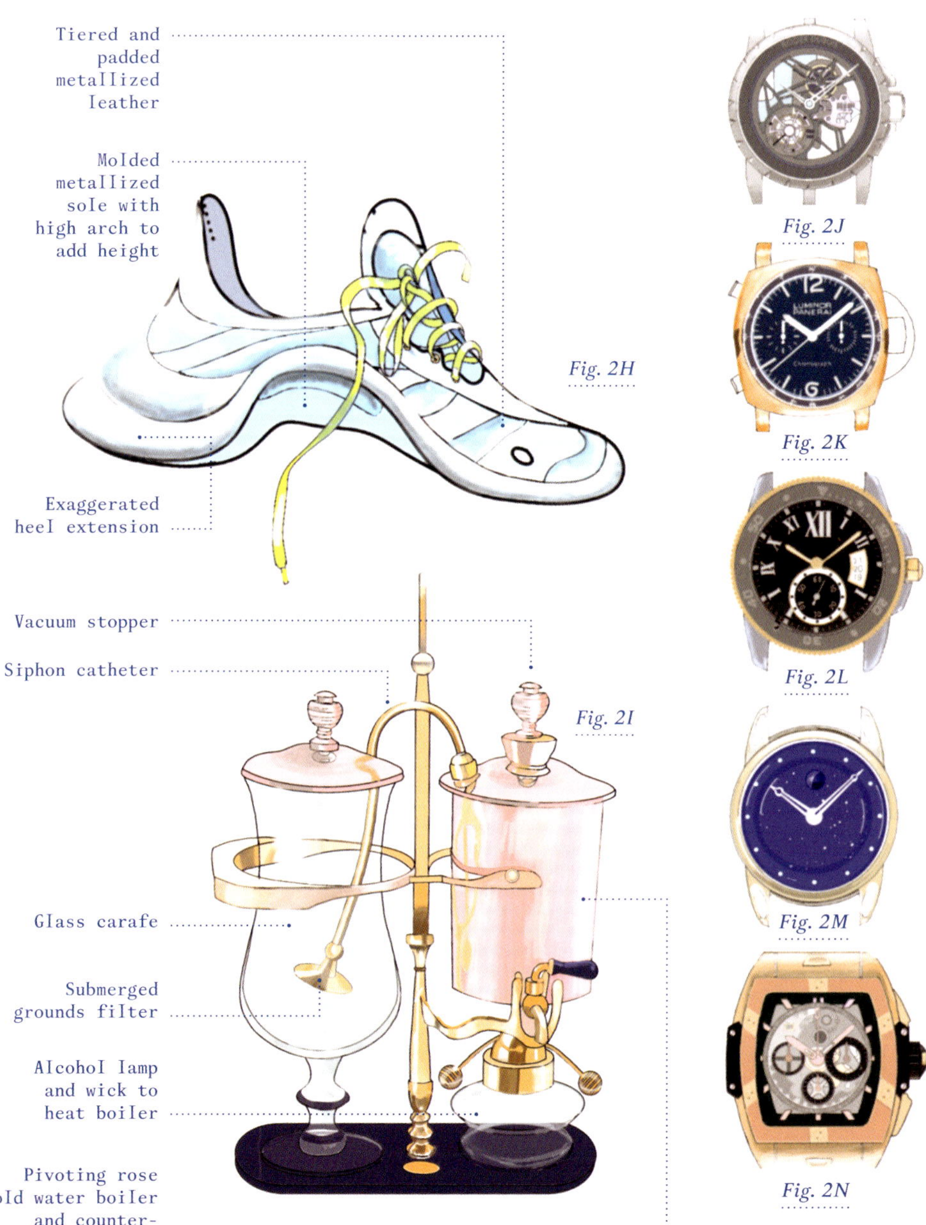

Fig. 2H

Fig. 2I

Fig. 2J

Fig. 2K

Fig. 2L

Fig. 2M

Fig. 2N

LV ARCHLIGHT SNEAKER (*Fig. 2H*),
AVANT GARDE ROYAL COFFEE MAKER (*Fig. 2I*),
EXCALIBUR FLYING MONOTOURBILLON TITANIUM WATCH (*Fig. 2J*),
LUMINOR CHRONO GOLDTECH WATCH (*Fig. 2K*),
CALIBRE DE CARTIER (*Fig. 2L*), DB25 MOON PHASE STARRY SKY (*Fig. 2M*),
KING GOLD, SPIRIT OF BIG BANG (*Fig. 2N*)

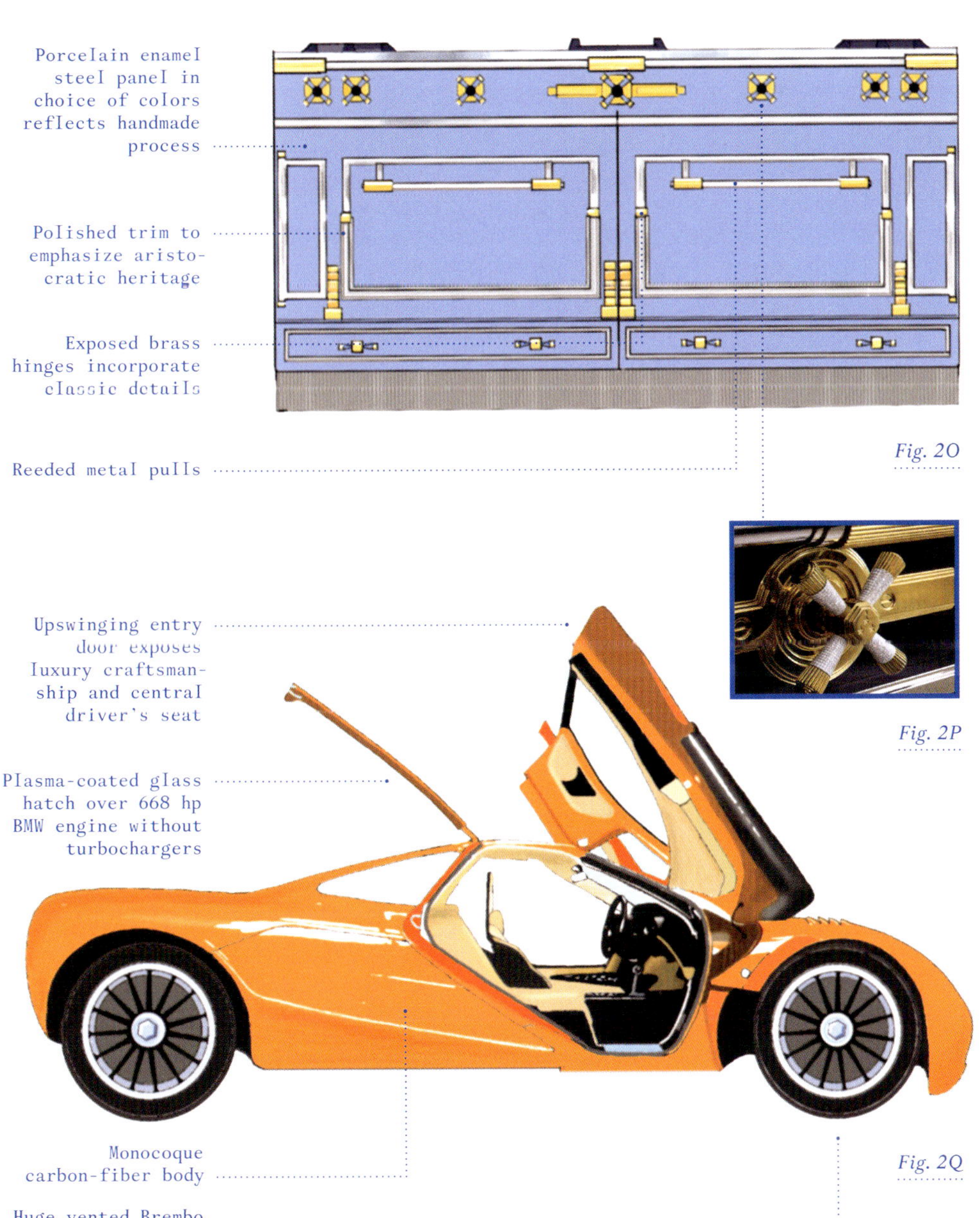

CHÂTEAU SUPRÊME GRAND PALAIS 180 RANGE (*Fig. 2O*), CONTROL KNOB (*Fig. 2P*), MCLAREN CAR F1 LM (*Fig. 2Q*)

Chapter 3

Fig. 3A–3J

MESSAGE

"TEASE
THE EYES TO
MAKE YOU
LOOK HARDER."

ATTRIBUTES

SHEER, FROSTED, PERFORATED MATERIALS,
GLIMPSES OF STRUCTURE AMID
REFLECTIONS AND HIGHLIGHTS SUGGEST
MYSTERY AND SEDUCTIVE APPEAL.

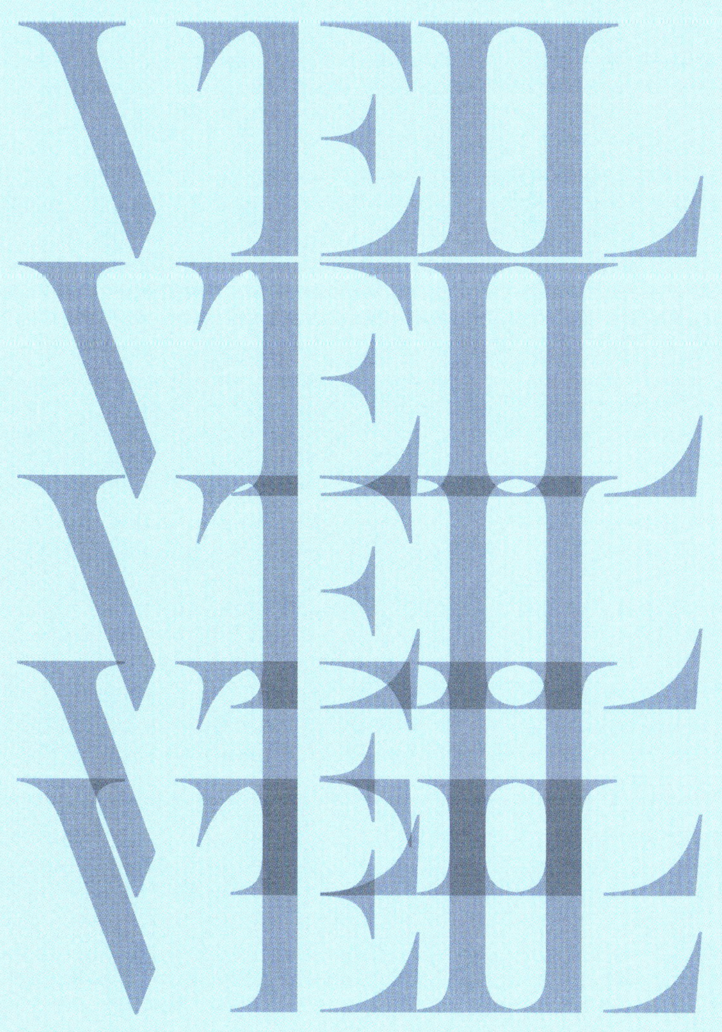

Some ability to look deep inside of things has long existed—through the anatomical etchings of Vesalius, glass mason jars and beer bottles, the X-ray vision of comic-book heroes, and the exploded diagrams in instruction manuals—but views into the inner workings of common-place items were not ubiquitous until the advent of transparent plastic products in the nineteen sixties.

Of course, variants on the theme of transparency or translucency had already, from the time of Solomon, provided a medium for seduction and erotic display. From the diaphanous robes depicted in ancient mosaics to the veils popularized by movie stars like Greta Garbo, peek-a-boo optics have enriched surfaces and flirted with the eye, implying, yet denying, visual access.

Architecturally, veiling has long been an essential part of buildings like the Taj Mahal and other Islamic structures, particularly in hot climates, reflecting the cultural and climactic importance of modesty, layers of privacy, and shading. But it took on a somewhat different language in the '50s and '60s, when concrete breeze-block screens, fretwork, and parades of slim columns – as in the work of Wallace Harrison and Edward Durell Stone – began to wrap more and more buildings, notably in places like Palm Springs, California, the desert where Mid-Century Modern design flourished.

In the first half of the 20th Century, Bakelite, a precursor to see-through materials like Plexiglas, Lucite, and Styrene, was widely molded into costume jewelry, cutlery handles, and objects like stylish streamlined radios, but it was darkly opaque and brittle. There had already been exotic applications of Plexiglas, first introduced in 1933, in the blow-molded canopies of fighter aircraft and the occasional bespoke starlet's dressing table, but it wasn't until reality caught up with the future that the material's true potential came into everyday use.

By the 1980s, the technical means to replace multiple parts of a traditional tool or appliance with a single, molded-plastic component, serving as both interior framework and exterior shell, made it possible to use the inner parts as design elements. That sensibility – backed by advances in chemistry that enabled plastics to assume reliable, structural roles – led to the transformation of nearly everything from skylights to sports helmets. Soon, the wood or metal casework of radios and automotive interiors were replaced by one-piece, injection-molded parts that were not only less expensive, but also outperformed their ancestors.

The aesthetic revolution that followed led to widespread applications, which exploited the material's transparency and fluidity, generating a spectrum of sometimes colorful, smoothly contoured versions of everything from toys and dinnerware to furnishings. Of particular note were Erwin and Estelle Laverne's application of vacuum-forming techniques to produce voluptuous, see-through domestic furniture in the sixties. The subsequent decade brought its own explosion of transparent design: the Accutron watch with tiny transistors and a miniature tuning fork audibly pulsing beneath a plastic crystal; inflatable furniture; and clear umbrellas and rainwear by prominent, avant-garde fashion designers. Transparency was in the air!

Soon, the sheathing of ubiquitous, high-rise, corporate architecture went from relatively small panes of glass with gridded mullions to continuous, wrap-around skins of glass, visibly bound only by lustrous metal bands, as in SOM/Gordon Bunshaft's design for the Pepsi-Cola Building (c.1960), in New York City.

Spurred by the inherent beauty of printed circuit boards – which had advanced in the mid-1950s with revolutionary etching and lamination techniques – designers began to explore the potential of exposed electronic parts. Quite beautiful in their own right, with their near-microscopic patterns of digital circuitry, they soon became integral design elements, often revealed through clear plastic casework. Particularly influential, the transparent Swatch watches and telephones of the early 1980s – picking up where the pre-electronic Accutron watches left off – exposed intricate, color-coded parts that had previously been hidden away. This approach fueled a long-dormant interest in the inner workings of even quite ordinary things.

Architecturally, that sensibility was persuasively expressed in the tiny façade of Toshiko Mori's Pleats Please (1998) in New York City. Passersby were intrigued by a seductive game of hide and seek achieved by a glass storefront treated with a special optical film that becomes transparent or translucent depending on one's point of view.

On yet another scale, this trend peaked with Apple's translucent, multi-hued iMac G3 computers in the late 1990s and early 2000s. Emotionally and visually distanced from the inscrutable black (or taupe) boxes associated with corporate dominance, they offered the ability to peer *inside*, helping demystify the implicit inequality of the human-machine interface. With that single gesture, they won the trust of wary homemakers and hobbyists. Later, Apple began to feature transparency in its retail stores, originally designed by Bohlin Cywinski Jackson and later, in even more unprecedented designs, by Foster + Partners/Norman Foster, pioneering the concept of retail spaces with crisp, white surfaces, floors of polished concrete, and vast expanses of glass unbroken by a single support. Structurally daring – and destined to remain in sketchbooks until engineering and manufacturing innovations conspired to enable their realization – they have offered wondrous examples of the seductive power of transparency. In erasing the visual boundaries between public space and retail activity, blurring the lines of propriety, a new kind of liminal volume emerged, which invites even casual passersby to partake in its environment.

Veil Observations

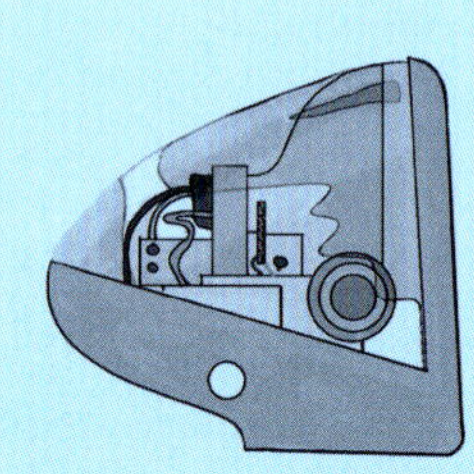

Fig. 3A BONDI BLUE IMAC (p. 96)

YEAR 1998
DESIGNER
Apple Industrial Design Group, Jonathan Ive
MANUFACTURER
Apple Computer Inc., USA

As a streamlined, transparent techno bubble, the iMac broke from the design assumptions of the traditional form of office equipment with a view to reposition the computer as a consumer product. Using a form language that had long been a staple of the automotive industry, the design went one step further (no doubt inspired by the instant success of the Swatch watch) to reveal the inherent beauty of the electronics within.

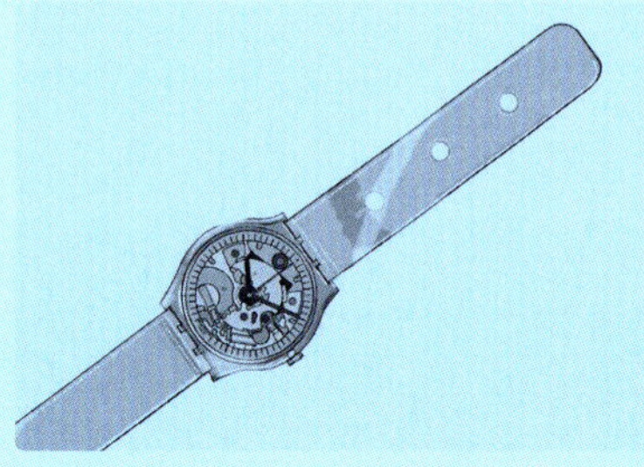

Fig. 3B JELLYFISH WATCH, GK 100 (p. 96)

YEAR 1983
MANUFACTURER
Swatch AG, Switzerland

The tremors in the Swiss watch industry that followed the introduction of the SWATCH still reverberate throughout the world of design, as it was arguably the first consumer product to feature brightly colored components encased within a transparent body. As such it became a world-wide phenomenon within a few months and is still a durable collectible in the age of the Apple watch.

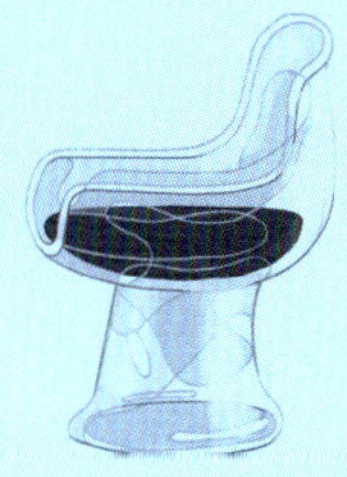

Fig. 3C DAFFODIL LOUNGE CHAIR FROM INVISIBLE GROUP (p. 97)

YEAR 1957
DESIGNERS
Erwine and Estelle Laverne
MANUFACTURER
Laverne International, USA

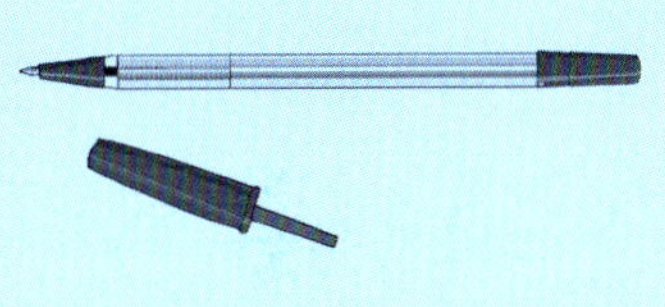

Fig. 3D BIC CRISTAL (p. 98)

YEAR 1950
DESIGNER
Décolletage Plastic Design Team
MANUFACTURER
Société Bic, France

An industrial process generally applied to consumer packaging, aircraft canopies, and other sheet-molding operations was adopted to create this nearly invisible line of furniture in the late '50s. Perfectly aligned with the emerging pop culture which embraced ready-made, novel forms and images, it enjoyed both critical and commercial success until the demise of its manufacturer.

The traditional components of the fountain pen have been discarded in this ball-point pen design that appropriates the structure of an ordinary wood pencil, with an ink gel reservoir in place of graphite and a clear plastic shaft in place of a wooden casing. Visual inspection of the remaining gel helps to estimate the lifespan of the pen.

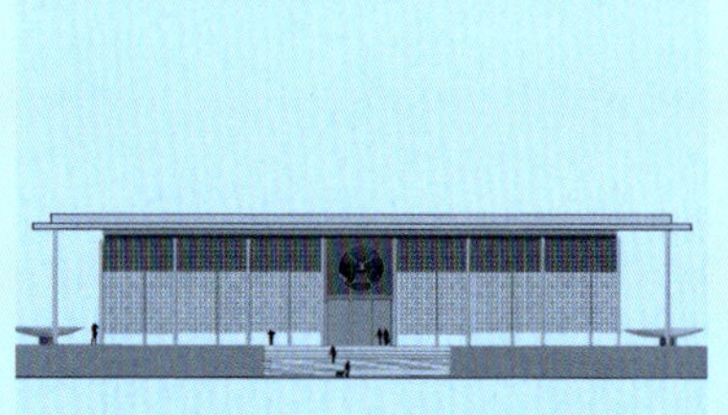

Fig. 3E U.S. EMBASSY (p. 98)

YEAR 1959
ARCHITECT
Edward Durell Stone
LOCATION
New Delhi, India

At a time before security concerns forced US embassies to become impregnable fortresses, the transparency and elegance conferred by this US Embassy's vocabulary of slim golden columns, lace-like walls, and pure, uncompromised geometry reinforced an idealistic version of America's commitment to peace and prosperity.

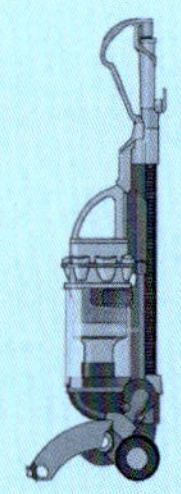

Fig. 3F UPRIGHT VACUUM CLEANER, DC14 (p. 99)

YEAR 2004
DESIGNER
Sir James Dyson
MANUFACTURER
Dyson Limited, Singapore

By capturing, then displaying, the collected spoils from an ordinary floor, the Dyson vacuum was the first to consider the debris itself as a design element and thereby launched a revolution in consumer appliances. Key to its success was to replace the traditional collection bag with a transparent cylindrical container within which the spiraling refuse could be seen.

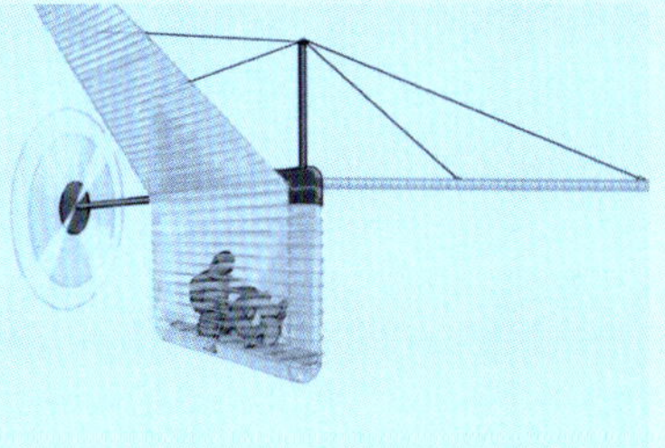

Fig. 3G GOSSAMER ALBATROSS (p. 100)

YEAR 1977
DESIGNER
Paul MacCready
LOCATION
California, USA

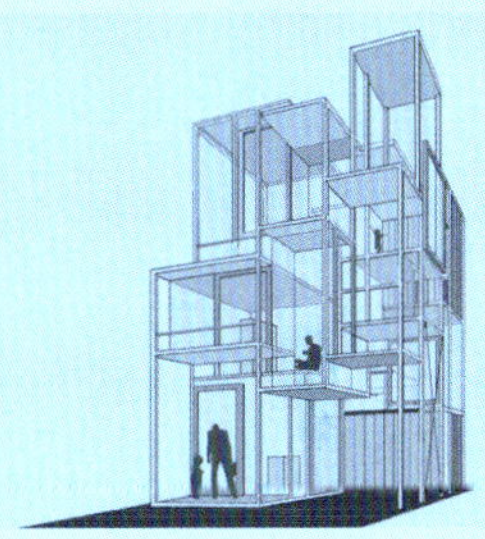

Fig. 3H HOUSE NA (p. 100)

YEAR 2011
ARCHITECT
Sou Fujimoto Architects
LOCATION
Tokyo, Japan

Paul MacCready's quest for human powered flight was dependent on the creation of an airframe with an eye-popping ratio of weight to the area of lifting surfaces. Every element, including the "skin" on the wings was scrutinized for opportunities to save weight. A material very much like clear household wrap was finally identified and applied, which gave the "Albatross" its distinctive, and revolutionary, see-through appearance. Coincidently, designers in the fashion industry had discovered a similar material and began showcasing it in avant-garde designs.

Crystalline glassed-in rooms with minimum structure have been arranged in a sculptural array to create vertical domestic spaces linked by stairs, sliding doors, and open terraces. Equally sized slim steel columns throughout emphasize the minimalist design ethic, while sliding and hinged doors featuring wide wooden stiles act as rhythmic punctuation marks.

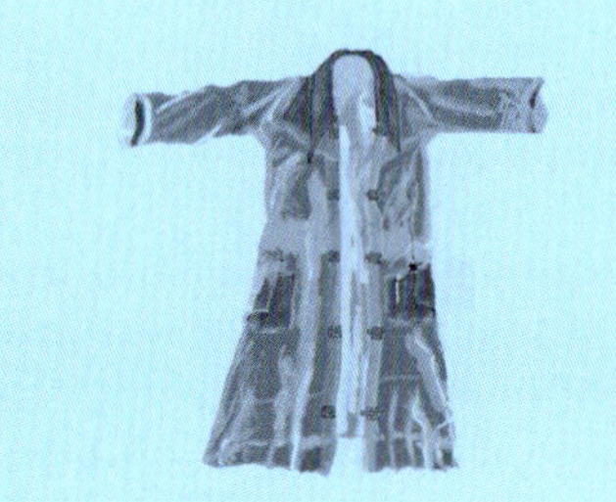

Fig. 3I VINYL RAINCOAT
(p. 101)

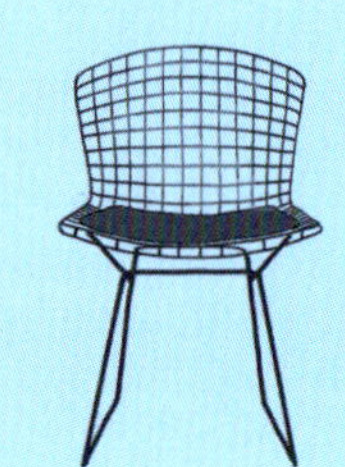

Fig. 3J SIDE CHAIR
(p. 101)

DESIGNER
Betsey Johnson
MADE IN
London, England

YEAR 1952
DESIGNER
Harry Bertoia
MANUFACTURER
Knoll
International,
Inc., USA

Flexible, waterproof plastic film was often utilized for stylish clothing by radical designer Betsey Johnson who sometimes utilized military-style hardware on the transparent surfaces of dresses to add decorative detail. In the years since, the supple material has evolved into an instant dose of future fashion.

Although the idea for a functional outdoor seating surface made of a wire grid was well established, the sculptor Harry Bertoia, who was highly regarded for the decorative screens he had installed in prestige buildings around the world, took advantage of the grid's ductility to mold a sturdy organic form which was comfortable as well as transparent, and thus able to adapt easily to a myriad of environments.

Veil Illustrations

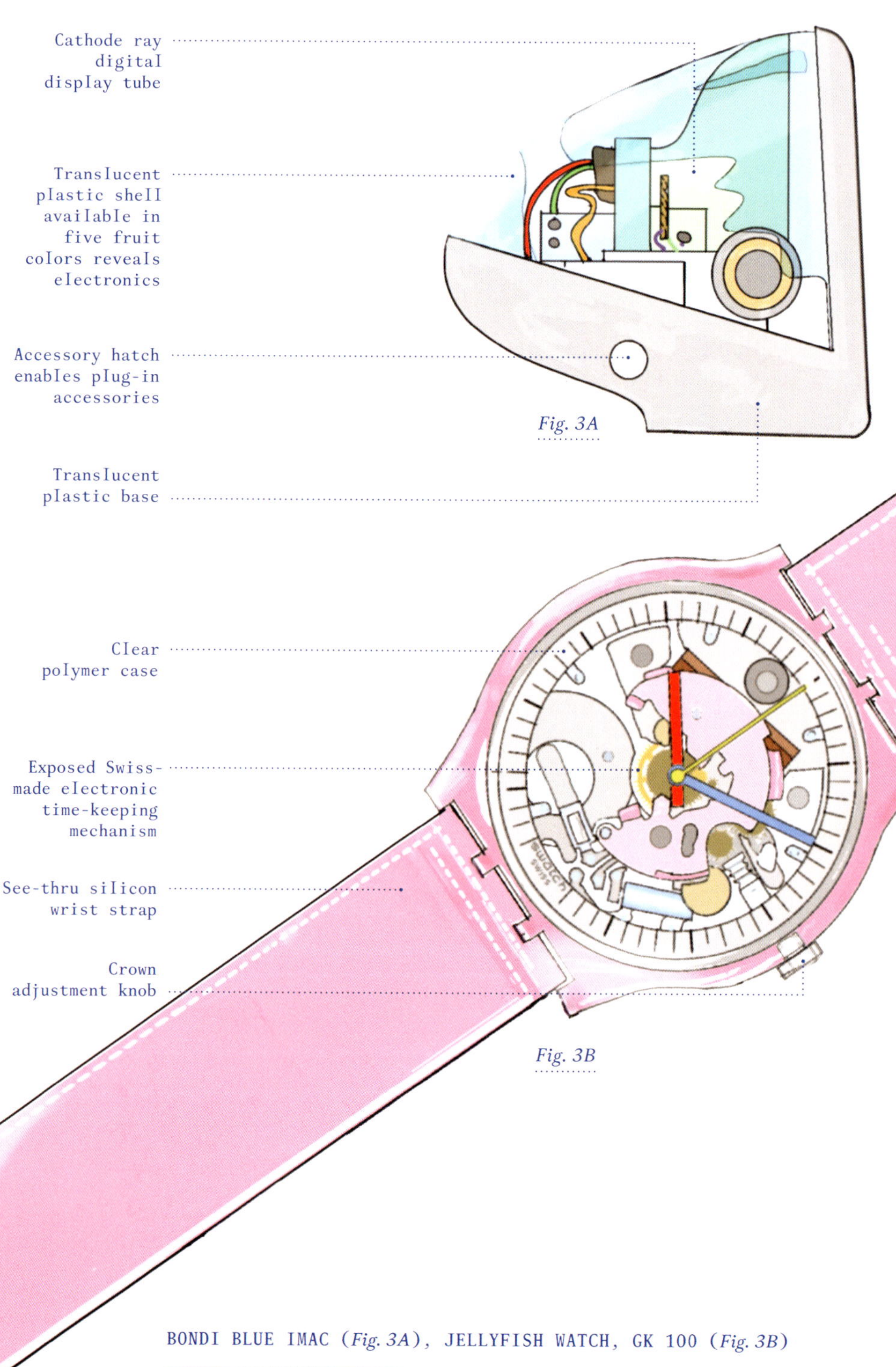

BONDI BLUE IMAC (*Fig. 3A*), JELLYFISH WATCH, GK 100 (*Fig. 3B*)

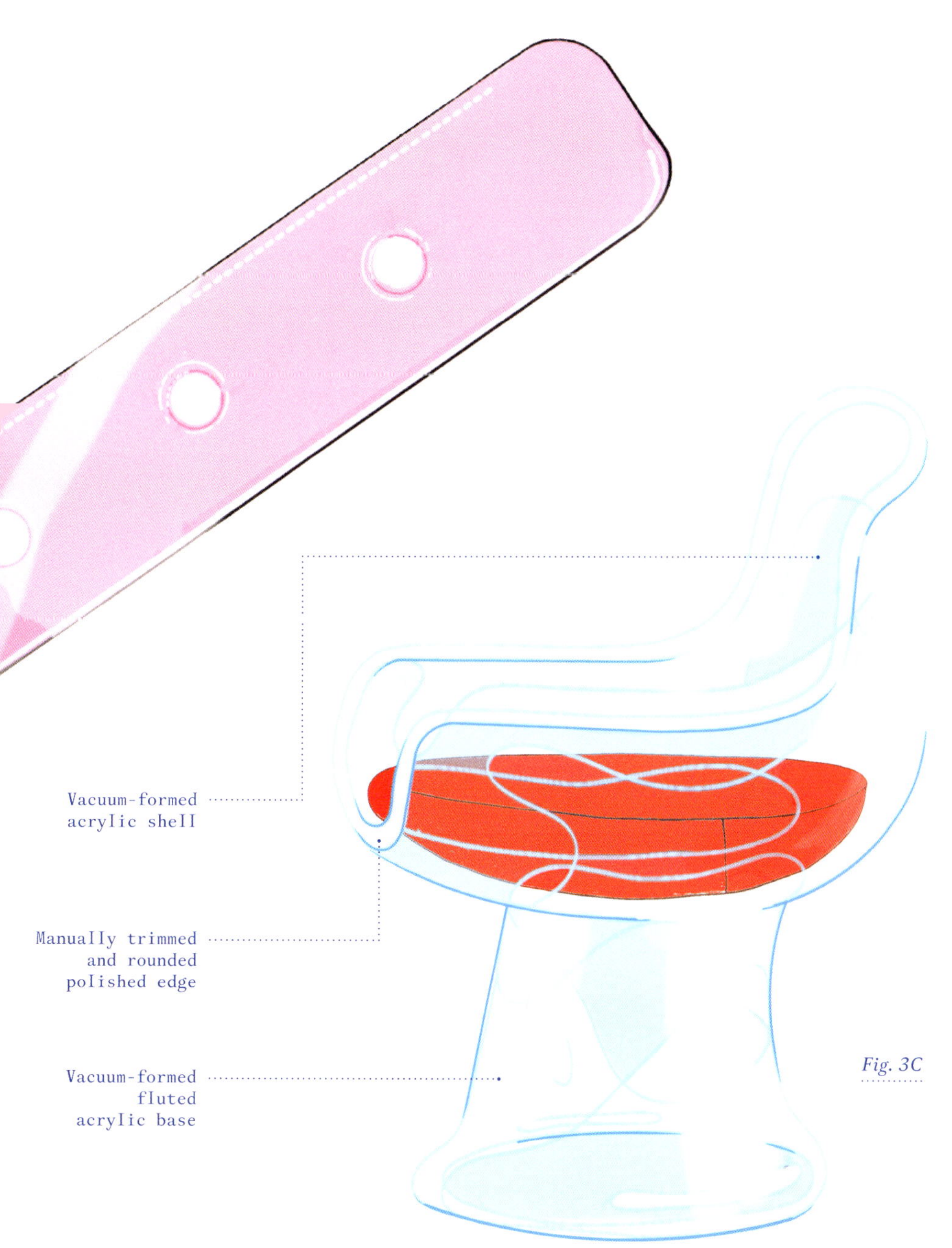

DAFFODIL LOUNGE CHAIR FROM INVISIBLE GROUP (*Fig. 3C*)

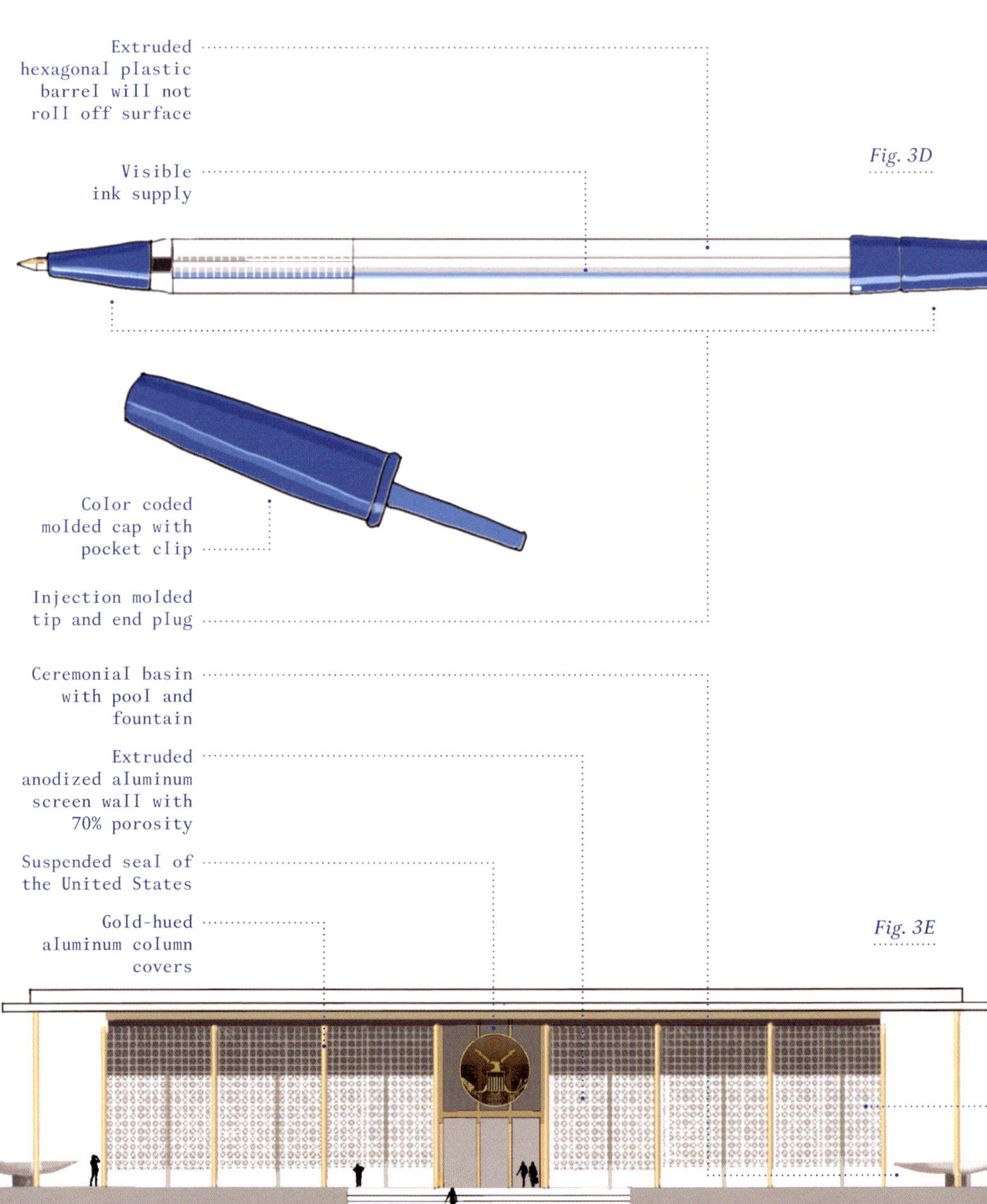

BIC CRISTAL (*Fig. 3D*), U.S. EMBASSY (*Fig. 3E*)

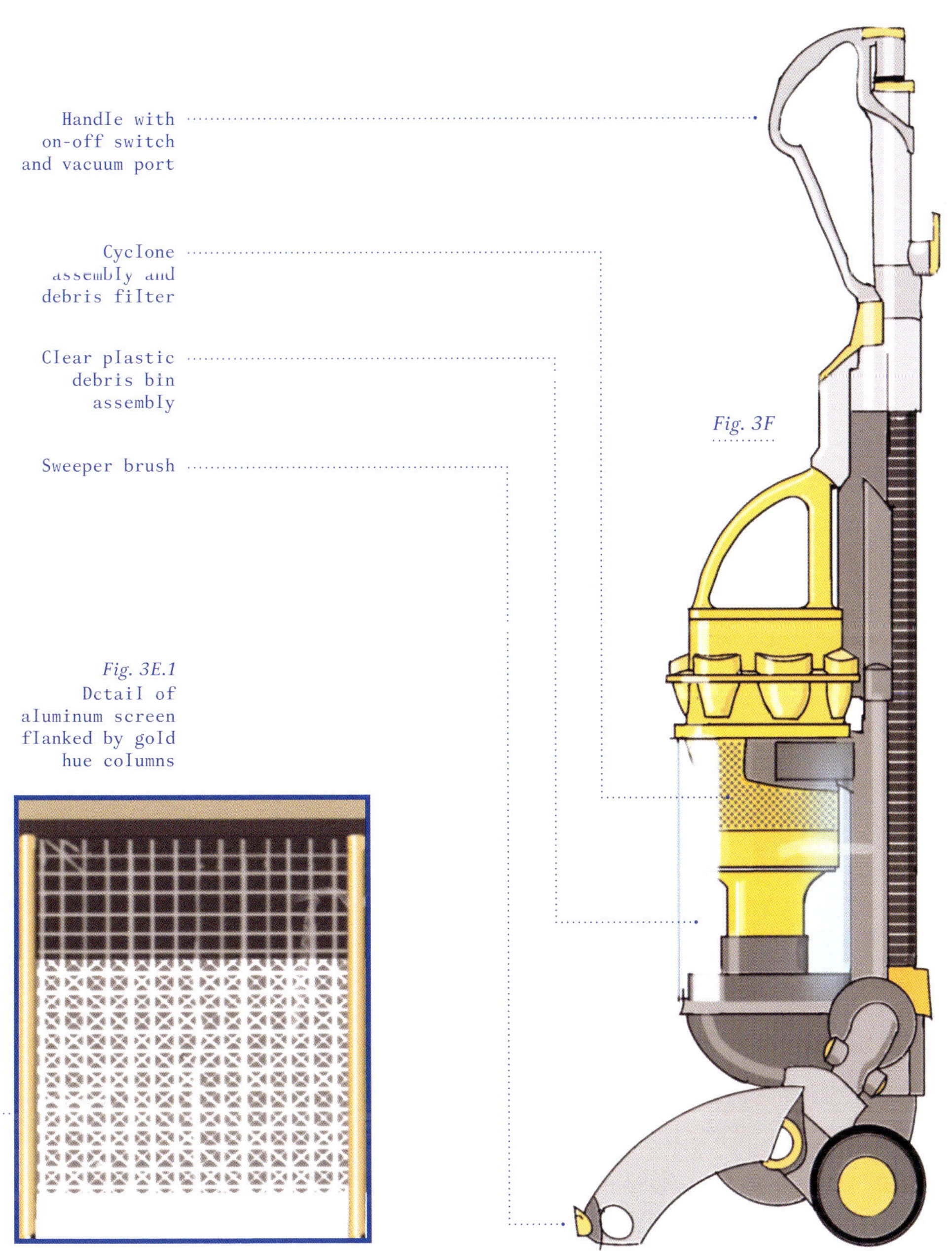

UPRIGHT VACUUM CLEANER, DC14 (*Fig. 3F*)

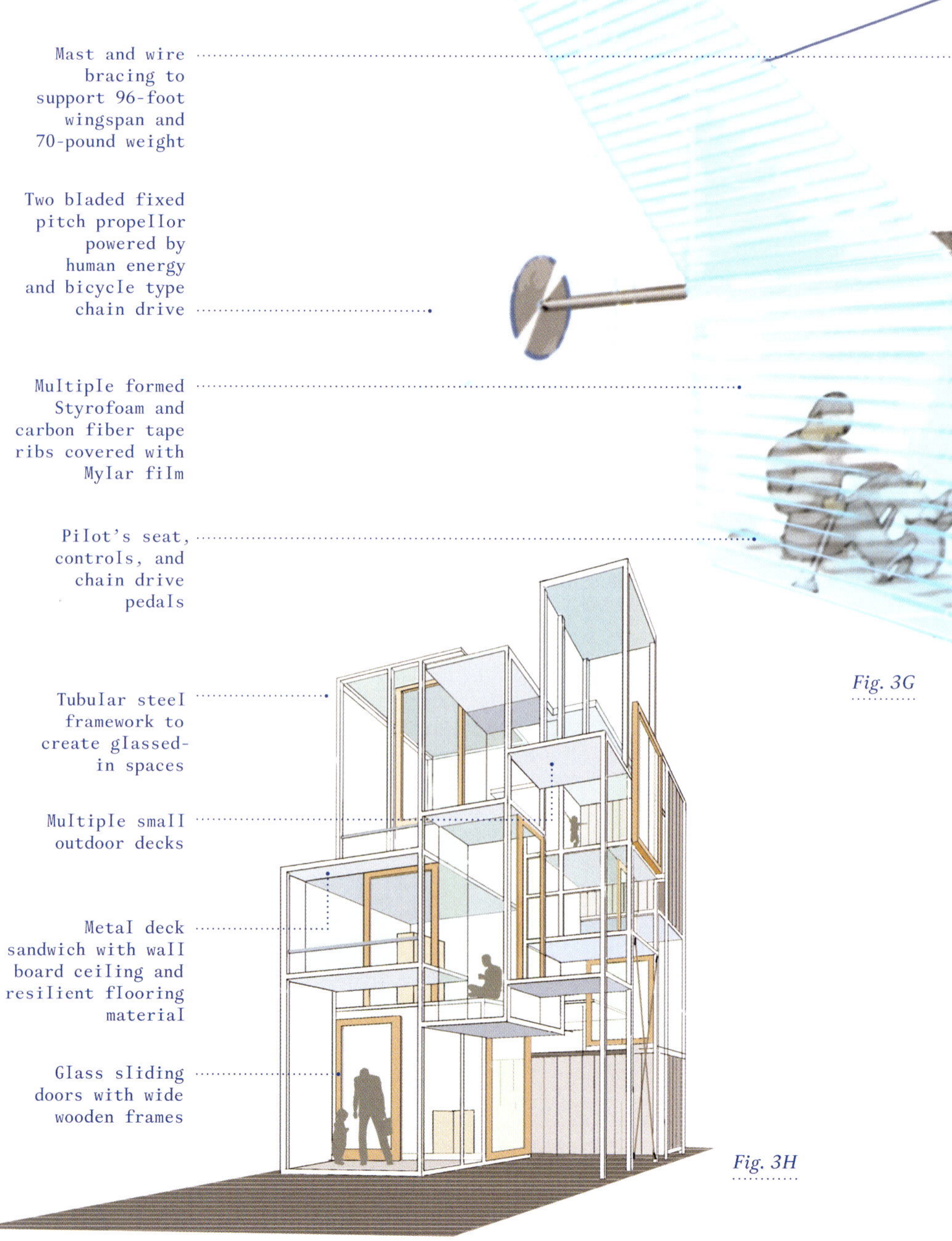

Fig. 3G

Fig. 3H

GOSSAMER ALBATROSS (*Fig. 3G*), HOUSE NA (*Fig. 3H*)

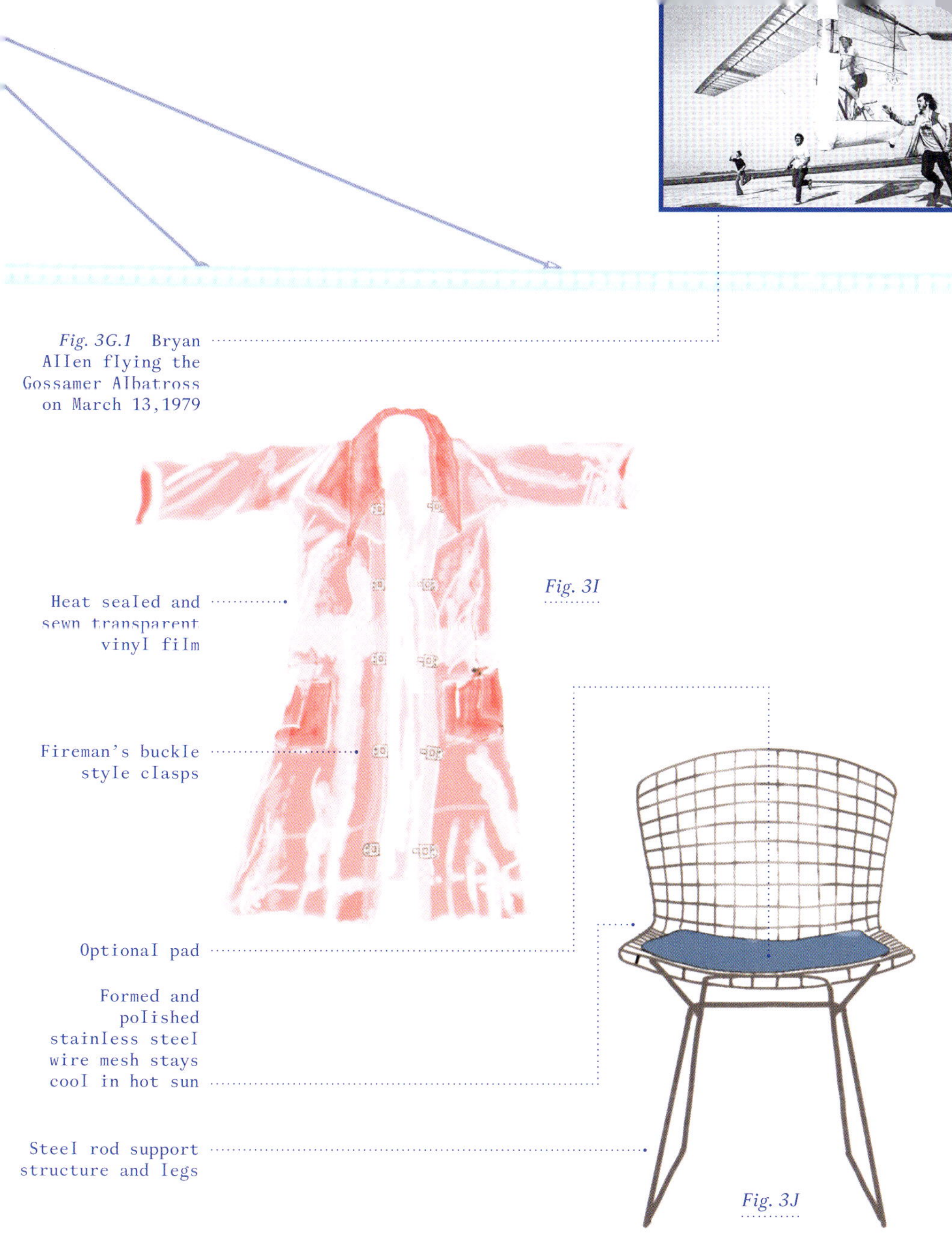

VINYL RAINCOAT (*Fig. 3I*), SIDE CHAIR (*Fig. 3J*)

Message:
"Brandish what's inside and show off their innards."

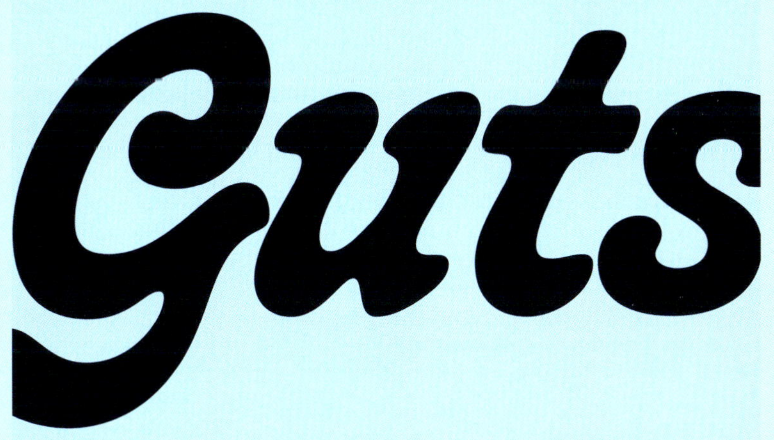

Attributes:
Out in the open forms featuring parts responding to function, touch, control, and capacity with finishes ready for prime time.

Exposure of the "intimate" parts of a device would have been considered rude, even scandalous, during Victoria's reign, when it was deemed immodest even to reveal the stubby legs supporting a divan. But, with the arrival of contraptions like the motorcar, for which there was originally no remedy but to expose the chains and gears of propulsion, the prohibition began to lift.

However, it was to return gradually first with Henry Ford's Model A (1927), with many of its mechanical necessities hidden beneath a sheet-metal carapace. Later, Norman Bel Geddes, who transformed brutish steam locomotives into sleek, metallic, futuristic icons, proposed teardrop-shaped, streamlined vehicles, during the '20s and late '30s, that set the tone for the unified designs that would henceforth conceal mechanical bits from prying eyes.

Thus, the intimate parts of objects, furnishings, and buildings remained more or less covered up through successive waves of 20th Century design – Bauhaus, Streamline Moderne, Art Deco, and so on – until 1977, when the winning design for Paris's Centre Pompidou, by architects Renzo Piano and Richard Rogers, exposed the building's mechanical systems, even on the facade, applying liberal swaths of comic book color and establishing the style now known as "high tech."

The shock waves that followed have reverberated ever since through the worlds of fashion, music, and transportation design, but the object that most exemplifies the aesthetic rewards of naked mechanical parts had already been gleaming in plain sight for nearly a century: the motorcycle and its pedaled companion, the bicycle. Both bring out a fetish-like desire to groom each component, no matter how obscure, with the care usually reserved for fine jewelry.

Consider also the dune buggy, with its chromium-and-aluminum power plant peeking out impolitely from beneath its fiberglass skirt (or shell), or Marilyn Monroe's iconic duet with a subway vent in the *Seven Year Itch* (1955), watched with a mix of innocence and scandal, or much later and more provocatively, the snaps, buckles, elastic bands, and exaggerated brassiere cups visibly corseting Madonna's frame during performance.

All these (wink-wink) inadvertent exposures have become normalized, some even reveling in what was once, at best, taboo or, at worst, highly sexualized transgression – much of it now strutted by rap performers and paraded by celebrities on the red carpet.

Whether in the fins of the air-cooled petrol engines of motorcycles or Volkswagens, or in the rhythmic visual staccato of spot welds or louvers on exotic automobiles, or even in the concentric stitch lines on 1950s "torpedo" bras, pure functionality optically reinforces the geometry of form, accentuating, sometimes even fetishizing, the object itself. The seams on early nylons and, later, fishnet stockings – like the pronounced, riveted dorsal seam splitting the rear window of a Bugatti Type 57 – imply their removal, and thus the exposure of the secrets within.

The craftsmen that spend their weekends building hot rods or their cousins, the "rat rods," take pride in displaying the transformation of aluminum billets into polished superchargers, exhaust manifolds, and controls – all components increasingly hidden from view in contemporary cars.

And now the widespread use of 3D digital modeling tools has revolutionized tasks that were once best left to specialized illustrators or renderers, revealing, for example, views under the skin of racing cars, fighter aircraft, or other complex machinery, even as they are being designed. For architecture, such technology has made it common practice to integrate within a single document all the building systems, including electrical conduits, ductwork, and plumbing, combining in great detail and laying bare all the information required to construct a project.

In medical science, the ability to map relationships of various organs within the body, or view myriad thin slices of them, with magnetic resonance (MRI) and other imagining can quickly render what took Leonardo Da Vinci years to begin to document – while similar technology enables engineers to detect structural flaws, in buildings and bridges, that are invisible to the eye.

But it is in the realm of musical wind instruments, and manually adjusted mechanisms, such as string instruments, that complex analog devices still prevail in a convergence of technical finesse and human dexterity that has yielded many satisfying artifacts, most of which have endured centuries of use without perceived change. The baroque twists and turns of brass wind instruments, the knurled knobs of microscopes, and the escapements of analog timepieces all provide some respite from the increasingly hermetic innards of digital devices, continuing to unite function and visual intrigue with direct physical interaction.

Guts Observations

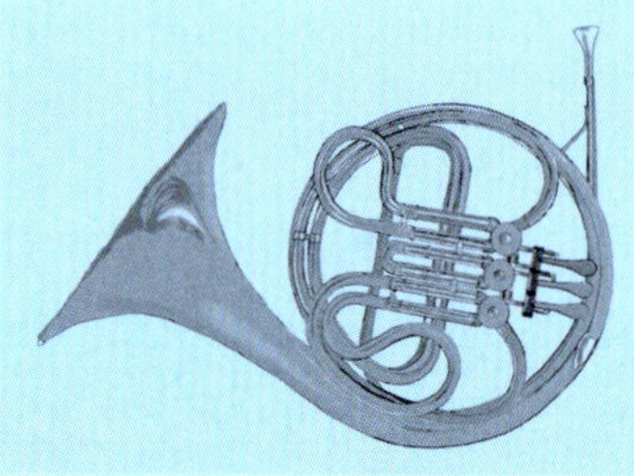

Fig. 4A

STANDARD F SINGLE HORN, YHR-314II
(p. 118)

MANUFACTURER
Yamaha Corporation, Japan

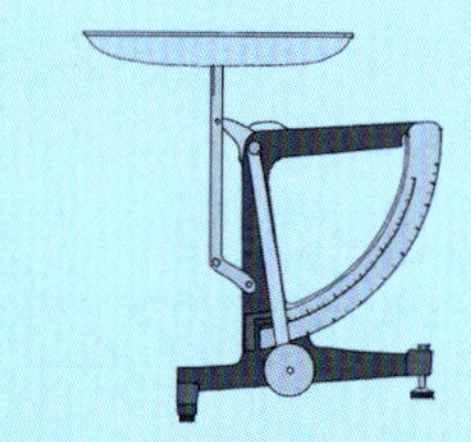

Fig. 4B

PENDULUM KITCHEN SCALE
(p. 118)

MANUFACTURER
Kikkerland Design Inc., USA

Of all the musical instruments, the French Horn offers the most alluring combination of curves and polished metal. A miracle of early nineteenth century sonic engineering, it is featured in innumerable adverts and album covers and has been transformed into logotypes from which its silhouette announces musical events of all kinds.

The elegant simplicity of this scale lies in the careful articulation of each of its components, which are arrayed as if in a constructivist, minimal, sculpture.

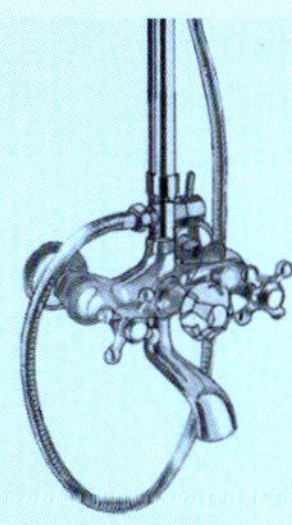

Fig. 4C

BRASS RAIN DUAL SHOWER HEAD
(p. 119)

MANUFACTURER
Juno Showers, USA

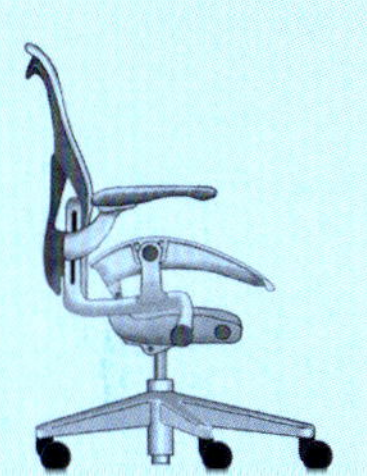

Fig. 4D

AERON CHAIR B
(p. 119)

YEAR 1994
DESIGNERS
Don Chadwick and Bill Stumpf
MANUFACTURER
Herman Miller, Inc., USA

An elaborate tangle of taps, leads, and a flexible hose enables precise control of water temperature and volume in this tour de force of plumbing ingenuity. Perhaps overly complicated by modern standards, it offers visual intrigue rather than touchscreen convenience.

In the years since Herman Miller provided a high-end precedent for the use of die-cast aluminum in office furniture, the Aeron chair was the first to refine and expose the multiple mechanisms that enable a wide range of convenient adjustments which are essential contributors to comfort for those bound to a desk. Now the standard in office furniture, it is widely imitated by manufacturers around the world.

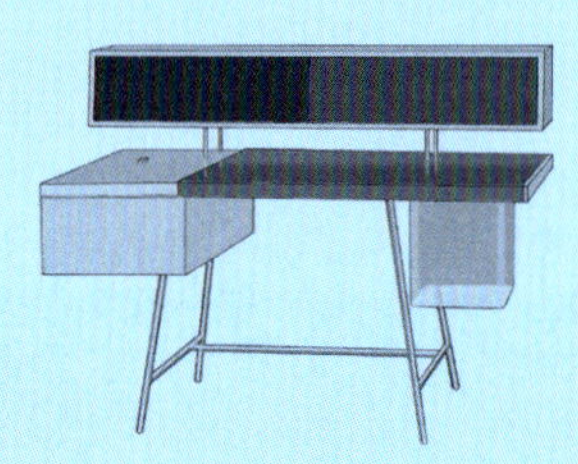

Fig. 4E HOME DESK
(p. 120)

YEAR 1946
DESIGNER
George Nelson
MANUFACTURER
Vitra,
Switzerland

It appears that a process of design by sorting through a parts bin to hack together a functioning desk was responsible for this syncopated essay on material properties and appropriate uses. Far ahead of its time, when nascent design veered toward simple, digestible forms, it was an outlier which had never enjoyed either commercial success or critical appreciation. Nelson's creed that "total design is nothing more or less than a process of relating everything to everything" might be better recognized today as a sophisticated "hack."

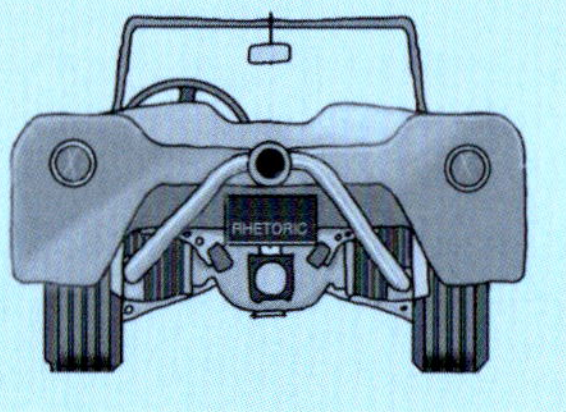

Fig. 4F VW DUNE BUGGY KIT KAR
(p. 120)

YEAR 1964
MANUFACTURER
Meyer Manx,
LLC, USA

This most basic of vehicles, single-minded in its pursuit of a lightweight, nearly indestructible beach toy, dispenses with the usual automotive parts bin. There are *no* doors, *no* hinges, *no* gauges, *no* glove box, *no* cup holders, *no* bonnet and *no* boot. The Volkswagen chassis, engine, and wheels rescued from a donor car and nakedly displayed beneath a fiberglass shell are impolite reminders of the origins of what remains the defining free-spirited image of surfing culture.

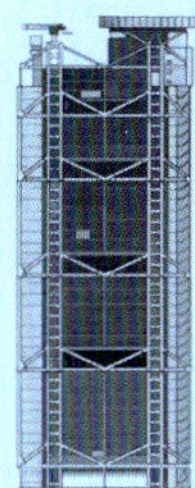

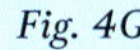

Fig. 4G

HONG KONG AND SHANGHAI BANK HEADQUARTERS
(p. 121)

YEAR 1986
ARCHITECT
Foster + Partners
LOCATION
Hong Kong, China

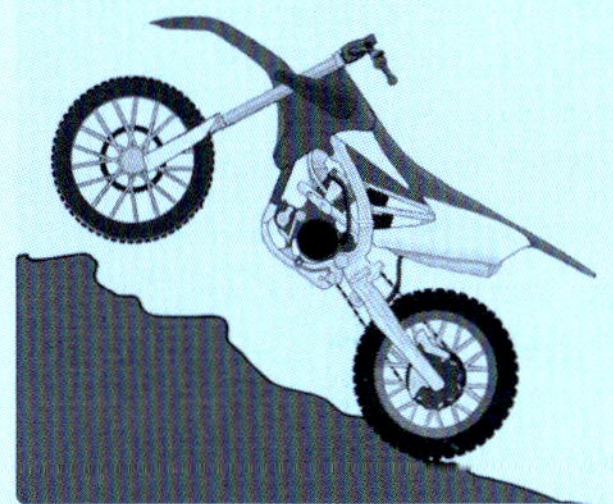

Fig. 4H

YAMAHA MOTORBIKE, YZ450F
(p. 122)

YEAR 2017
MANUFACTURER
Yamaha Motor Co., Ltd., Japan

With an exposed exoskeleton that incorporates bridge-like trusses piled one above the other while suspending a stack of office floors beneath each, the Hong Kong bank is perhaps the most iconic of the “high-tech” structural extravaganzas of the last Century. Like the Eiffel Tower, the Golden Gate Bridge, and the Apollo Assembly Building, it has become the defining example of a feat of pure ultra engineering and a centerpiece of the congested downtown area due to its elevated unobstructed ground floor and no compromises silhouette.

As the rear suspension pivots on the swooping exterior frame members that cradle the engine assembly, the elements of this bike’s design are both visible and poetic, expressing each function with flair and structural integrity.

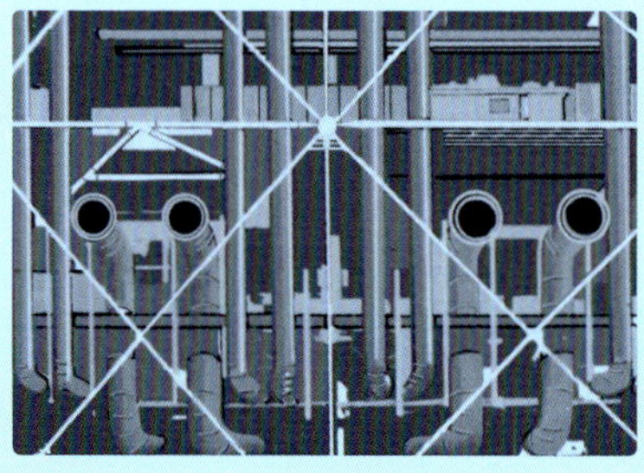

Fig. 4I THE CENTRE POMPIDOU (p. 123)

YEAR 1977
ARCHITECTS
Renzo Piano and Richard Rogers
LOCATION
Paris, France

The winning scheme from a competition organized by the City of Paris, the inside-out architecture of the Centre Pompidou, like a mammoth industrial machine, deploys meticulously designed functional parts in lieu of cladding, fenestration, and add-ons like louvers and screens. Normally internal functions, such as ducts for air conditioning are arranged for maximum efficiency, color coded, and cantilevered from the exterior structure of the building on forged steel gerberettes.

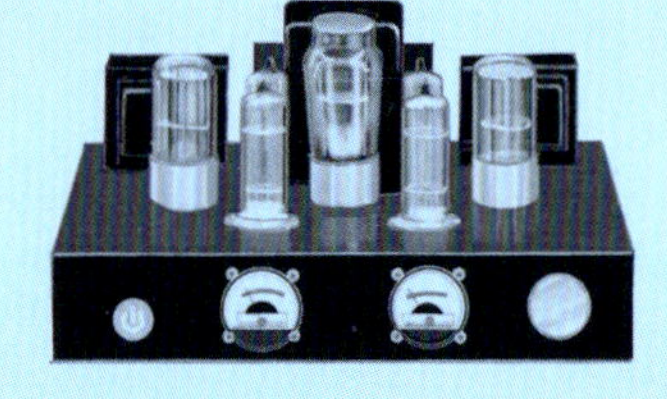

Fig. 4J HIFI VACUUM TUBE AMPLIFIER SOUND AMP (p. 123)

MANUFACTURER
Branwish, China

Usually draped with spider-webs, these units were secreted in heavy wooden cabinets until Sony's first transistors began to replace vacuum tubes with circuit boards. Now prized by connoisseurs of recorded music for their warm sonic timbre, and still in production, such units hark back to a time when technologic novelty was at its apogee.

Guts Illustrations

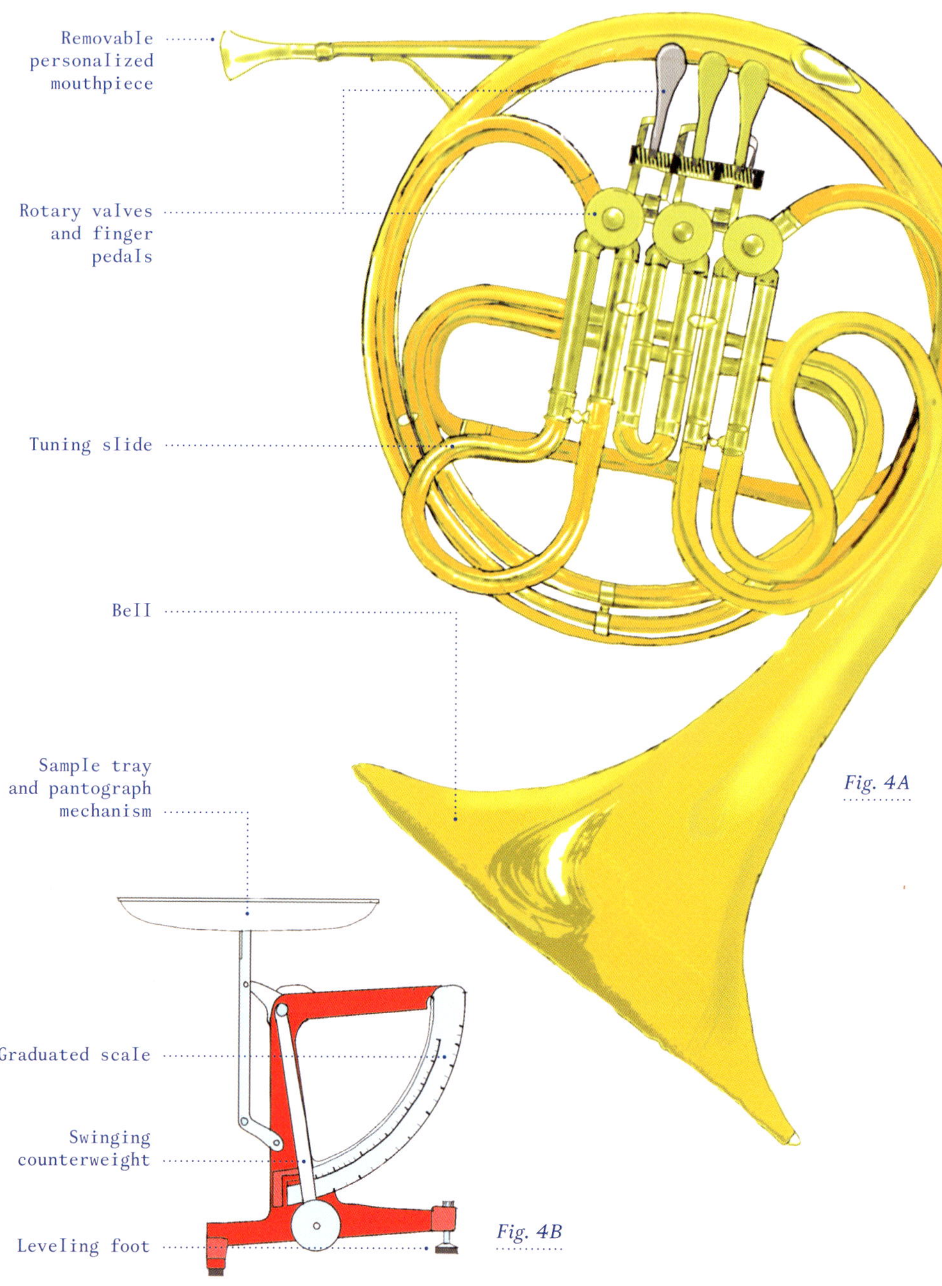

STANDARD F SINGLE HORN, YHR-314II (*Fig. 4A*),
PENDULUM KITCHEN SCALE (*Fig. 4B*)

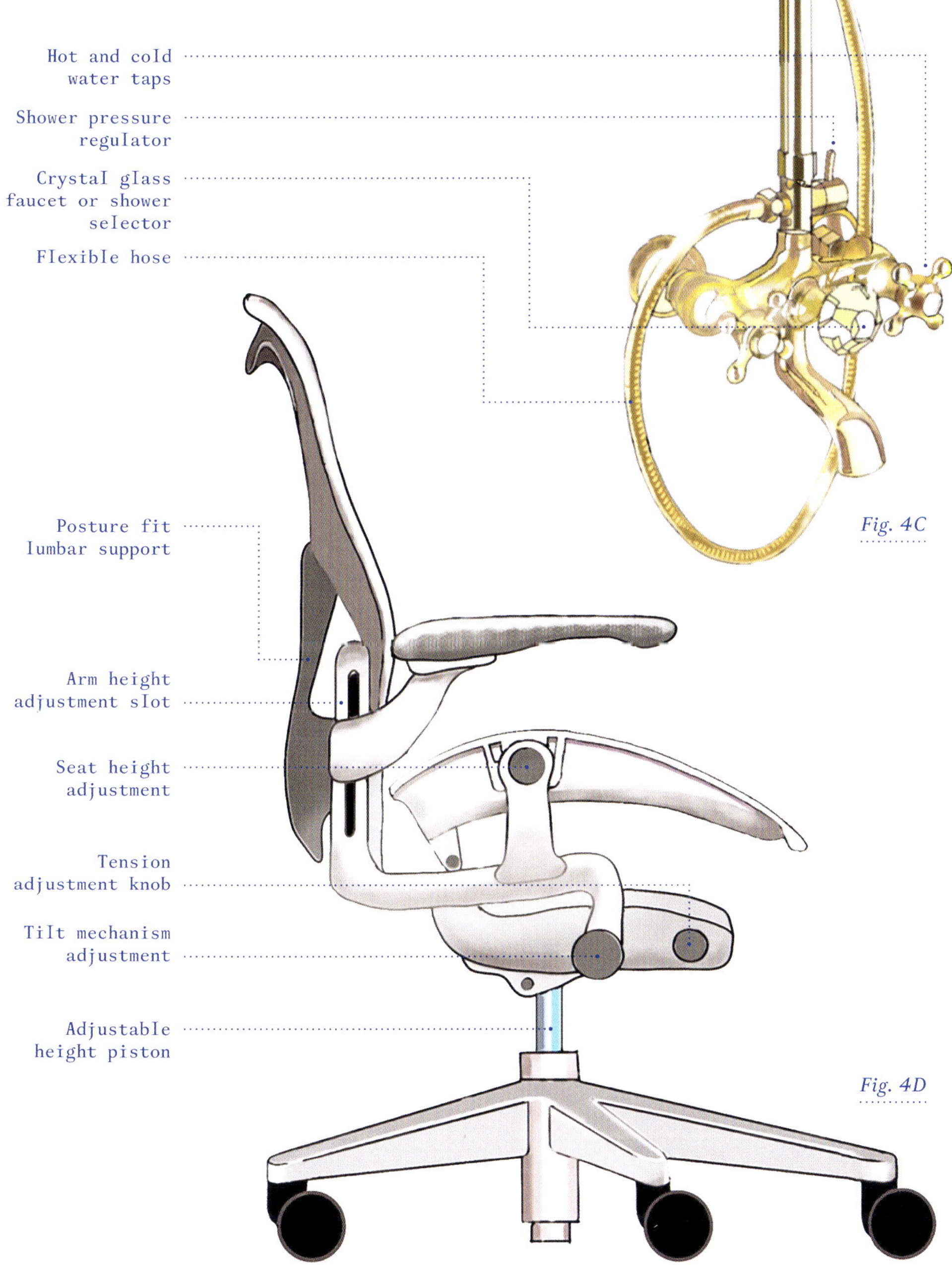

BRASS RAIN DUAL SHOWER HEAD (*Fig. 4C*), AERON CHAIR B (*Fig. 4D*)

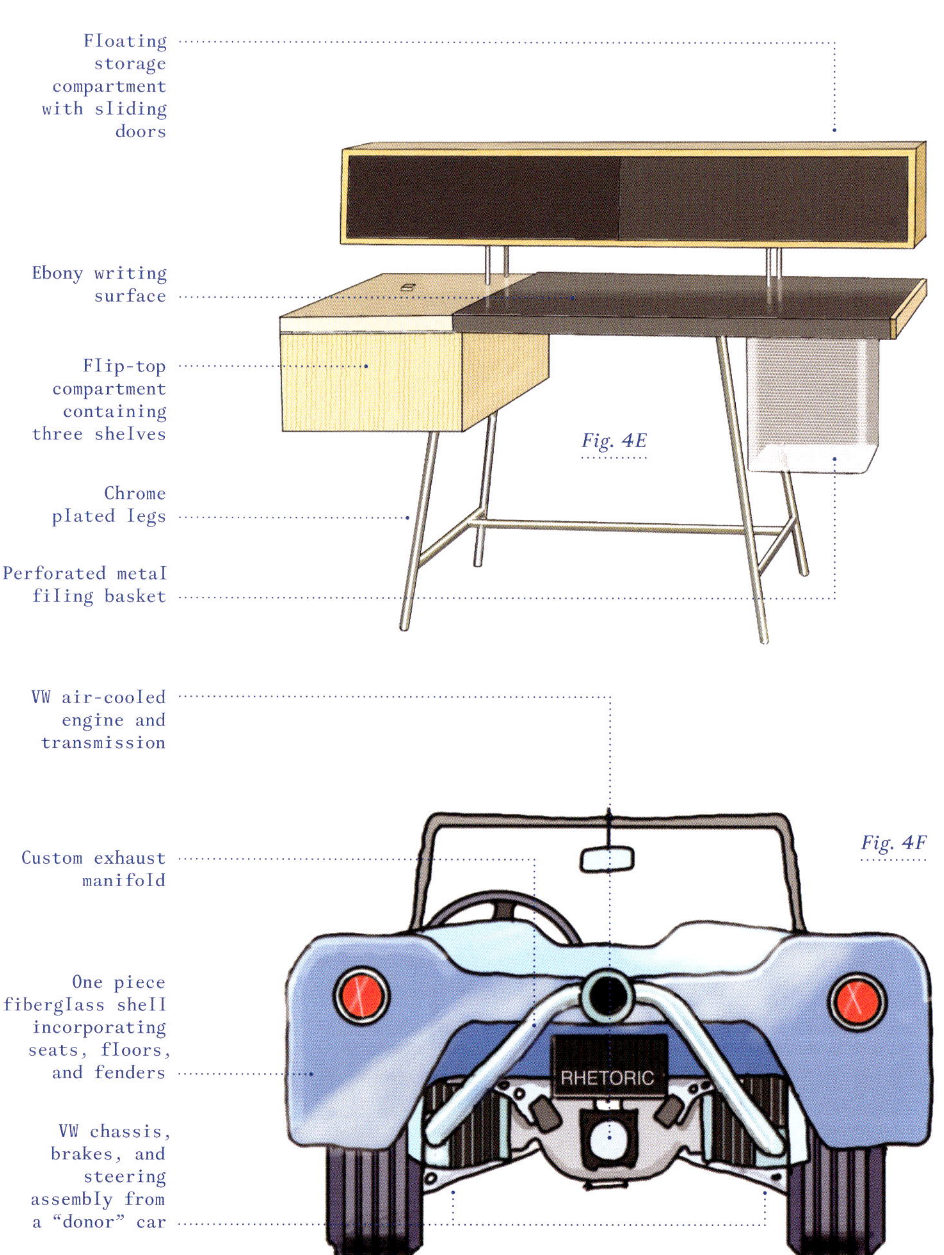

HOME DESK (*Fig. 4E*), VW DUNE BUGGY KIT KAR (*Fig. 4F*)

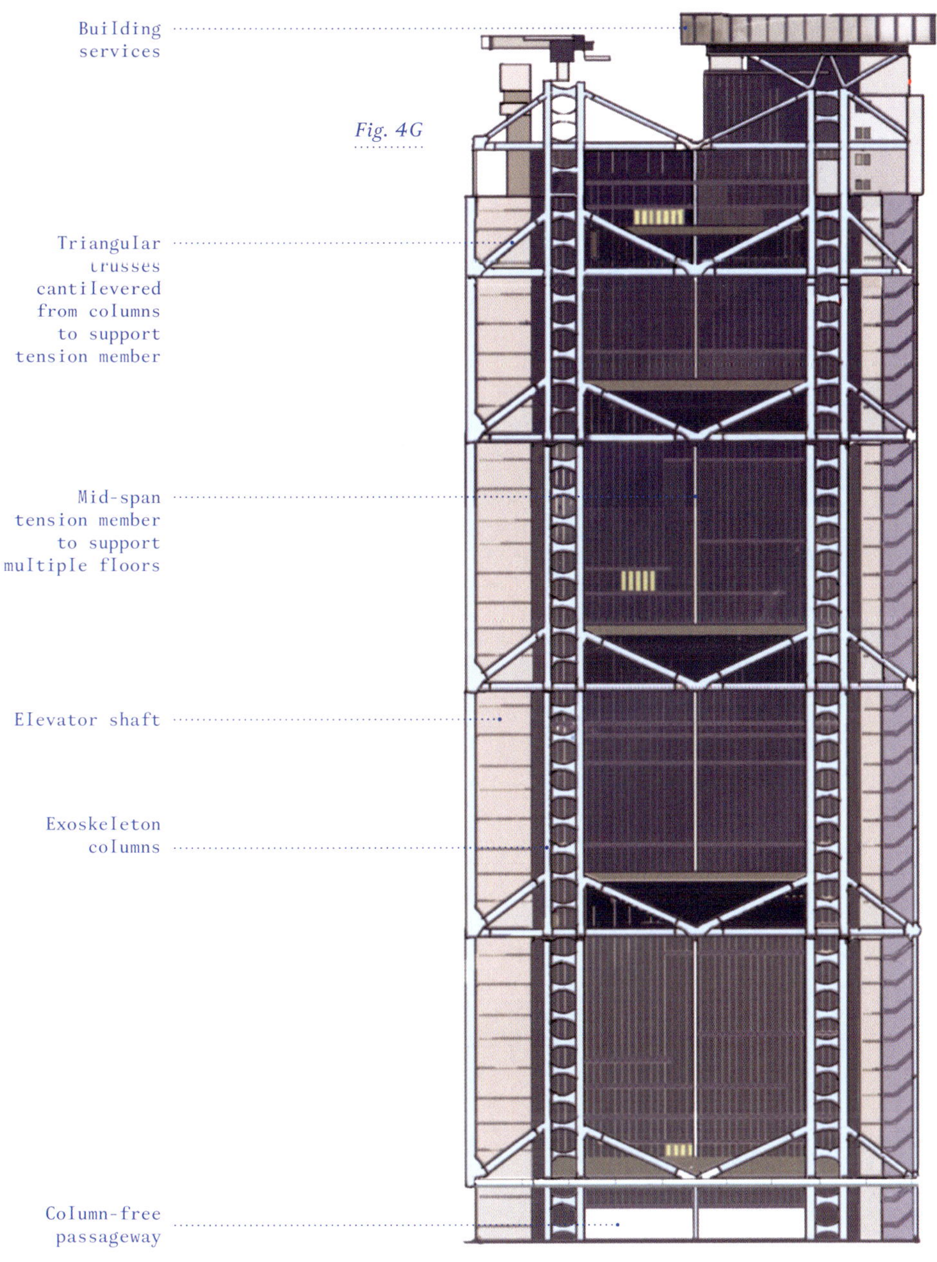

HONG KONG AND SHANGHAI BANK HEADQUARTERS (*Fig. 4G*)

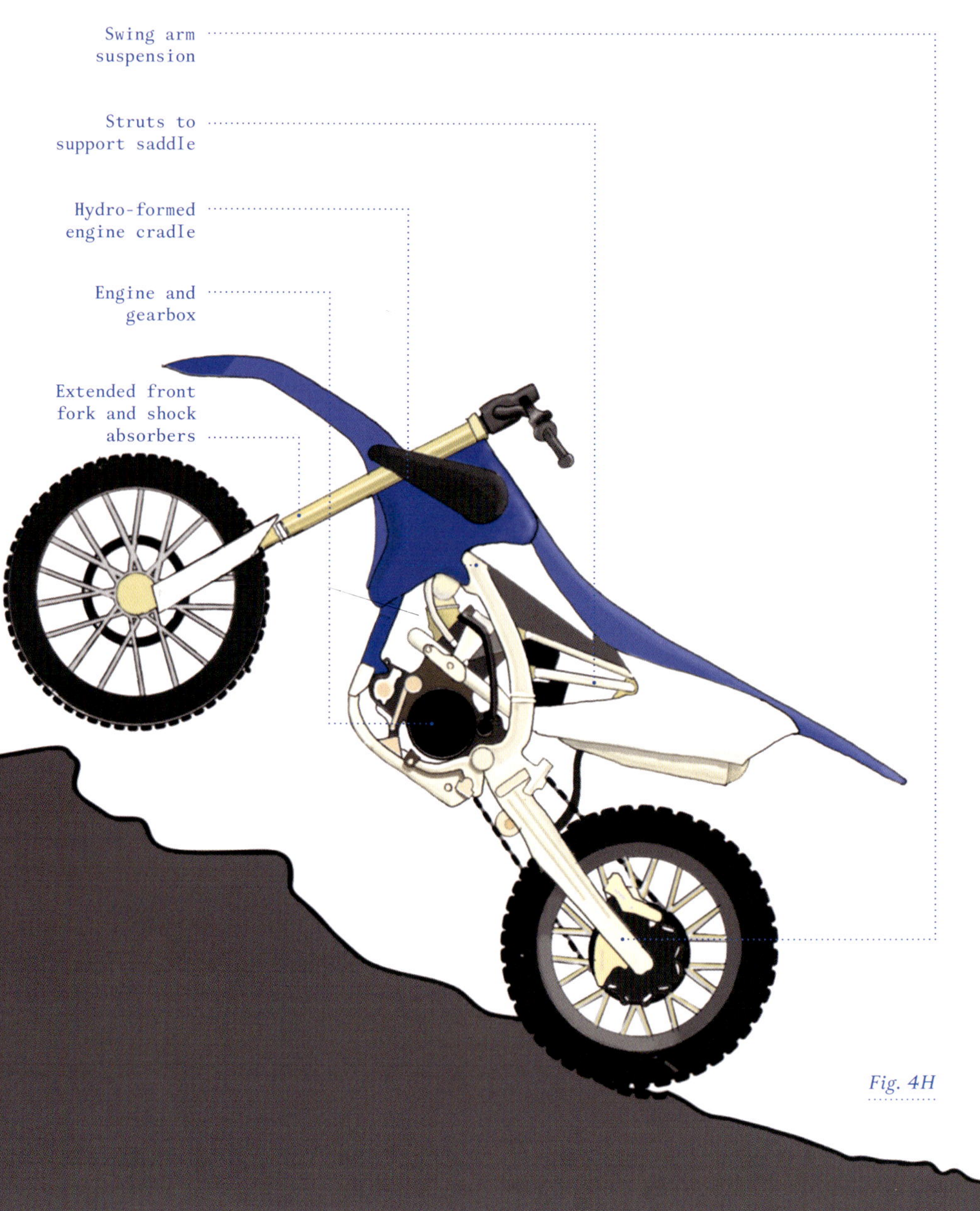

YAMAHA MOTORBIKE, YZ450F (*Fig. 4H*)

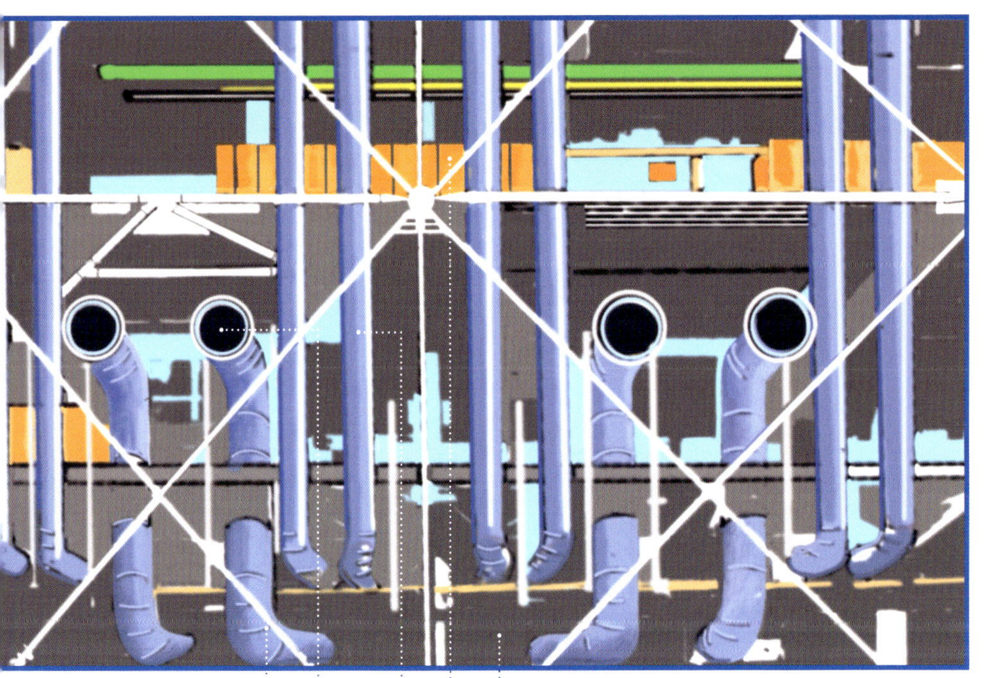

Fig. 4I

Power transformer
Output transformer
Power amplifier
vacuum tubes
with electrode
Pre-amplifier
vacuum tubes
with electrodes
Output gauges

Fig. 4J

THE CENTRE POMPIDOU (*Fig. 4I*),
HIFI VACUUM TUBE AMPLIFIER SOUND AMP (*Fig. 4J*)

Message
"I'M CLASSY,
A BIT FRAGILE,
SO BE SURE TO HANDLE ME WITH CARE."

Attributes
GRACIOUS, CON-
FIDENT DESIGN,
UNDERSTATED
ALLURE WITH
SIMPLE LINES &
SUPERB CRAFT
CONTRIBUTE
TO ELEGANT, SOPHISTICATED SETTINGS.

Beauty, especially if relaxed and alluring, is perhaps the ultimate design challenge. Whether delicate and fragile with ineffable qualities or lithe and powerful with compelling proportions, a beautiful object often imposes special responsibilities. Consider the profile of a fine violin or an elaborate vessel for rare perfume. Value and sentiment combine to extract maximum emotional engagement from those fortunate enough to possess or interact with such objects.

These qualities imply white-glove handling and conferring quasi-curatorial status on the owner or user. Such objects presuppose a sophisticated, observant audience with cultivated tastes, curiosity, and a willingness to seek out the subtleties of fabrication, materials, and form. In contrast to a bold, aggressive statement, a design with subtle *élan* typically avoids overt, attention-grabbing features – epitomized by the way a Dior ensemble exudes understated elegance, bolstering confidence and stature in the wearer.

In that context, unnecessary distrations – such as visible underpinnings or fasteners, including rivets, flanges, and zippers – are suppressed (unless they are themselves customized, fine-tuned design elements) with an emphasis on refined craftsmanship and careful articulation of materials and seams.

Achieving such refinement, especially in consumer goods – or on the scale of architecture – requires painstaking attention to detail, as well as holistic integration of motifs within a single, governing aesthetic discipline. Purity of form, as in the Jony Ive-designed series of iPhones or the Jaguar E-Type, can occasionally be achieved in buildings – witness Oscar Niemeyer's Niterói Contemporary Art Museum (1996) in Rio de Janeiro, Brazil or the proposed Hermitage Museum (2016) in Barcelona by Toyo Ito. But embarrassing lapses in execution – as seen in the irregular surface development of the ill-fated Bricklin SV-1 (c.1975) sports car, or the clumsy, generic detailing of the LAX Theme Building (1961), which over-promised on a futuristic imagery, are more the rule than the exception.

Flaws in execution, often excused by the limitations of technology, are no more acceptable than blemishes in the complexion of a cover model. Many designs, particularly poorly engineered consumer plastics, betray their pedestrian origins through warping or misalignment, although such flaws are far less common today with advanced computer modeling.

True precedent-setting masterworks, or breakthrough designs, often become instant classics in their own right – as with Phillipe Starck's Louis Ghost Chair (2002), which transformed the staid archetypical Regency dining chair into a seamless, transparent, useful object, or Artimede/Richard Sapper's Tizio Lamp (1972), borne of an insight that eliminated the burden of conventional wiring.

The precise and precious character of beautiful objects can induce an elevated sense of proprietorship, even arousing a protective demeanor among owners and users, who might, for instance, only reluctantly surrender their personal smartphones to someone they know just slightly. The proliferation of protective cases for *fragile* objects, especially iPhones, is a further demonstration of a collective, instinctive response, often incorporating enhancements meant to transform them into bauble-encrusted jewel-boxes. Gilding the lily – adding gratuitous decoration or "improvement" to something that is already perfectly beautiful, often to the point of tainting or ruining it – is an expression that describes precisely such "enhancements." The propensity to *dress-up* minimalist designs with personalized accessories has many precedents, as when the second owner of Craig Ellwood's elegant Case Study House #17 (1955) remodeled it in 1962, encasing its slender steel supports in Classical fluted Doric columns and adding a frilly peaked roof – a transformation that underscored the fragility of the type, and the boorish character of the owner.

As jousting for market share becomes the *raison d'être* of many millennial brands in search of identity, the subtleties of more sophisticated designs are rapidly being supplanted by ones that scream for attention. This is especially true of automotive design, where many current models are dolled up with faux air intakes and unnecessary, meaningless recesses in the contours of their body work. Fortunately, numerous start-ups in various design disciplines are finding niches by reviving sidelined Minimalist principles and making them stylish again. Outstanding among them is a line of men's urinals by Niagara, which demonstrates that even the most generic of things can benefit from a fresh return to an essential mission.

ELAN OBSERVATIONS

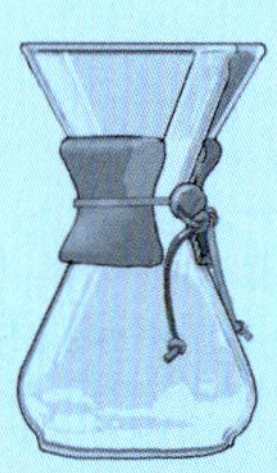

Fig. 5A CHEMEX COFFEE MAKER (p. 142)

YEAR 1941
DESIGNER
Peter Schlumbohm
MANUFACTURER
Chemex Corp., USA

With an hourglass figure, a leather tassel, and a wooden bustier, the Chemex is the epitome of elegant design while remaining fully functional. Each component is perfectly suited to perform a primitive yet technically sophisticated aspect of the brewing process, whether funneling hot water through the filter, or providing an insulated hand hold. Mechanical fastenings are eliminated at the waist by the use of a leather thong to secure a pair of contoured wooden grips to the basic glass vessel.

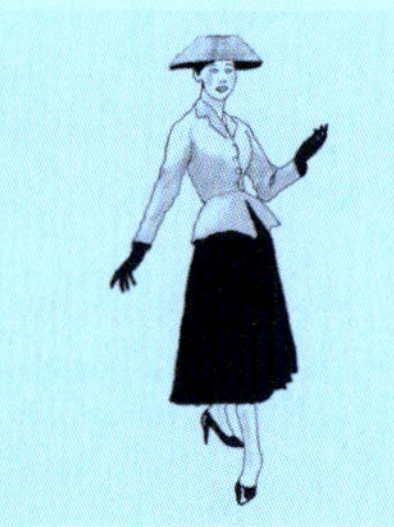

Fig. 5B BAR SUIT (p. 142)

YEAR 1957
DESIGNER
Christian Dior
COMPANY
Dior, France

The impact of this suit in 1957 cannot be overstated. It's simple palette of well-made but subtly elegant fabrics tailored to narrow the waist by padding the hips caught the exclusive world of couture fashion off guard. It was *the* silhouette for many years, as it elevated the House of Dior to cult status among *fashionistas* around the world.

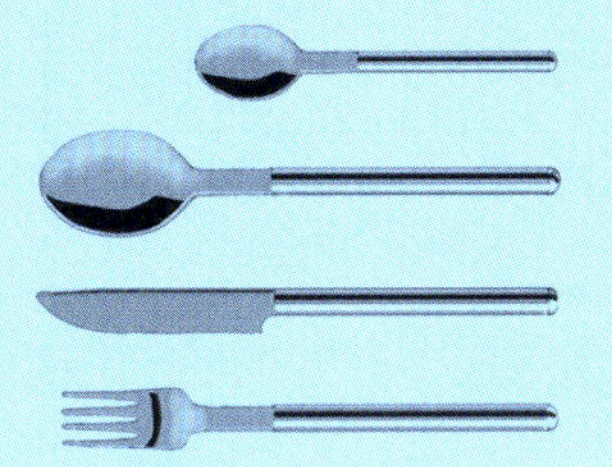

Fig. 5C MONO OVAL FLATWARE (p. 143)

MANUFACTURER
Mono GmbH, Germany

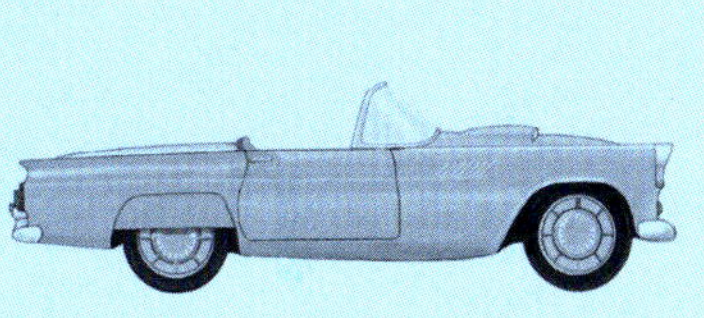

Fig. 5D THUNDERBIRD (p. 143)

YEAR 1955
DESIGNERS
George Walker and Louis D. Crusoe
MANUFACTURER
Ford, USA

There is not a hint of pretension in the form language of this flatware, that unifies elegance, impeccable workmanship, and pristine geometry. The proportions of each piece, articulated by a sharp transition from cylindrical to planar, create a lyrical ensemble able to lend structure to any place setting.

Now unrecognizable after decades of corporate overhauls, the 1956 Thunderbird was Ford's retort to GM's 1955 Corvette, with a decidedly romantic, boulevardier twist. Much too dainty to race, with an eyeliner sharp silhouette, and fashionable colors, it was to the automotive world what Chanel was to fashion: simple, seductive, and aspirational. However, those qualities were soon to be derided as the rise of the American muscle car all but reset the boundaries of decorum.

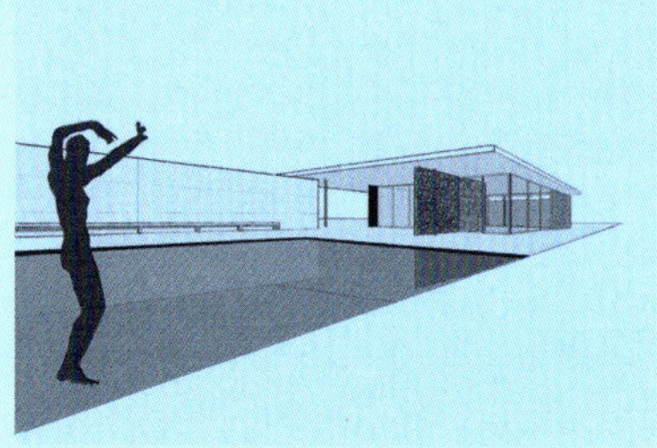

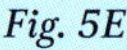

Fig. 5E BARCELONA PAVILION (p. 144)

YEAR 1929
ARCHITECTS
Ludwig Mies van der Rohe and Lilly Reich
LOCATION
Barcelona, Spain

Reduced to its essentials: a roof, a floor, figured stone planar walls, and slim cruciform columns, the Pavilion is both a diagram and an intoxicating environment. An extraordinary assembly of simple yet evocative parts arrayed precisely in order to create an almost liquified space, it has served, like its ancient Greek counterpart the Parthenon, as the embodiment of modern architectural aspirations since its unveiling at the Barcelona World's Fair.

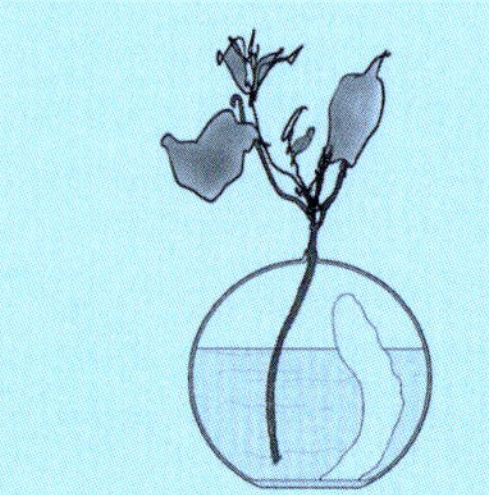

Fig. 5F TSUGARU GLASS VASE (p. 144)

DESIGNER
Tsugaro Vidro
MANUFACTURER
Ishizuka Glass Co., Ltd., Japan

The visual pleasure of framing a single bud in a nearly invisible vessel is both elegant and practical, revealing a refined sensibility and fastidious habits. Geometry, clarity, and purity combine to create an understated iconic presence with an ideal form.

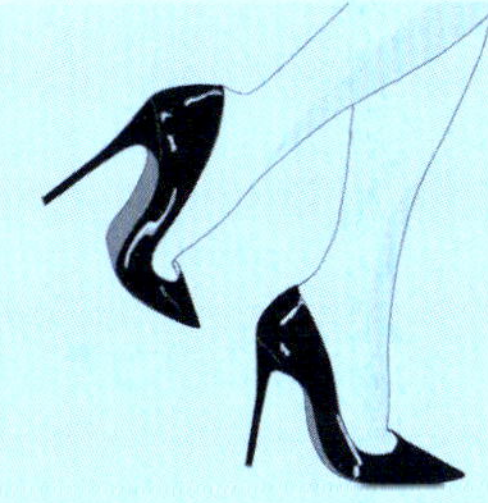

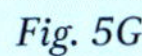

Fig. 5G SO KATE STILETTO PUMPS (p. 145)

DESIGNER
Manolo Blahnik
COMPANY
Manolo Blahnik International Ltd., UK

That the presence of such a slender heel, balanced by a perfectly proportioned upper has become the *sine qua non* of stylish footwear. With its ability to affect both poise and posture, and to project an image of dainty, proto-feminine traits, the omnipresent classic pump is an indispensable part of business attire.

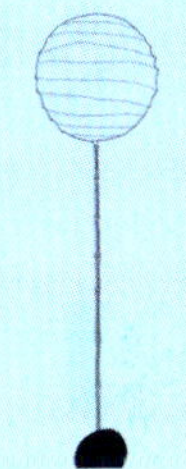

Fig. 5H AKARI LIGHT SCULPTURE (p. 145)

YEAR c.1951
DESIGNER
Isamu Noguchi
MANUFACTURER
Ozeki Workshop, Japan

Anchored by an unadorned “found” stone, and held aloft by a bamboo reed, the fragile paper sphere is illuminated from within to cast a gentle light on its surroundings. Its design, by sculptor Isamu Noguchi, is derived from a philosophy that values the variability of natural materials, while celebrating the essence of traditional craft.

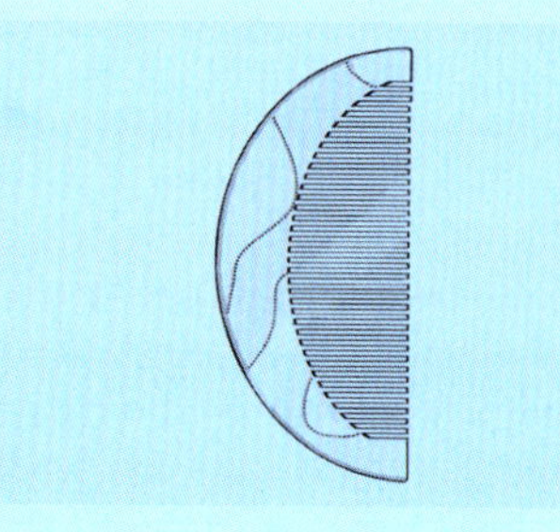

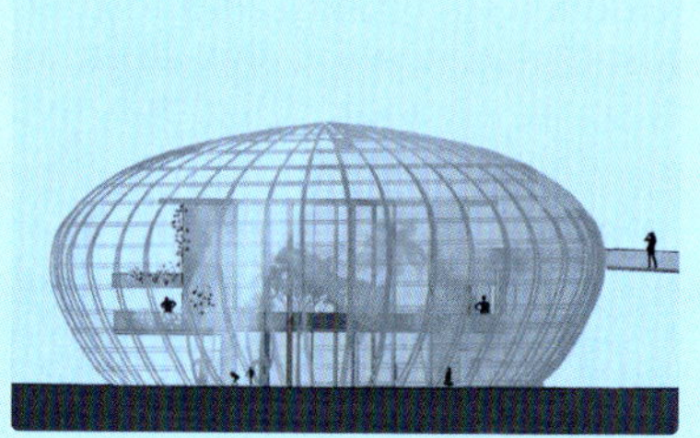

Fig. 5I TOKIGUSHI COMB
(p. 146)

MADE IN
Japan

Fig. 5J FRUIT MUSEUM
(p. 146)

YEAR 1997
ARCHITECT
Itsuko Hasegawa
LOCATION
Yamahashi, Japan

Manifestly simple, yet complex in form and utilization, the iconic Asian comb combines a poetic visual language with evocative materials such as bone, stone, or wood. Its presence on dressers and in make-up cases conveys admiration for traditional, simple, luxury.

A refined tracery complements a purity of form appropriate to the rarified purpose of these gossamer structures in Yamanashi Japan. Designed by esteemed architect Itsuko Hasegawa, the delicate structure creates a crystalline bubble so seemingly light and fragile that a sudden gust might send it aloft. Yet the meeting of form and function is so explicit, with a heritage going back to Paxton's cast-iron Crystal Palace and Buckminster Fuller's geodesic American Pavilion at the '64 Montreal World's Fair, that it may be the final episode of a centuries-old search for a diaphanous structural expression.

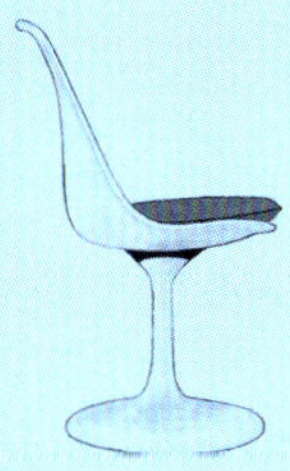

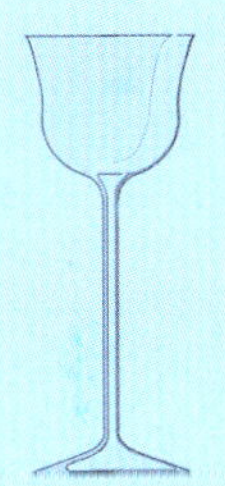

Fig. 5K TULIP CHAIR (p. 147)

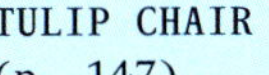

YEAR 1956
DESIGNER
Eero Saarinen
MANUFACTURER
Knoll, USA

Fig. 5L GRACE CRYSTAL WINE GLASS (p. 147)

DESIGNER
Ann Demeulemeester
MANUFACTURER
Serax, Belgium

By replacing the four legs of a conventional chair with a single, smoothly integrated stem, Eero Saarinen echoed and ultimately consummated a popular appetite for futuristic household necessities. Besides being visually comfortable in nearly any environment, the design offered a gracious, unobtrusive presence in contrast to the visual noise of its conventional peers.

A traditional slender stem lends an air of elegance mixed with fragility that fosters restrained gestures by hosts and guests alike. Notable for inclusion in traditional as well as contemporary settings, the essence of its form has survived cultural and economic change over centuries with little or no revision, largely because it helps to keep wine from warming. The addition of various minerals by George Ravenscroft in 1670 to increase the strength and clarity of glass enhanced its role as a sparkling addition to festive occasions.

ELAN ILLUSTRATIONS

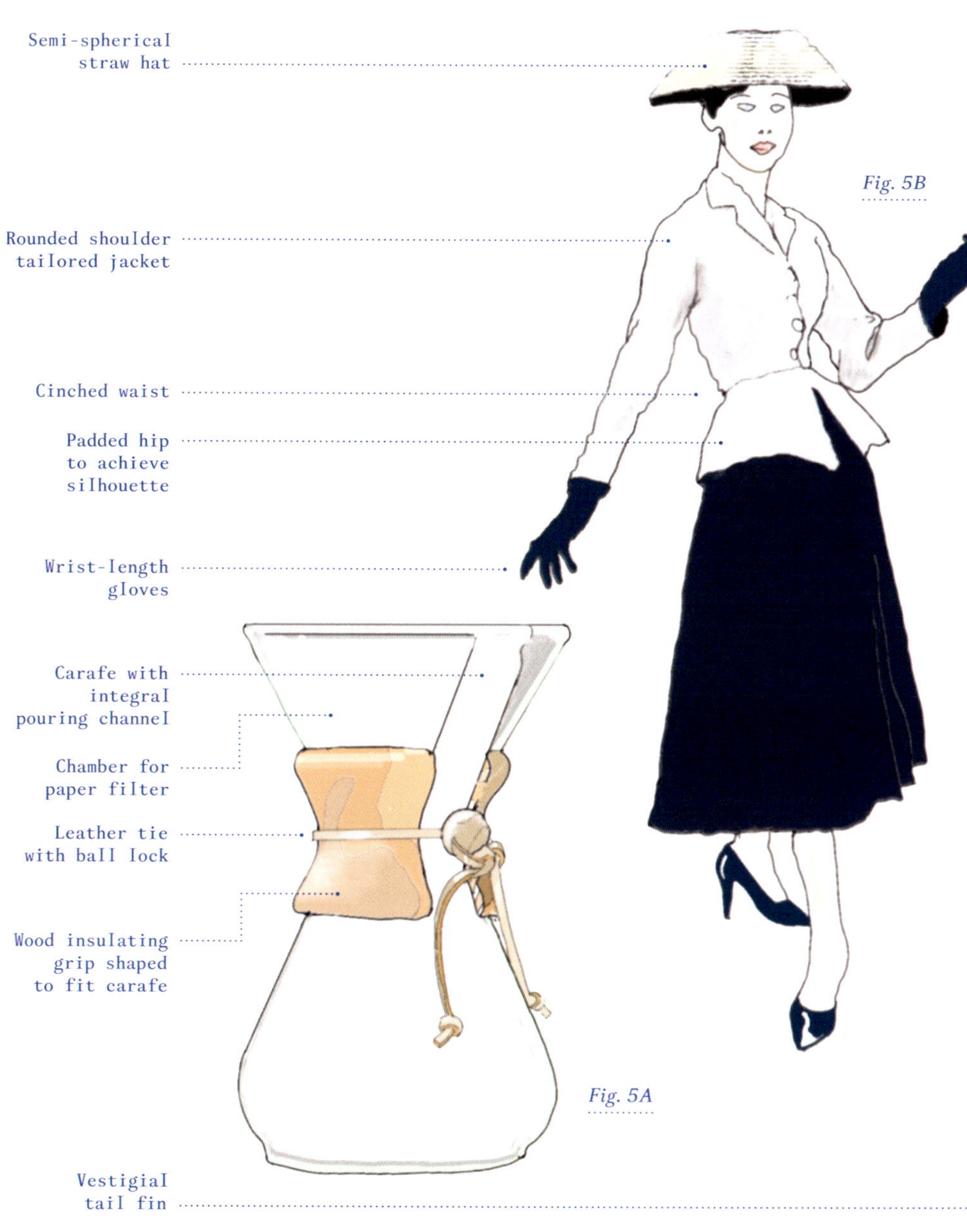

CHEMEX COFFEE MAKER (*Fig. 5A*), BAR SUIT (*Fig. 5B*)

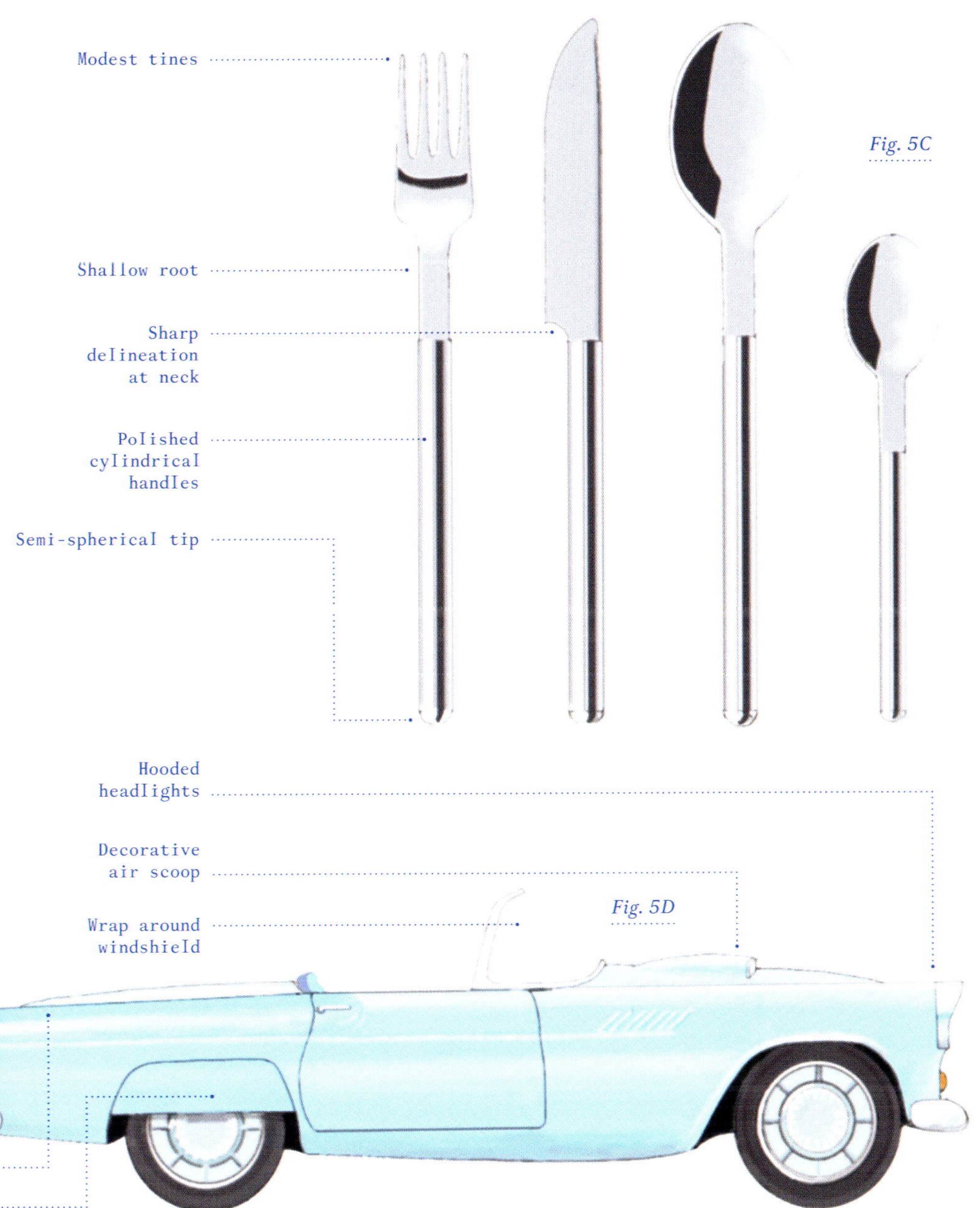

MONO OVAL FLATWARE (*Fig. 5C*), THUNDERBIRD (*Fig. 5D*)

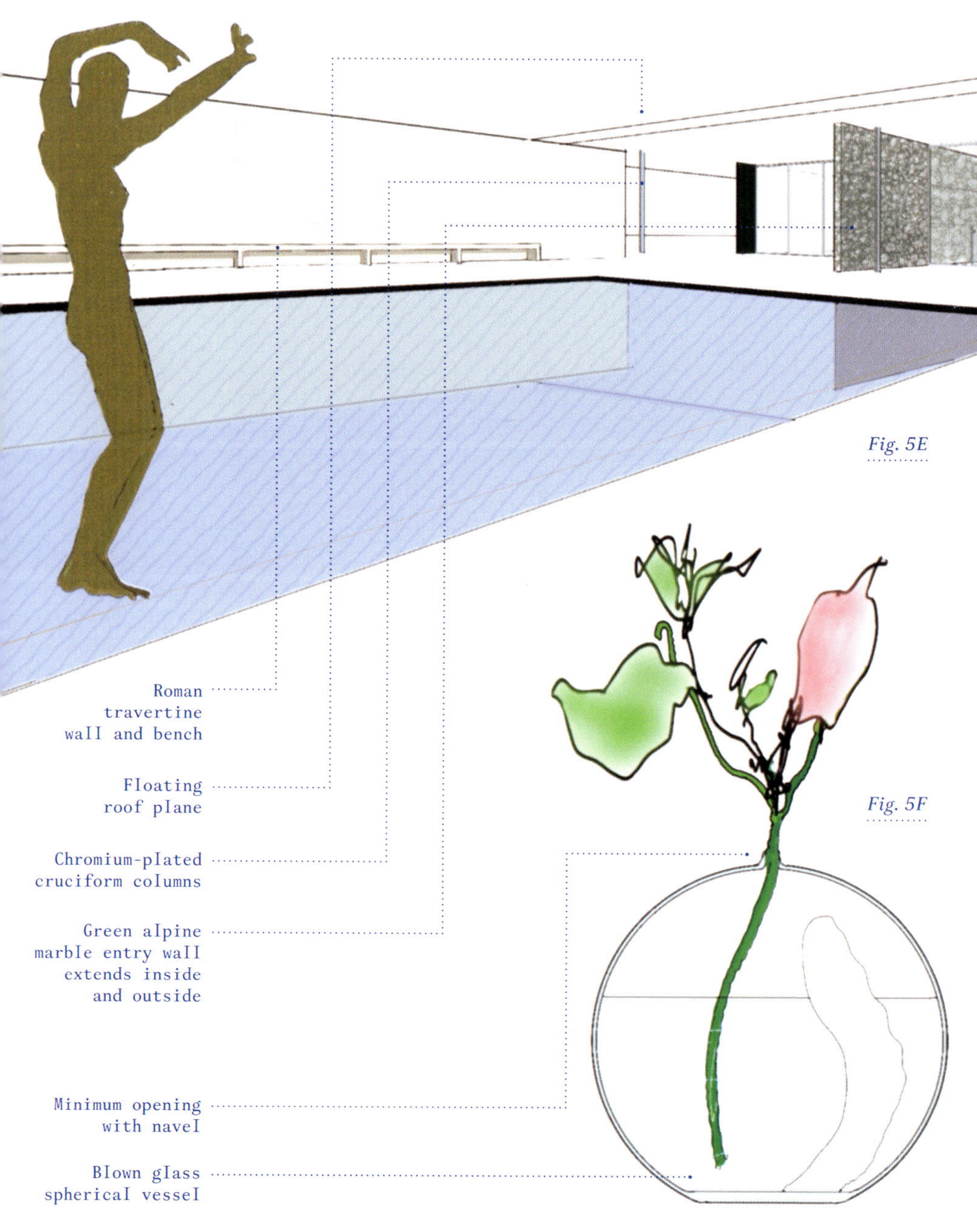

BARCELONA PAVILION (*Fig. 5E*), TSUGARU GLASS VASE (*Fig. 5F*)

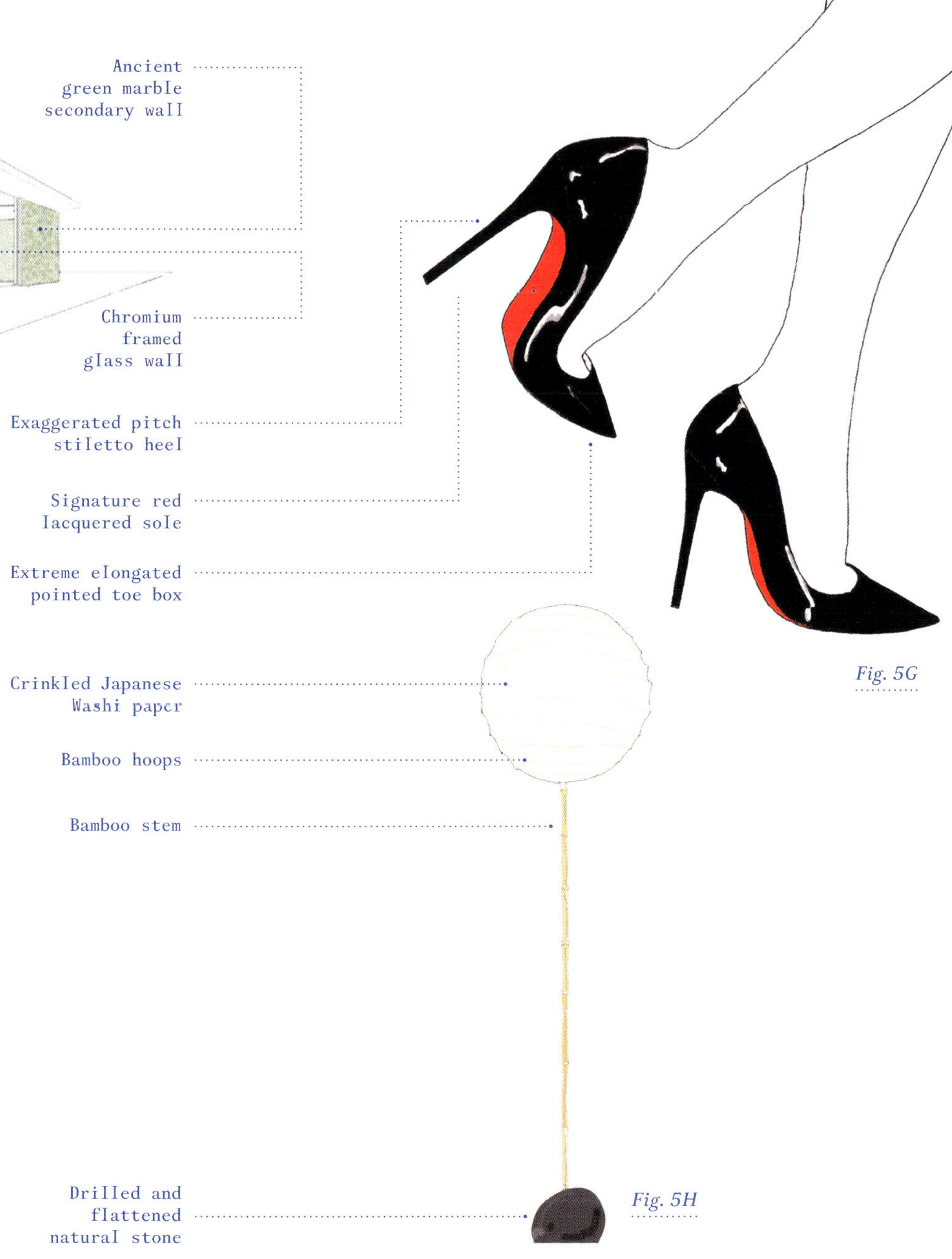

Fig. 5G

Fig. 5H

SO KATE STILETTO PUMPS (*Fig. 5G*), AKARI LIGHT SCULPTURE (*Fig. 5H*)

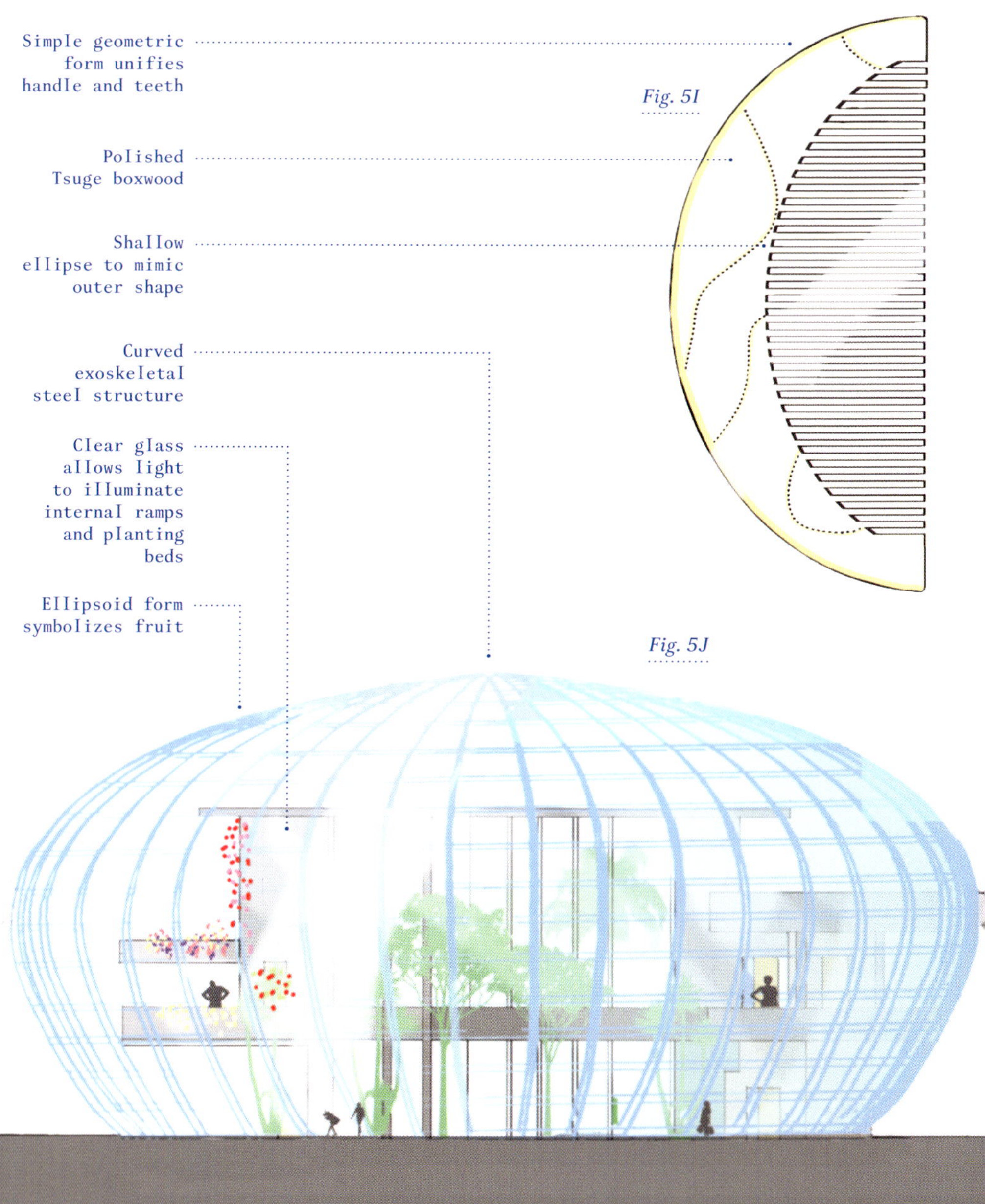

TOKIGUSHI COMB (*Fig. 5I*), FRUIT MUSEUM (*Fig. 5J*)

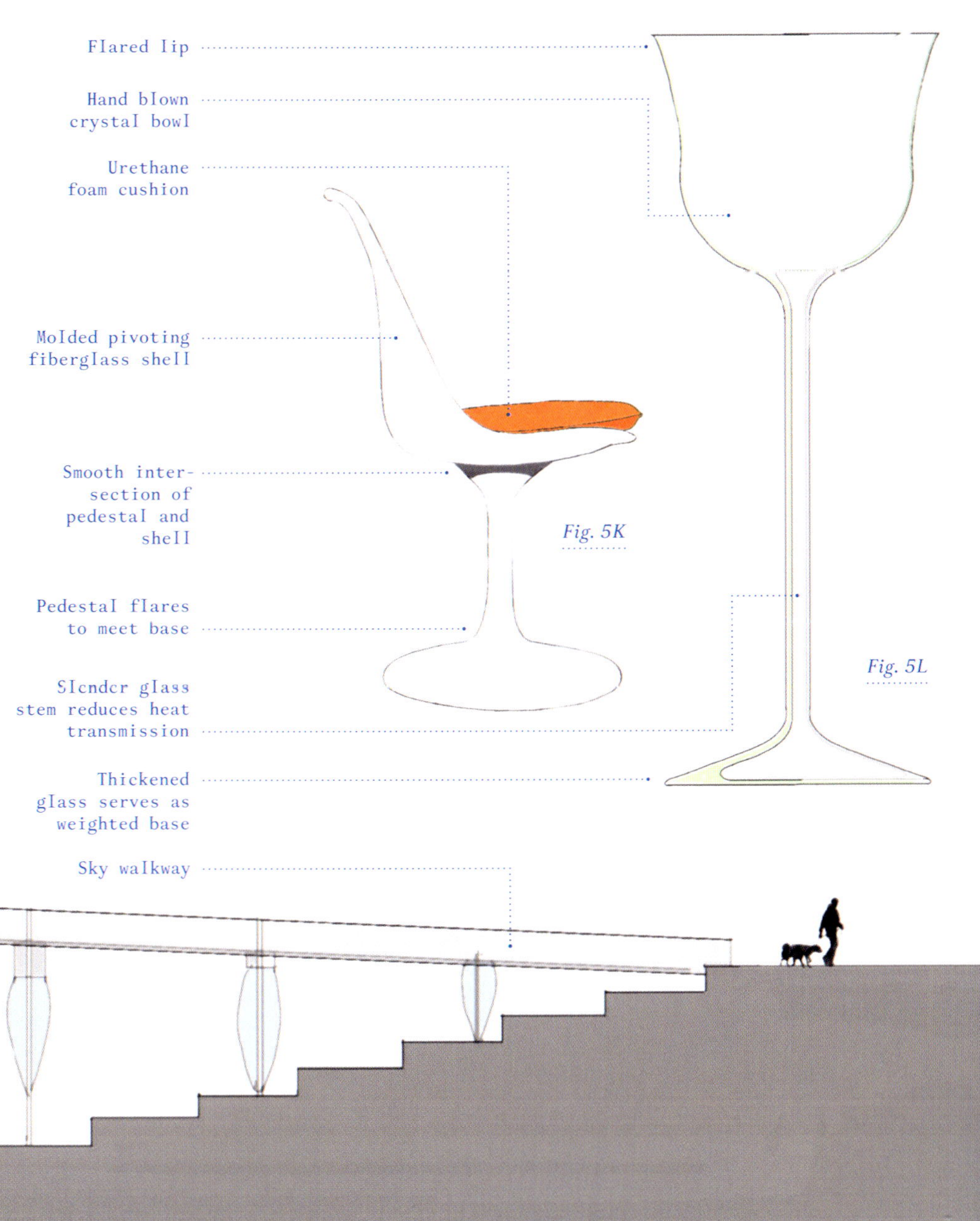

TULIP CHAIR (*Fig. 5K*), GRACE CRYSTAL WINE GLASS (*Fig. 5L*)

● **MESSAGE**: "GET RID OF ANYTHING THAT PROTRUDES TO MAKE A SHAPE THAT SLIPS SILENTLY INTO VIEW."

● **ATTRIBUTES**: SMOOTH AND SLIPPERY, UNBROKEN SURFACES, SUBDUED DETAILS BLENDING IRREGULARITIES INTO A SINGULAR NUBILE FORM WITH ALLUSIONS TO MOVEMENT.

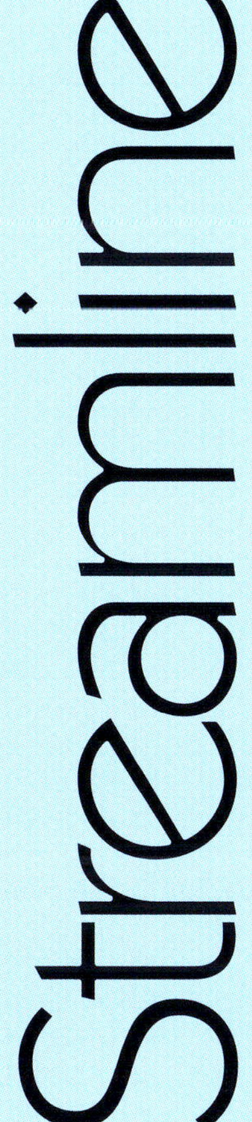

Introduction

The nubile, hairless object, featureless yet definitive in shape, evokes strong, visceral reactions, tactile sensations, and the desire to stroke, whether it's an automobile or an appliance. That appeal and the reactions elicited are amplified when the smooth object is at architectural scale, inviting the eye to wander freely over the surface without encountering a discordant feature.

The overall impression is of a nascent, self-contained object that titillates, teases, and refuses to be interrogated. Although plastics, sheet metal, and more recent materials, such as carbon fiber, are now uniformly and commonly employed to achieve such effects, it wasn't always so. In fact, until the late 19th century, when sheet metal first became widely available, complex curved forms were commonly created by subtraction – by carving into a base material, such as wood or stone. Although sheet metal had been produced since the prior century, most often it was just bent or cut into simpler, less voluptuously contoured shapes. Or sometimes nuanced sculptural curves, as in a breastplate, could be achieved with a wooden mold, or buck, over which a skilled craftsperson would gradually hammer the metal sheet until it settled comfortably over the form. It wasn't until much later, with the advent of mass production, that giant stamping equipment, capable of producing and readily reproducing even more complex shapes, came into common use. From that point, the ability to quickly form thin, self-supporting, three-dimensionally curved steel or aluminum skins would revolutionize the design of automobile bodies, washing machines, aircraft, and more.

The creation of a formed steel envelope to contain and consolidate the disparate parts of appliances and automobiles was first achieved by designer Norman Bel Geddes, in the early 1930s, for his refrigerator and stove designs. In the automotive industry, the idea first took root in Italy, resulting in the precedent-setting, streamlined design of the 1946 Cisitalia 202 GT, which soon became the template for cars worldwide and is now represented in the permanent collection of New York's Museum of Modern Art.

Portraying humans and animals in motion through sequential, locomotion-capturing photographs, Eadweard Muybridge's late 19th Century photography provided a pioneering model for still images that express speed. In a similar vein, motion interrupted and reassembled in overlapping sequence animates Marcel Duchamp's 1912 painting *Nude Descending a Staircase*, establishing a language of representation that is still valid today. In more recent times, architect Massimo Iosa Ghini's elongated furniture designs recalled Philippe Halsman's "stop-action" photographs, most notably his surreal 1948 *Dalí Atomicus* portrait of artist Salvador Dalí, with a visually "frozen" arc of flung water suspended in mid-air across the room, lending a sense of motion to otherwise static conditions. And the "Forward Look" automotive design by Virgil Exner for Chrysler – first introduced in 1955 to invigorate the floundering Chrysler brand – employed visual devices, including dynamic vectors, exaggerated fins, and other dart-like silhouettes, to convey power and speed. Those qualities soon imbued countless radios, dining sets, and even washing machines with gestures implying velocity.

This widespread emphasis on motion, sometimes characterized as a psychodynamic phenomenon, powerfully reflected the optimism of the post-World War II era, when industry, culture, and lifestyle seemed locked in a common aspiration to move forward rapidly toward a brighter future. The nearly simultaneous development of the Interstate Freeway system, the Salk Polio vaccine, television and the TV dinner, and the home dishwasher heralded an age later celebrated by Thomas Hine in his 1986 book *Populuxe* – an era of Googie restaurants, boomerang logos, and swept-back hairstyles, all thrusting the entire country into a fast-moving, future-oriented frenzy.

Although Streamline Moderne design, beginning in the 1930s, had celebrated speed, fluidity, and motion in everything from buildings and furniture to airplanes, ships, and automobiles, it wasn't until the turn of the 21st Century that technology advanced enough to enable architects to take it even further, with the completion, in 1997, of Frank Gehry's Guggenheim Bilbao Museum. The building's metal skin designed using CATIA 5, computer software originally developed for the complexities of aircraft design, departs from streamlined fluidity, in favor of windswept, dynamically undulant, but disconnected, swaths of titanium.

Ever since, significant projects around the world have been dressed in titanium in ways that redefine the age-old vocabulary of construction. Now it has become possible to supplant conventionally flat surfaccs and angular intersections with a single, continuous, voluptuously curved surface, an exterior shell that eliminates corners altogether, turning the entire building into what architect Greg Lynn christened a "blob" in the mid-1990s. This non-traditional form making has also been enabled by advances in design software, as well as advances in construction technology. Such buildings rendered at an all-enveloping, immersive scale – strike a balance between the technological advancements of aircraft and racing cars and organic, natural forms such as seashells and dunes.

Streamline Observations

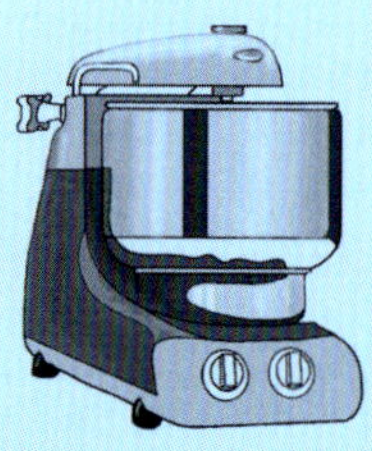

Fig. 6A ANKARSRUM ASSISTENT ORIGINAL MIXER (p. 172)

YEAR 1940-2024
MANUFACTURER
Ankarsrum Inc., Sweden

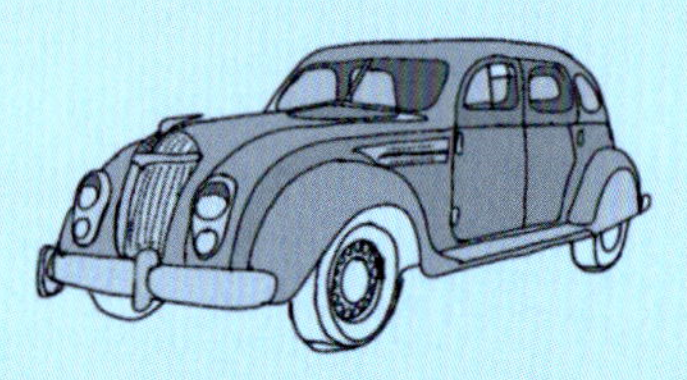

Fig. 6B AIRFLOW SEDAN (p. 172)

YEAR 1936
MANUFACTURER
Chrysler Corporation, USA

By locating the motor in the base, and rotating the bowl, this mixer design is able to reduce both the visual mass and weight of the mixing head, thus increasing access to the bowl in order to mix in additional ingredients. Its smoothly curved surface reduces cleanup chores while the placement of its control panel is both intuitive and ergonomically convenient.

A commercial failure but a noteworthy effort, the Chrysler Airflow is known as a pioneer in the concept of streamlining despite a bulky mass and clumsy production-driven detailing. Clearly hampered by a traditional ladder chassis and old-fashioned prewar manufacturing processes, it nevertheless introduced features that would become must-haves when automobile production resumed after WWII.

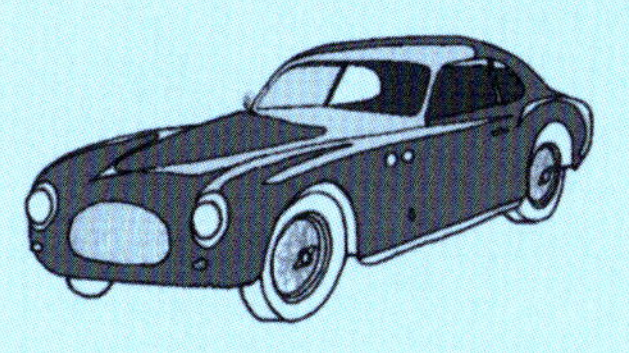

Fig. 6C CISITALIA COUPE, 202 GT (p. 172)

YEAR 1948
DESIGNER Pininfarina (Battista "Pinin" Farina)
MANUFACTURER S.p.A. Carrozzeria Pininfarina, Italy

Upon its selection for the initial design collection at Manhattan's Museum of Modern Art, this limited production Italian automobile became the inspiration for a whole generation of ordinary production cars which shed their pre-WWII running boards and fenders to adopt the Cisitalia's sleek, uncluttered form vocabulary.

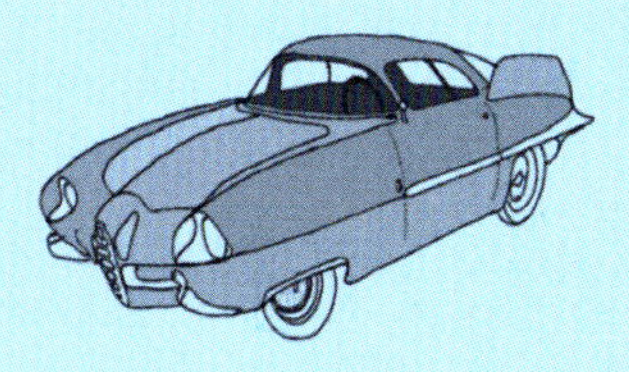

Fig. 6D ALFA ROMEO COUPE, BAT 9 OR BERLINA AERODINAMICA TECNICA (p. 172)

YEAR 1955
DESIGNER Nuccio Bertone
MANUFACTURER Alfa Romeo Automobiles S.p.A., Italy

One of three experimental aerodynamic bodies designed by Italian *Carrozeria Bertone* with a radical form that mimicked the flow of air in sheet metal form as a result of extensive wind-tunnel testing. In 2020, RM Sotheby's sold all three cars as one lot at their auction for US $14.84m.

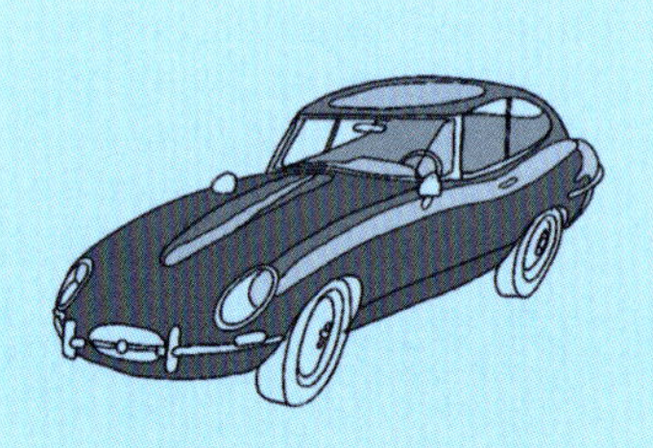

Fig. 6E

JAGUAR XK-E FIXED HEAD COUPE (p. 172)

YEAR 1967
DESIGNERS
Malcom Sayer and William Lyon
MANUFACTURER
Jaguar Cars Ltd., England

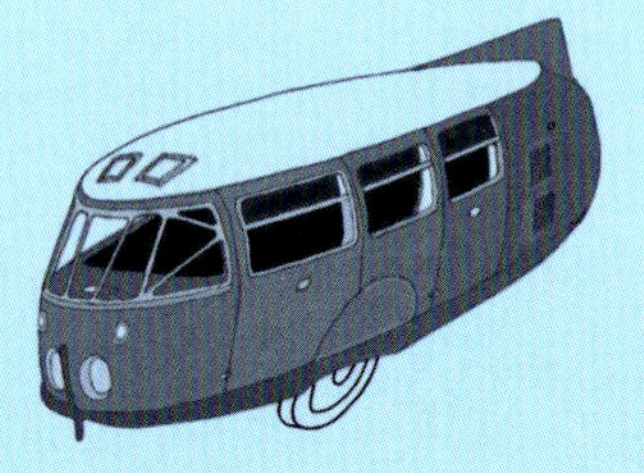

Fig. 6F

DYMAXION PROTOTYPE (p. 172)

YEAR 1933
DESIGNER
Buckminster Fuller
MANUFACTURER
The Dymaxion Corporation, USA

Designed by aircraft engineer Malcom Sayer and William Lyon and introduced at the Paris Auto Show on15 March 1961 to an unprecedented level of excitement, giving birth to a true automotive icon. With a monocoque structure and highly tuned engine it was capable of record-breaking speed and acceleration, and offered a unique mix of ultra-high performance, beauty, and affordability.

Futurist Buckminster Fuller's trend-bucking Dymaxion automobile was notable not just for its sleek, aerodynamic body work, but for its reliance on steering via the rear wheels, a design that allowed for exceptional maneuverability at low speed, but that was unstable at highway speeds, a fact responsible for its withdrawal from production after an accidental death.

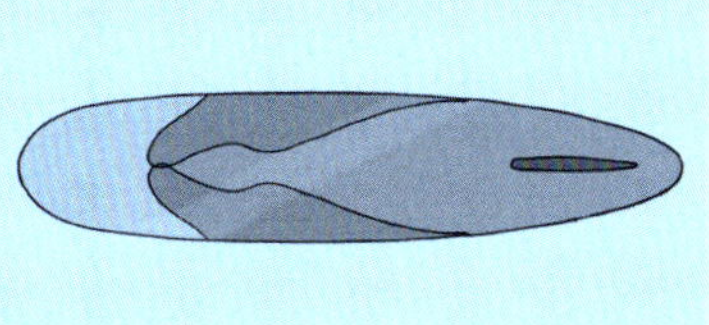

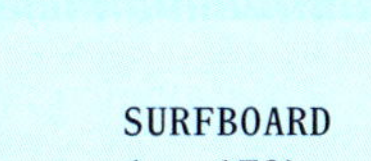

Fig. 6G SURFBOARD (p. 173)

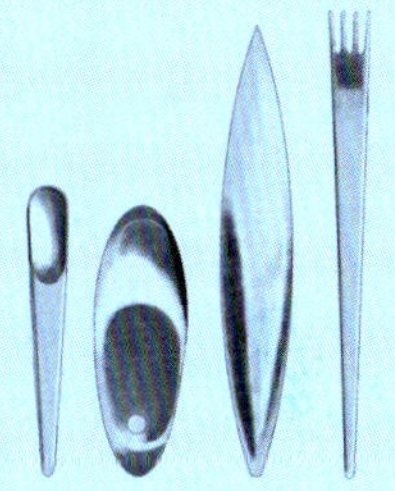

Fig. 6H MONO ZEUG FLATWARE (p. 173)

YEAR 1995
DESIGNER
Michael Schneider
MANUFACTURER
Mono GmbH, Germany

Intuitively shaped over centuries of interaction with waves and water, the classic surfboard epitomizes streamline design as derived from functionally meaningful experience and performance. Originally carved from soft woods such as Balsa, most of today's boards are made from polyurethane foam with a fiberglass skin.

Asserting the value of form over function, this place setting questions ergonomic preconceptions by discarding established conceptions of comfortable use and electing to challenge diners to reframe their habits.

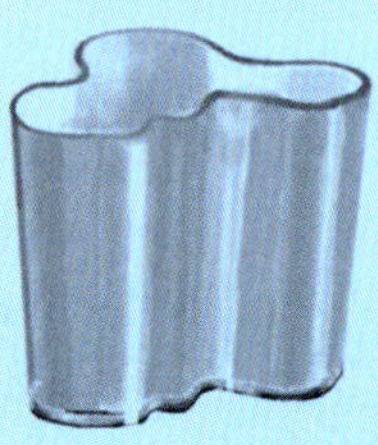

Fig. 6I VASE
(p. 174)

YEAR 1936
DESIGNERS
Alvar and
Aino Aalto
MANUFACTURER
Iittala
Glassworks,
Finland

First exhibited at the 1937 World's Fair in Paris, the sinuous form of this vase echoes a long fascination with lyrical form and was achieved by a unique process that allowed molten glass to assume its natural shape by blowing it into a cluster of vertical sticks, thus avoiding the inherent marks of a traditional mold.

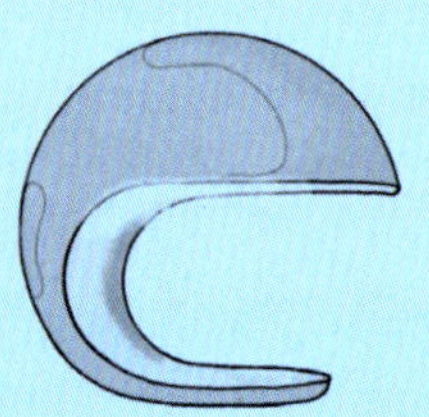

Fig. 6J FOGLIA LAMP
(p. 174)

YEAR c.1970
DESIGNER
Elio Martinelli
MANUFACTURER
Martinelli Luce,
Italy

Named in Italian for its resemblance to a leaf, the sleek organic shape of this lamp, and the soft luster of the light it emanates would not be possible were it not for Acrylic plastic's formability and calibrated luminosity.

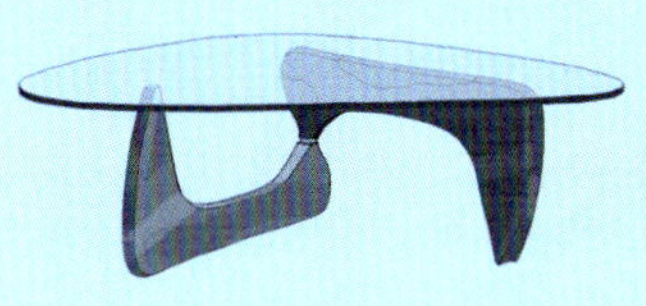

Fig. 6K

NOGUCHI
COFFEE TABLE
(p. 174)

YEAR 1944
DESIGNER
Isamu Noguchi
MANUFACTURER
Herman Miller, Inc., USA

A limpid line tracing disparate materials unifies the elements of this table. The muscular yet sleek wooden "shoulders" carry a contoured glass top in the shape of a pond. The sculpted design evolved from Noguchi's revenge for a copy of an earlier version marketed in England.

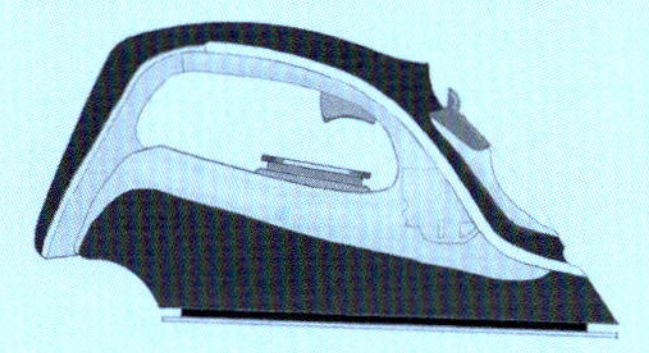

Fig. 6L

INTELLITEMP
IRON
(p. 175)

YEAR 2022
MANUFACTURER
Morphy Richards, England

With an ant-eater profile this steam iron noses smoothly through fabric and between buttons, while ready access to a trigger suggests a speedy way to deliver a shot of steam where and when required. A sinuous polished line separates the water reservoir from the control cluster before descending to become an insulated rest.

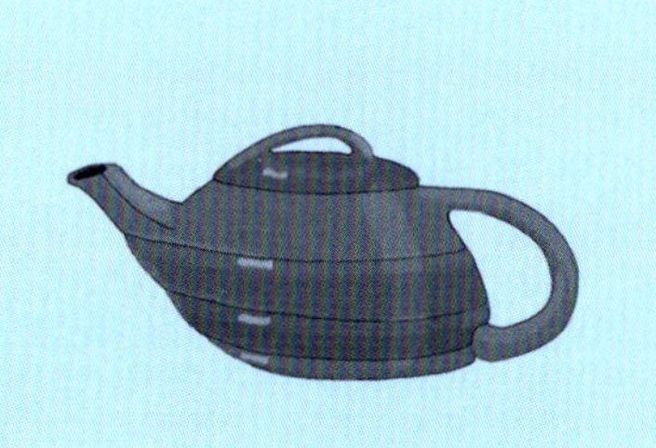

Fig. 6M BAUER TEAPOT
(p. 175)

YEAR c.1936
DESIGNER
Frederick
Hurten Rhead
MANUFACTURER
Fiesta Tableware
Company, USA

Characterized by fluid volumes articulated by subtle, rhythmic striations, and vibrant glazes, the Bauer designs animate table settings with a forward-looking attitude that redefines the traditional, static role of tableware. During World War II, certain glazes containing Uranium 235 were deemed strategic resources, curtailing production. Upon the end of the war, Bauer incorporated depleted Uranium as a substitute and were able to restore the brilliance of their glazes.

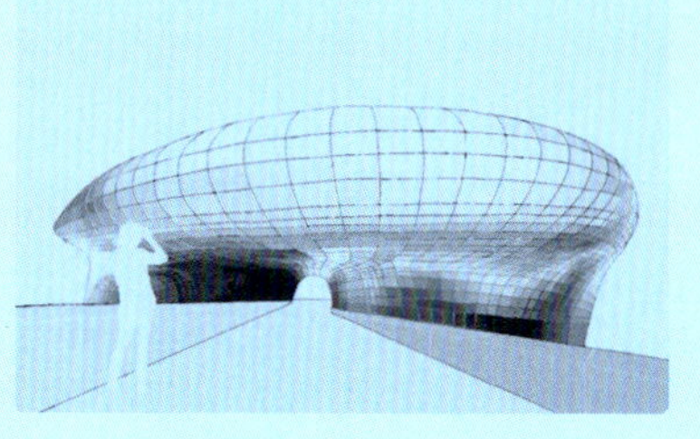

Fig. 6N DONGDAEMUN
DESIGN PLAZA
(p. 175)

YEAR 2014
ARCHITECT
Zaha Hadid
Architects
LOCATION
Seoul,
South Korea

The most comprehensive example of Zaha Hadid's vision remains this urban shopping, cultural center, and museum, with a floor area of nearly one million square feet. Designed according to Hadid's *Metonymic Landscape* philosophy and composed of multiple undulating surfaces, the seamless exterior, mostly devoid of windows, encloses a vast public courtyard defined by criss-crossing bridges and interpenetrating voids.

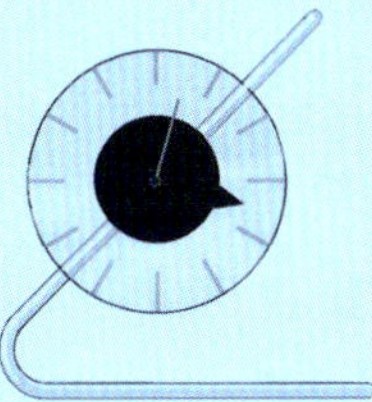

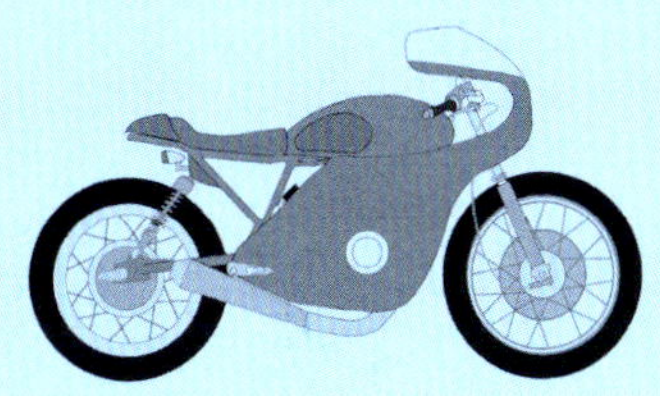

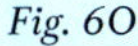

Fig. 6O AROODS CLOCK
(p. 176)

YEAR 1933
DESIGNER
Gilbert Rohde
MANUFACTURER
Herman Miller
Clock Co., USA

Fig. 6P HONDA CR500
HAILWOOD RACE
FAIRING
(p. 176)

DESIGNER
Auctmarts
Fairing
MANUFACTURER
Auctmarts
Trading Co.,
China

This clock, reduced to the asymmetric disposition of its parts, and the forward thrusting attitude, epitomizes the incorporation of streamline moderne principles into a static design vocabulary. By incorporating a bent tube containing the power cord as a support for the floating dial, the resulting design seems to float independently of its connection to the electrical mains.

In an aftermarket full of motorcycle accessories, the streamlined, retrofitted fairing is one of the most effective ways to increase speed as well as rider comfort with a single device. Generally made of fiberglass, with provisions for multiple accessories, the fairings became signature assets to what are known as café racers – loose groups of motorcycle enthusiasts who convene at various pubs and ride out together.

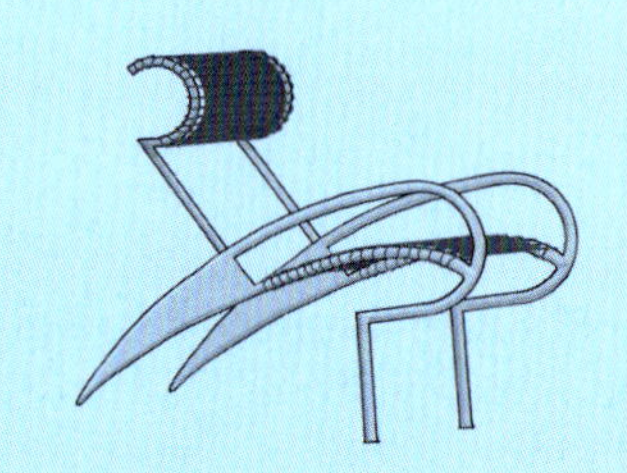

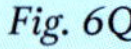

Fig. 6Q

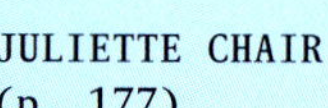

JULIETTE CHAIR
(p. 177)

YEAR 1987
DESIGNER
Massimo
Iosa Ghini
MANUFACTURER
Memphis
S.R.L., Italy

Looking as though it might leap forward at any moment, the coiled energy of this chair contrasts with the more relaxed design of many of its peers to inject a dynamic presence into the usually stiff world of interior design. Manufactured and inspired by Memphis, the radical design collective started by Ettore Sottsass, the chair lends its rakish behavior to a menage of quirky and outlandish mates.

Fig. 6R

CONUNDRUM
WINE GLASS
(p. 177)

MANUFACTURER
Conundrum
Wines, USA

Molded to conform to the fingers meant to encircle it, the Conundrum wine glass avoids platonic ideals, opting instead for a comfortable, molded grip. Although one could argue that the large contact area of the glass would rapidly warm its contents, the design offers a unique, more intimate drinking experience.

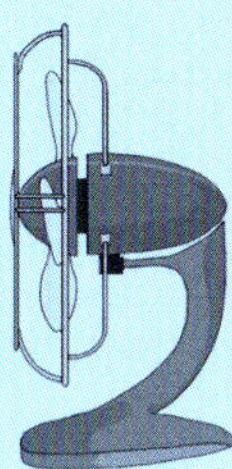

Fig. 6S AIRFLOW FAN
(p. 177)

YEAR 1937
DESIGNER
Robert Heller
MANUFACTURER
AC Gilbert
Company, USA

Although the purpose of both desk fans and airplane propellers is to move air, and their blades share similar constraints, the desk fan must remain rooted to a surface, while the propeller moves into the sky. This fan, taking its design cues from aerodynamic principles, combines typical aircraft features like its streamlined strut, sleek nacelle, and smooth base into a singularly graceful accessory for steamy weather.

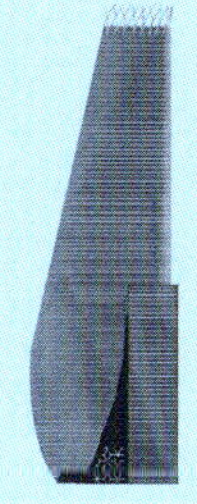

Fig. 6T PHARE TOWER
(p. 178)

YEAR 2006-2010
ARCHITECT
Morphosis
LOCATION
La Defénse,
Paris, France

This unbuilt design for a prestige office tower in Paris adopted a streamlined configuration as well as innovative ecological, structural and cladding ideas. With an aerodynamic profile and sleek physique, its design offered a sophisticated alternative to the growing taste for towers bristling with setbacks, tortured floor plates, and jutting cantilevers. If built, the hope was to become the symbolic heart of a new, multivalent mixed-use neighborhood.

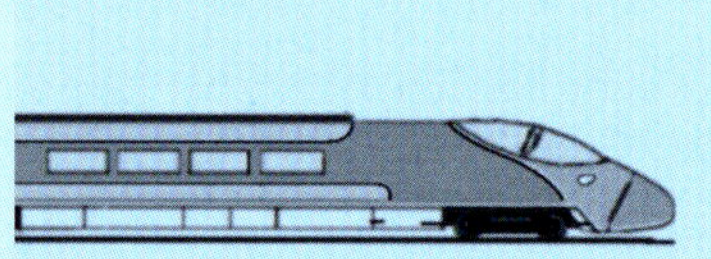

Fig. 6U HEXIE HARMONY HIGH SPEED TRAIN (p. 178)

MANUFACTURER
Bombardier Transportation, Kawasaki Heavy Industries, Alstom, Siemens, CRRC

In order to reach and maintain speeds up to 200 miles an hour, all new high-speed trains adopted a nearly unbroken aerodynamic design that largely eliminated the turbulent spaces between aircraft-inspired light weight carriages. Featuring extensive use of light-weight alloys and all electric motive power supplied by special pantographic collectors, they travel exclusively on well maintained,system integrated tracks.

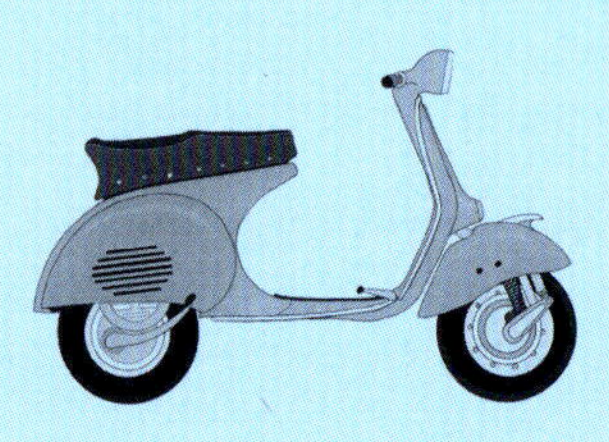

Fig. 6V VESPA GS 150 V2, BM410 (p. 179)

YEAR 1956
MANUFACTURER
Vespa, a subsidiary of Piaggio Group, Italy

Easy to straddle while maintaining one's dignity, easy to stay dry in case of puddles, with convenient storage, the Vespa was arguably the first urban scooter to appeal to riders of both sexes. Lightweight and nimble, it was soon to be found on college campuses, city streets, and backroads, helping to revive Italy's postwar economy with inspired engineering and design.

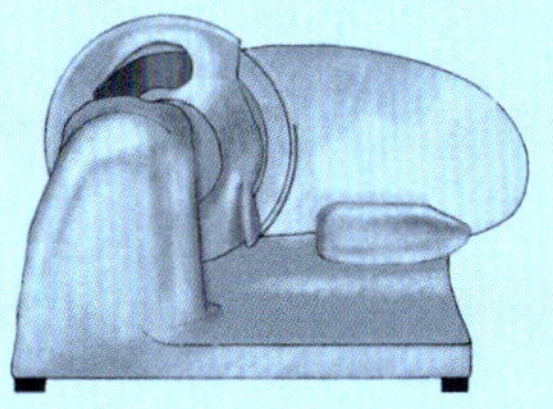

Fig. 6W

STREAMLINER MEAT SLICER, MODEL 410 (p. 179)

YEAR c.1940
DESIGNERS
Egmont Arens and Theodore C. Brookhart
MANUFACTURER
The Hobart Mfg. Co., USA

The svelte form of this meat slicer eliminates the difficult-to-clean nooks and crannies of its peer appliances. Smooth, functional design, attentive to the demands of professional butchers, led to an object that transcends its utilitarian role, and earned it a permanent place in the collections of major museums in the world.

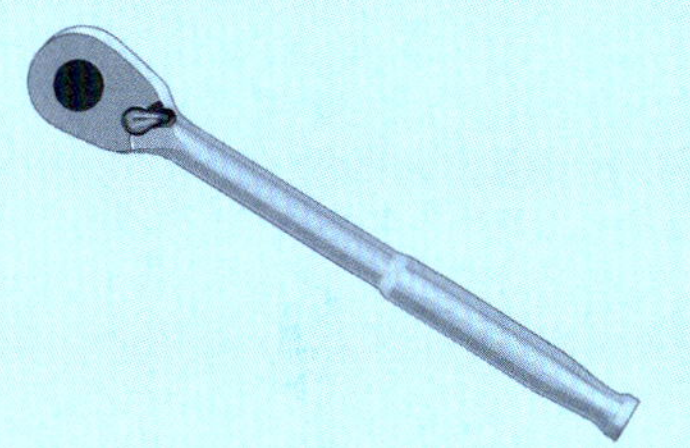

Fig. 6X

REVERSIBLE 1/2" DRIVE RATCHET HANDLE (p. 179)

MANUFACTURER
Wiha Tools, USA

The absence of visual embellishments, in keeping with this tool's immaculate form, emphasizes the left-to-right function of its ratchet control button, and avoids knurling and grip patterns in favor of smooth, easy to clean surfaces.

Streamline Illustrations

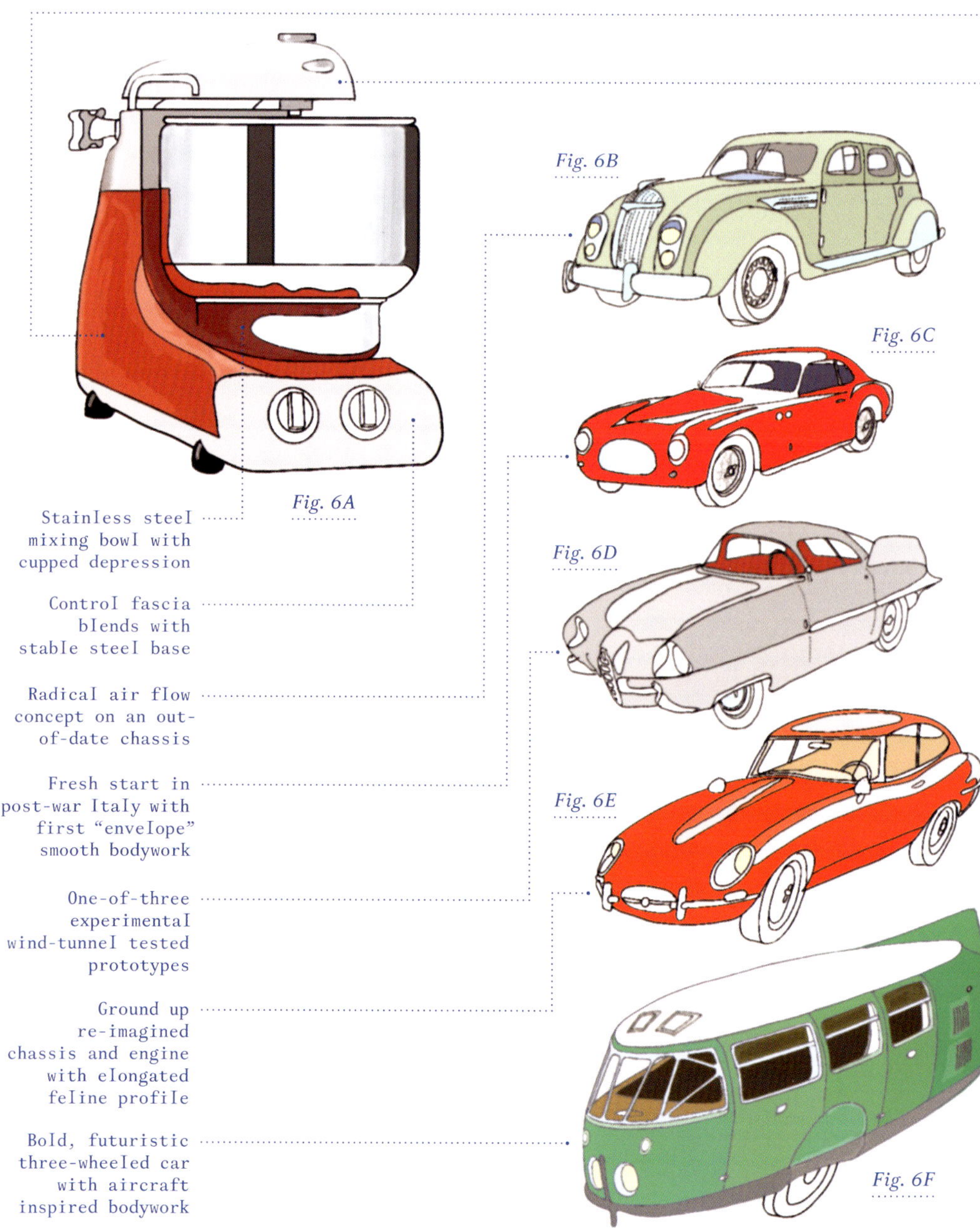

ANKARSRUM ASSISTENT ORIGINAL MIXER (*Fig. 6A*), AIRFLOW SEDAN (*Fig. 6B*), CISITALIA COUPE, 202 GT (*Fig. 6C*), ALFA ROMEO COUPE, BAT 9 OR BERLINA AERODINAMICA TECNICA (*Fig. 6D*), JAGUAR XK-E FIXED HEAD COUPE (*Fig. 6E*), DYMAXION PROTOTYPE (*Fig. 6F*)

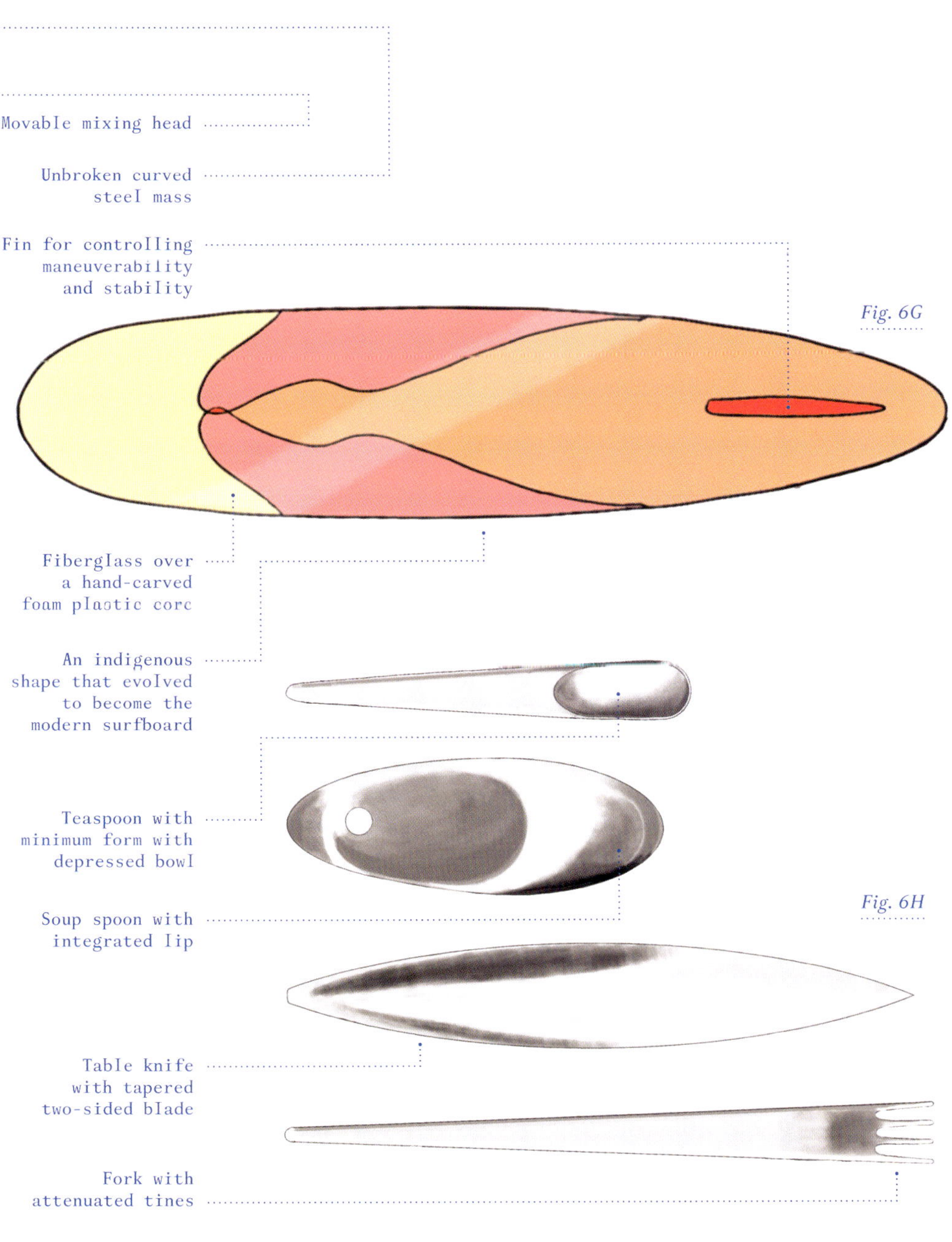

SURFBOARD (*Fig. 6G*), MONO ZEUG FLATWARE (*Fig. 6H*)

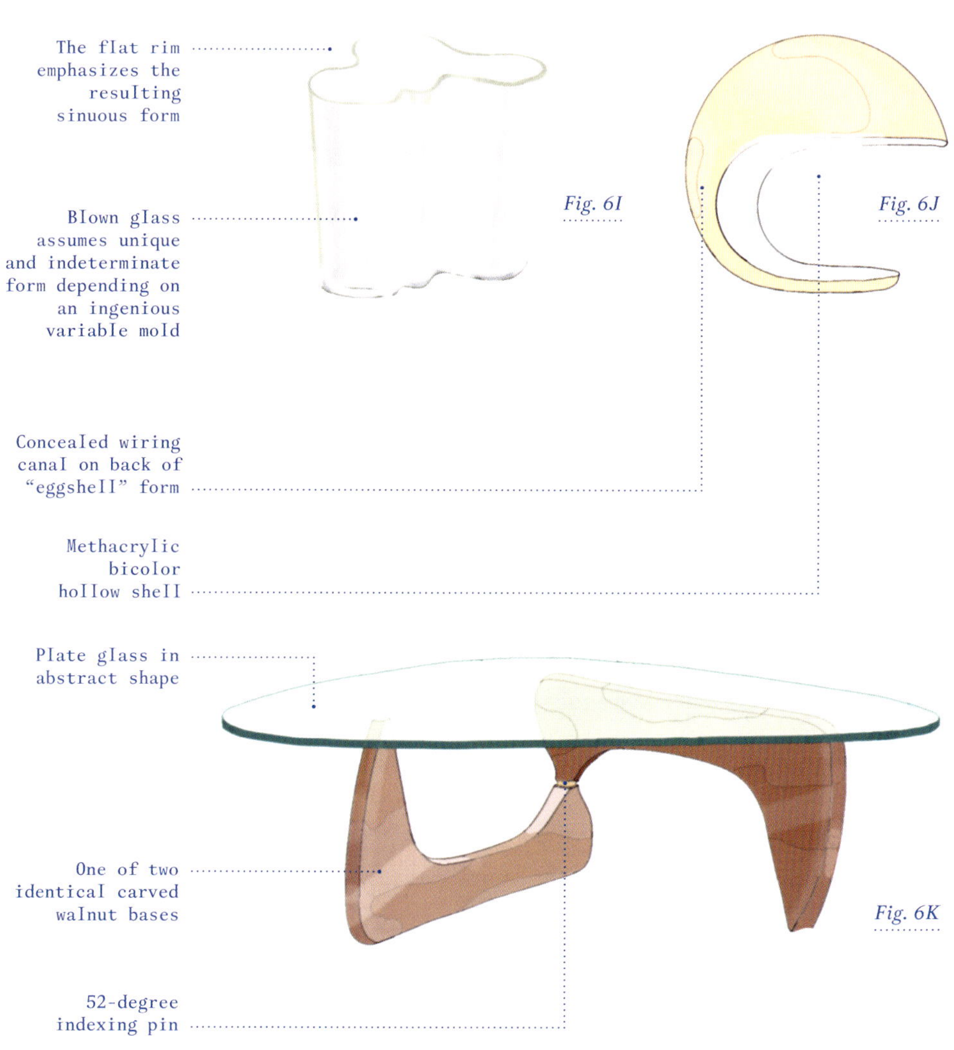

VASE (*Fig. 6I*), FOGLIA LAMP (*Fig. 6J*), NOGUCHI COFFEE TABLE (*Fig. 6K*)

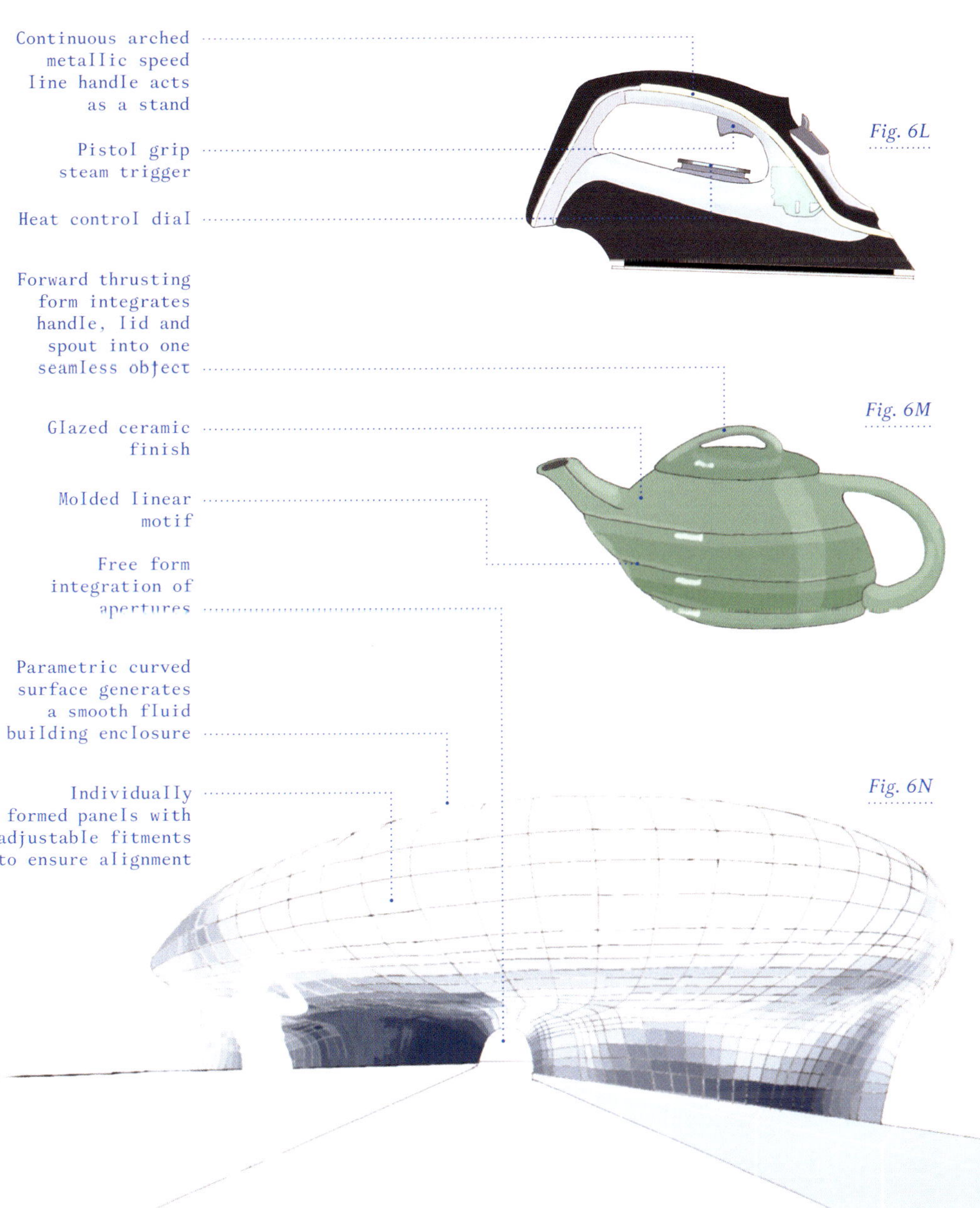

INTELLITEMP IRON (*Fig. 6L*), BAUER TEAPOT (*Fig. 6M*), DONGDAEMUN DESIGN PLAZA (*Fig. 6N*)

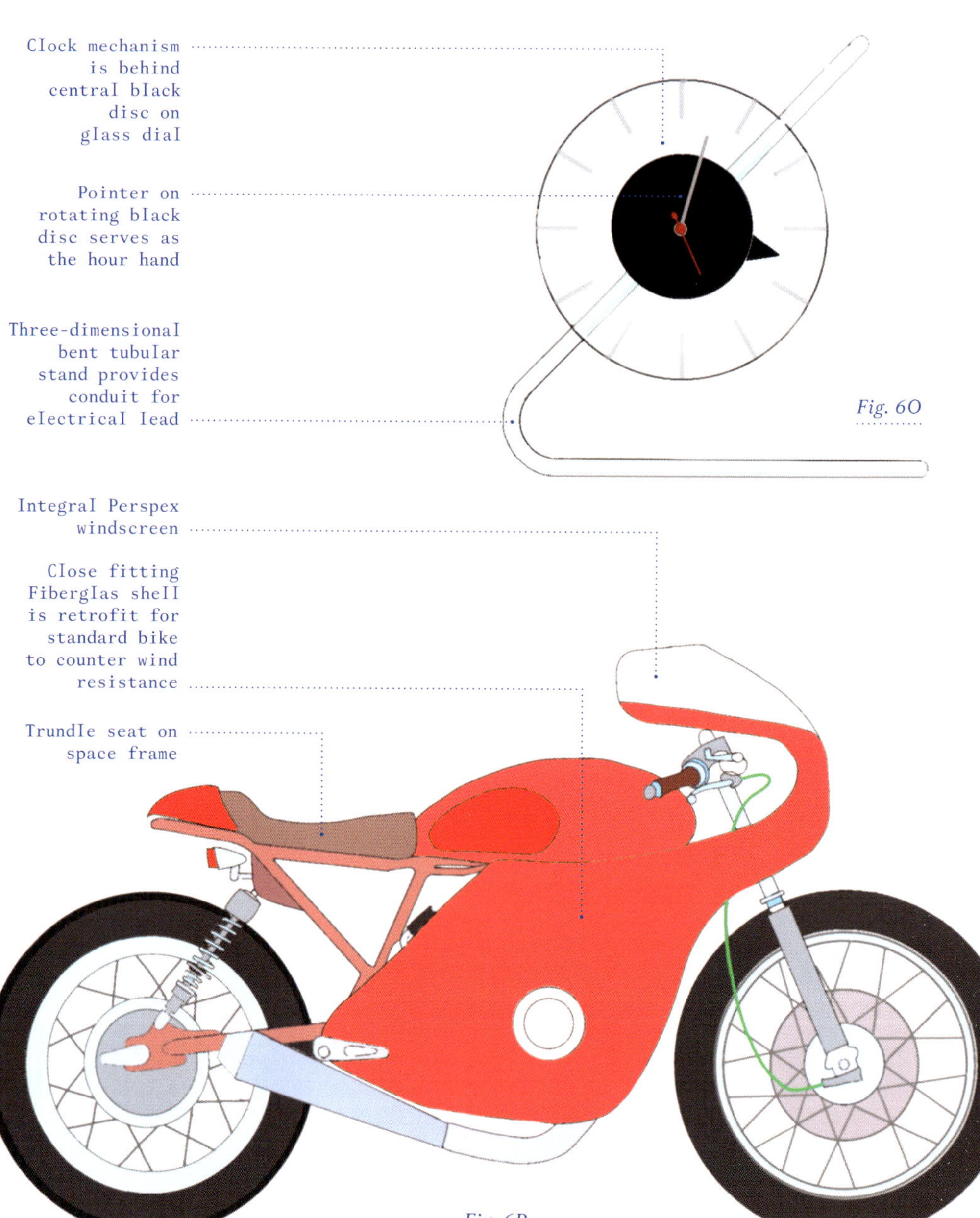

Fig. 6O

Fig. 6P

ARODS CLOCK (*Fig. 6O*), HONDA CR500 HAILWOOD RACE FAIRING (*Fig. 6P*)

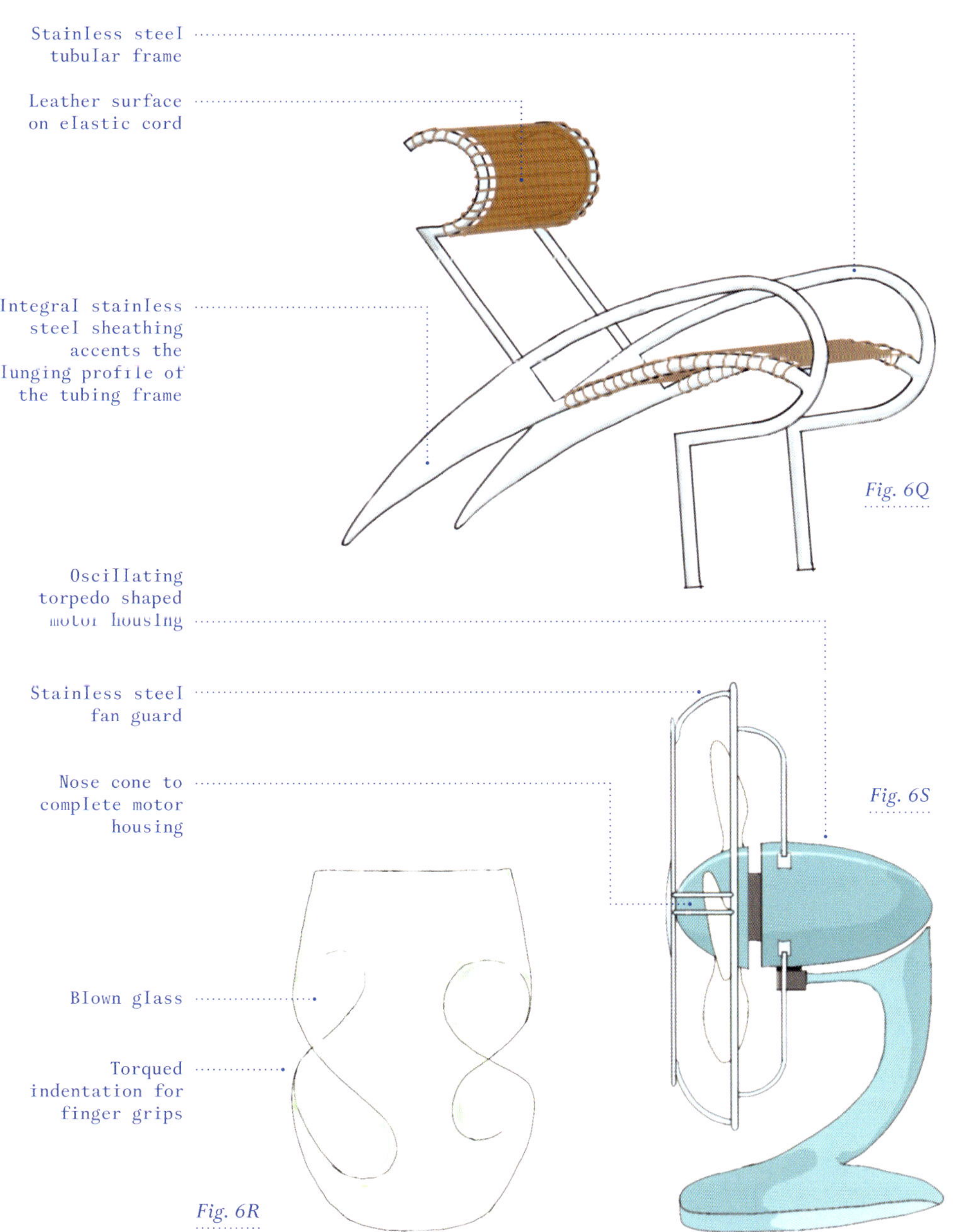

JULIETTE CHAIR (*Fig. 6Q*),
CONUNDRUM WINE GLASS (*Fig. 6R*), AIRFLOW FAN (*Fig. 6S*)

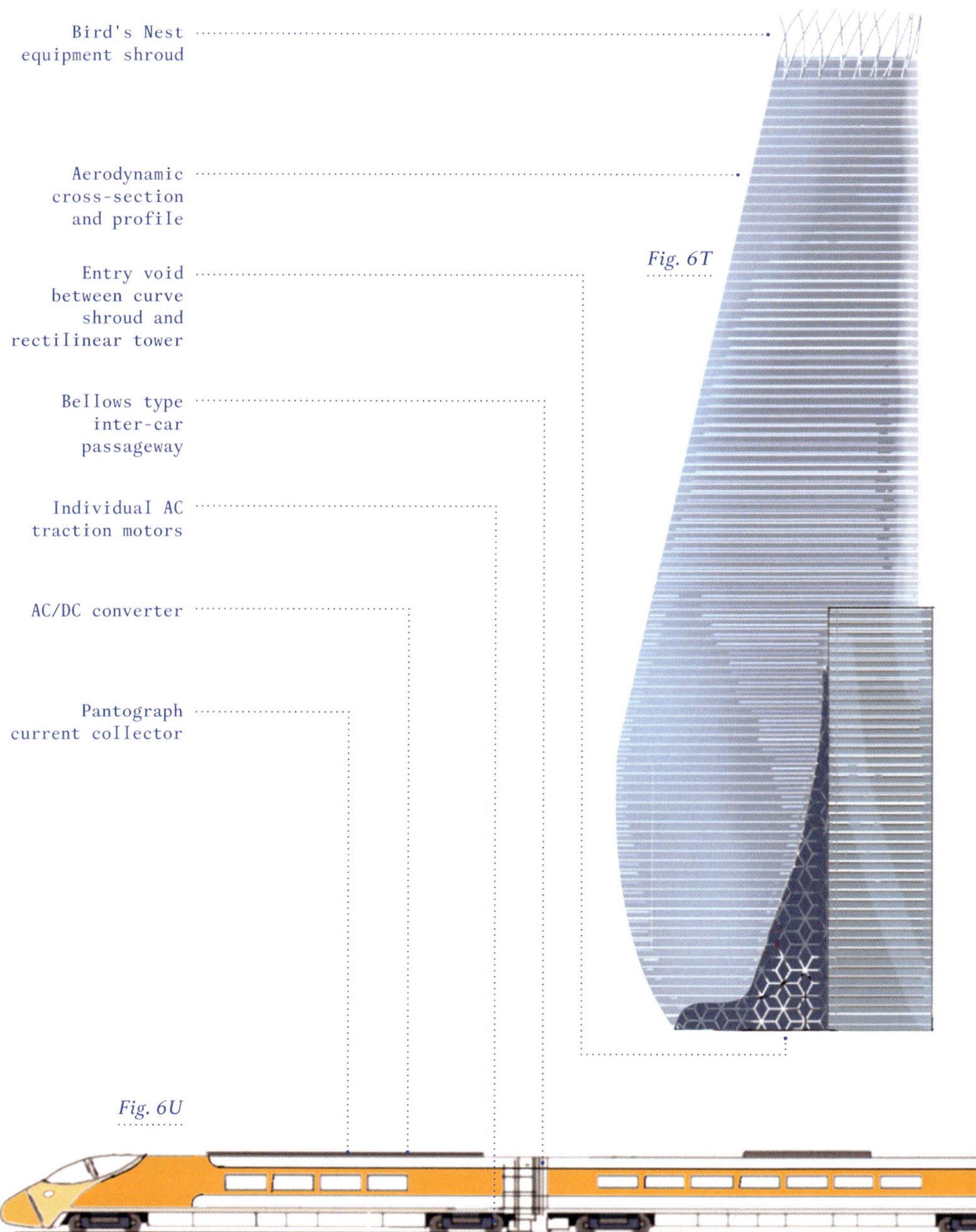

PHARE TOWER (*Fig. 6T*), HEXIE HARMONY HIGH SPEED TRAIN (*Fig. 6U*)

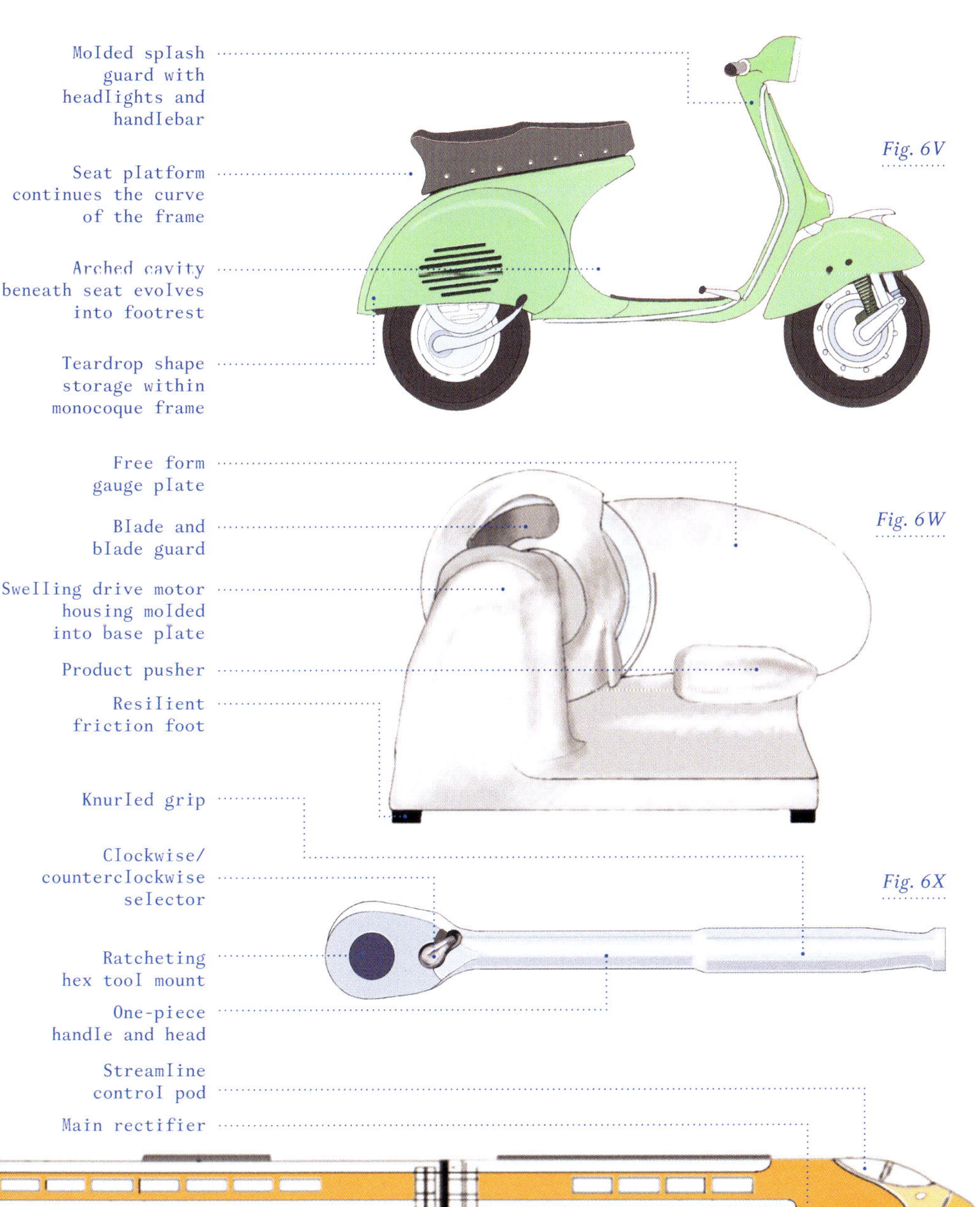

VESPA GS 150 V2, BM410 (*Fig. 6V*),
STREAMLINER MEAT SLICER, MODEL 410 (*Fig. 6W*),
REVERSIBLE 1/2" DRIVE RATCHET HANDLE (*Fig. 6X*)

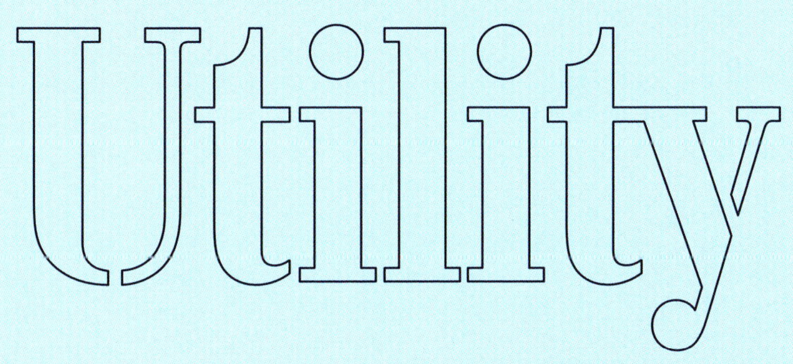

MEANING

"Don't be fooled by all the bells and whistles. All you need is this."

ATTRIBUTES

Straightforward expression of structure, fastenings, or parts and materials as necessary to achieve durability, usefulness and ease of function.

By the mid-20th Century, "absolutes" in design were challenged by the advent of radical new technologies and the evolution of new standards in response. Post-war surplus lots were full to bursting with never-before-seen cans of spray paint, plastic aircraft canopies, fiberglass, discarded instruments, and jeeps ripe for the picking.

It wasn't long before manufacturers, hobbyists, and amateur inventors noticed and began incorporating bits and pieces of the leftover objects – as well as technologies developed for the war effort – into a new generation of peacetime products. Charles and Ray Eames famously converted the process they had developed for their molded "plyform" military leg splint into a new generation of furniture – and popular appetites, eager for a fresh start, enthusiastically followed.

A second revolution in popular taste wasn't far behind when the first moon landing, in 1969, brought an unprecedented burst of visual and technical novelty – from the look of spacesuits to the Lunar Excursion Vehicle (LEV). Wrapped in gold foil, with functional bits protruding at odd angles and a goblin personality, the LEV had an unprecedented look – yet one that was emphatically pragmatic, shaped by outer-space safety measures, human factors, and aerospace engineering.

That it departed significantly from pre-moon landing conceptions of space travel, as featured in movies and magazines, revealed the limits of designers' imagination during an era of sugar-coated, chrome-loaded automobiles and Googie-styled restaurants, inspired by an imagined future. In fact, it wasn't until *after* the NASA moonwalk that movie designers and illustrators shifted from streamlined Star Trek imagery to the sensor-encrusted spaceships of *Alien* (1979) and its offspring. A new era had begun, dubbed "hi-tech" by the popular press. Houses featuring raw fastenings and steel girders proliferated, while appliance manufacturers rejiggered their offerings to eliminate the pastel colors that had characterized 50's and early 60's models in favor of the exposed, industrial-looking metal of function-driven design.

But the idea that *form "inevitably" follows function* is an astute, somewhat subversive reading of Louis Sullivan's dictum, suggesting an apparent lack of design intent. As pencil meets paper, certain details and choices will inevitably emerge, potentially giving shape, form, and style to functional necessities. It is then that screws are exposed or suppressed, that surfaces are polished, and corners are radiused. Whatever the discipline, such artful choices can create a classic or a flop. This is the realm where proportion, massing, and workmanship can elevate a merely useful object to a memorable icon.

Designs that eschew "niceties," such as comfort and ergonomics, in favor of blunt expression of required functions often lead to formally or aesthetically extreme solutions. But works that *celebrate* structural and operational necessities – such as fastenings, springs, and materials – also connote a certain "engineering pragmatism," thus distilling design to its essence. Such a bare-knuckles approach avoids the pitfalls of an obvious style, while suggesting that anything additional or ingratiating is excessive and impedes efficiency. In return, there is an implicit tolerance for sometimes incoherent, inconsistent *formal* relationships, which seek to validate each aspect of the design by prioritizing only the necessary and uncompromised elements.

Although this type of function-driven design surged after the 1969 moonwalk, notable examples of it had emerged in earlier periods, sometime before the very *idea* of industrial design, as opposed to engineering, was a recognizable activity. Palpable weight, no-nonsense form, and industrial machine-like controls are, for example, the defining characteristics of the KitchenAid Model K mixer – designed by Egmont Arens and patented well ahead of its time in 1937. Made of cast iron, with primitive geometry, it made no ingratiating compromises. Like the gruff cowboy heroes who epitomize the unyielding mythos of the Wild West, the design evokes traditional masculine values while also providing a focused, well-defined utilitarian function. Devoid of extraneous decorative elements and as bold in its way as much larger, more powerful machinery, it is as explicit as a Bukowski novel, a big cigar in a smoky saloon, or a fully loaded and exposed weapon. Its no-frills attitude exudes purpose and a capacity for big jobs, bringing a professional-league tool to a woman's traditional domain that, by its presence, elevates the role of the moms, housekeepers, and wives who swear by it.

In 1948, thc functional shape of the molded fiberglass chair that won MoMA's International Competition for Low-Cost Furniture Design was defended by its authors, Charles and Rae Eames, as designed for the way people actually sit, in contrast to the rigid posture demanded by traditional furniture. But to achieve success at that time meant convincing consumers to abandon the conventional decorative aspects of their cherished dining sets, in order to embrace the spare functionality of a new breed of seemingly utilitarian furniture.

The governing aesthetic of well-designed products in this style – the common theme that unites disparate offerings by legions of manufacturers – is the care with which the competing functional elements are resolved, and the resulting harmony of the parts that make up the whole.

Utility Observations

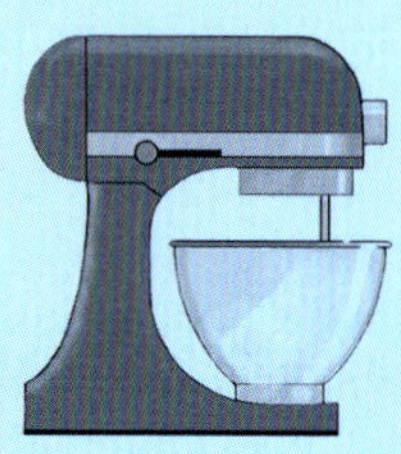

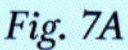

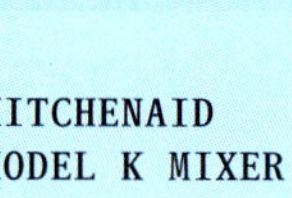

Fig. 7A KITCHENAID MODEL K MIXER
(p. 200)

Fig. 7B LATHE CONTROL CRANK
(p. 200)

YEAR 1937
DESIGNER
Egmont Arens
MANUFACTURER
KitchenAid,
The Hobart Corp.,
USA

Patented in the late thirties, and offering a unique double-action mixing head, suited to heavy-duty chores, the sturdy cast-iron KitchenAid Model K mixer weighs nearly 11 kilos, or 23 pounds. With robust mechanical controls and an iconic presence, its hefty, no-frills design established it as a tool for professional bakers that was swiftly adopted by proud housewives as a must-have kitchen accessory. Easy to clean, with no nooks and crannies and requiring no other maintenance, it is a prime example of utilitarian design.

The Kitchen Aid mixer's control knobs utilize typical manual controls for industrial machinery, which often feature sliding or ratcheting levers with ball-shaped tips to give oil-soaked handles and slippery hands a sure grip.

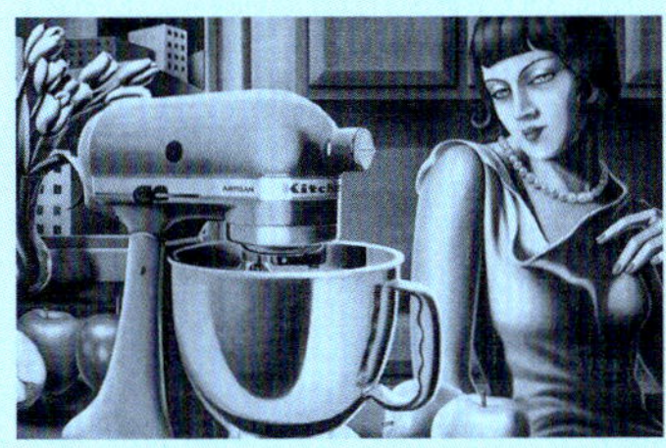

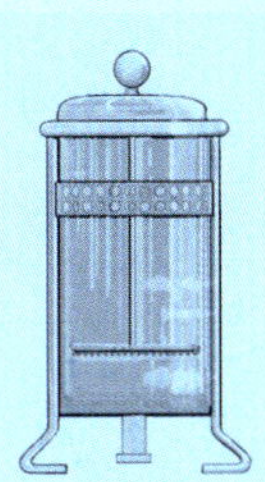

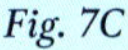

Fig. 7C KITCHENAID BY ART DÉCO 1925 (p. 200)

YEAR 2011
AD CAMPAIGN BY
DDB Brazil

Fig. 7D CHAMBORD FRENCH PRESS (p. 201)

YEAR 1928
DESIGNERS
Attilio Calimani and Guilio Moneta
MANUFACTURER
Bodum Inc., Denmark

In this 2011 ad, the jarring juxtaposition of a hunky KitchenAid mixer with a woman in seductive evening wear – with its echoes of Stanley Kowalski and Blanche DuBois – suggests the psychological pull that bonds many chefs to the brand.

Long before our brewing experience was aided by electrically powered pumps, forcing hot water through a shot-glass-sized coffee pod, the French Press performed much the same task utilizing human muscle to push a fine filter through coffee grounds submerged in boiling water in a cylindrical vessel. To connoisseurs, the resulting brew excels in aroma as well as taste and has become a reliable part of millions of morning routines.

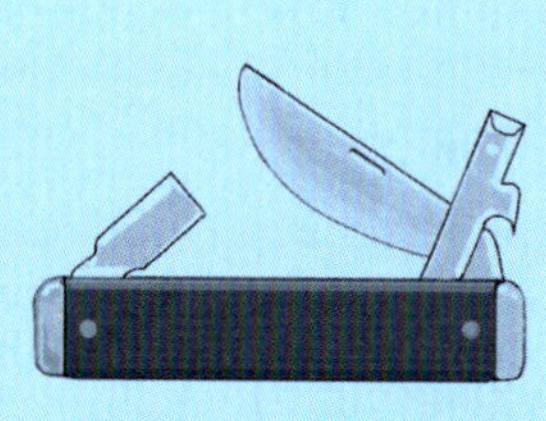

Fig. 7E VICTORINOX SWISS OFFICER'S KNIFE CHAMPION (p. 201)

YEAR 1968
DESIGNER
Karl Elsener
MANUFACTURER
Victorinox, Switzerland

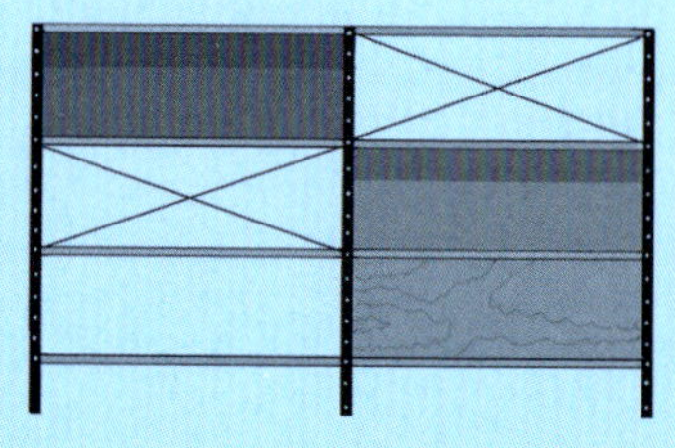

Fig. 7F EAMES STORAGE UNIT (p. 202)

YEAR 1950
DESIGNERS
Charles and Ray Eames
MANUFACTURER
Herman Miller Inc., USA

Elegant functionality, driven by the need to address multiple tasks in a simple, easy-to-access package, the smooth, streamlined form slips easily in and out of a pocket or purse and is readily identified by its bright red color. Small fingernail-ready incisions on the retractable blades enable the user to deploy each of the many tools individually, without adding to the device's overall weight or size. A triumph of intelligent design, unchanged for many decades.

With their signature storage unit, Charles and Ray Eames gave character, design intent, and flexibility to what might otherwise have been an anonymous stack of shelves. Where ordinary furniture *concealed* construction details, the Eames's went to great pains to *accentuate* the nuts and bolts. Where ordinary furniture attempted to project a spirit of *gravitas,* the Eames's created an "Erector Set" of colorful components, much like those in the classic children's toy. And where ordinary shelving units achieved stability with stout joints and solid backs, the Eames' braced each frame with a visually delicate, piano wire "X."

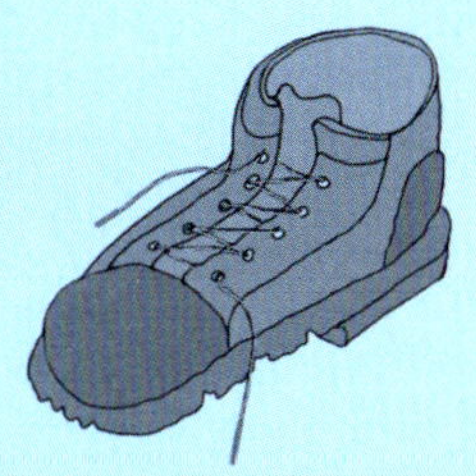

Fig. 7G WORK BOOTS (p. 203)

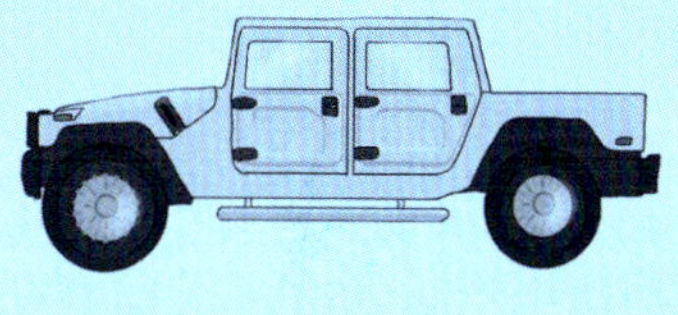

Fig. 7H HUMMER H2 (p. 203)

YEAR c.2004
MANUFACTURER
AM General,
General Motors,
USA

Is there a more frequently abused, tortured, and neglected object of clothing than the ordinary work boot? Subjected to multiple indignities and expected to keep the wearer's feet warm and dry no matter the circumstance, the work boot, if it could talk, would say "Bring it On!" Rugged, practical materials display their readiness to absorb rough treatment, husky eyelets can clog with sand and mud and still function, while steel reinforced toes and heels can shed heavy blows that would crush more refined materials. No bows to fashion distort their sense of purpose or obscure their rational construction.

With massive rubber straps to hold it together, an assortment of visible buckles, exposed hinges, and deeply embossed door panels, the civilian version of the legendary military Humvee parroted the gnarly details of its combat-ready progenitor while taming its no-holds-barred qualities. Elimination of military priorities resulted in a 30 percent reduction in scale and weight, while other modifications stopped just short of a gentrified take-over, trading the original raw mil-spec Humvee interior for an upscale SUV version with vague appeals to the hyper alpha-male libido thought to be its primary customer.

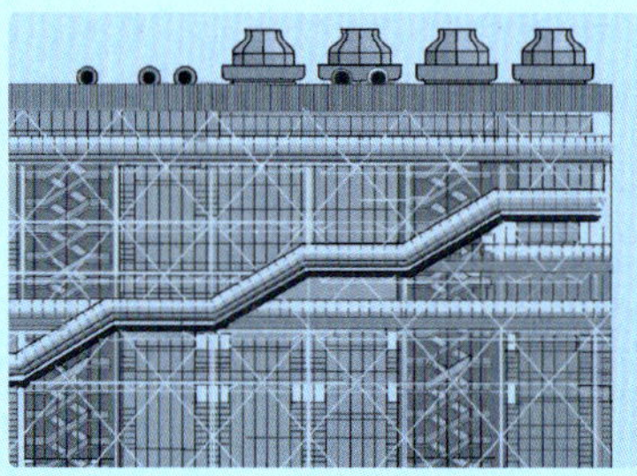

Fig. 7I THE CENTRE POMPIDOU (p. 204)

YEAR 1977
ARCHITECTS
Renzo Piano and Richard Rogers
LOCATION
Paris, France

Fig. 7J PLUG-IN CITY DRAWING (p. 204)

YEAR 1965
ARCHITECT
Archigram, Sir Peter Cook

Based unapologetically on the visionary concepts of Archigram – the avant-garde British architects known for their provocative unbuilt projects of the 1960s and 1970s – the inside-out architecture of the Centre Pompidou suspends meticulously designed functional parts in front of conventional cladding and fenestration, evoking the character of a well-maintained petroleum refinery teleported to the center of the city. Usual internal functions, such as air-conditioning ducts, escalators, and corridors are arranged for access, color coded, and hung on trapeze-like exterior suspenders, where their colorful jumble inspires innumerable selfies.

Archigram's colorful visualizations of "Plug-in City" proposed an ever-changing urban landscape, in which brightly colored apartment modules could be positioned nearly anywhere on massive frames, with overhead cranes which straddled older, decrepit buildings to create a new, vibrant way of urban life. By exposing the framework, as well as the individuality of the models, this visionary proposal stripped away non-functional "skin," highlighting dynamic relationships among component parts.

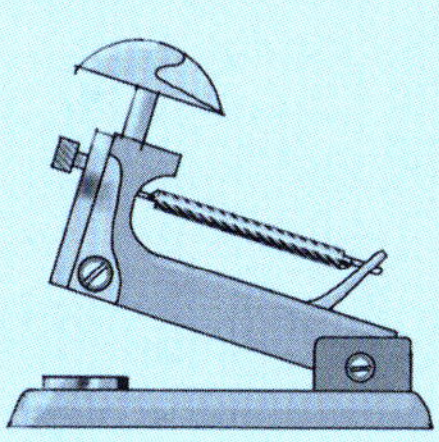

Fig. 7K EL CASCO STAPLER M-1 (p. 205)

YEAR c.1932
MANUFACTURER
El Casco, Spain

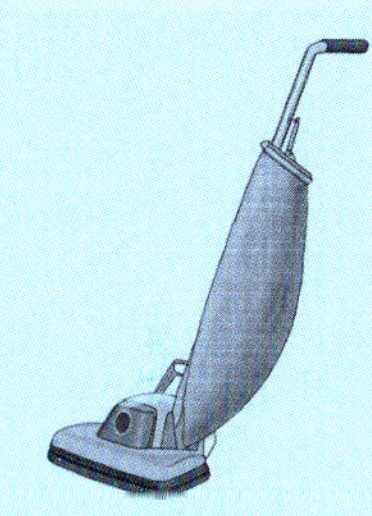

Fig. 7L HOOVER LARK UPRIGHT VACUUM (p. 205)

YEAR 1956
MANUFACTURER
Hoover, USA

On occasion, exposing the constituent parts of a simple, functional object can elevate its visual vocabulary to an intriguing assemblage, in which each part assumes an individual identity without sacrificing its essential operation. This stapler flaunts its springs, knurled knobs, and guillotine-like mechanism in a carefully arranged composition of coordinated components. With echoes of larger-scale engineering works, like Bugatti sports cars or steam locomotives, the components are robust, purposeful, and elegantly composed.

Conceived in an era when in-person demonstrations of home appliances were *de rigueur*, the Hoover vacuum cleaner was a pitch-perfect assemblage of practical, visible parts, each expressing its specific functional attributes. Such an ideal subject enabled the salesman to describe in detail the superior attributes of what was not yet a fixture in every home. After demystifying the working parts, and thus gaining the trust of the housekeeper, the sales demonstration climaxed with a scattering of debris, to the horror of the customer, followed by a dignified pick up.

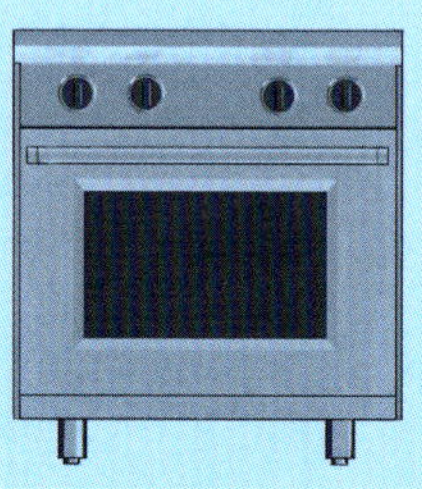

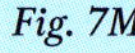

Fig. 7M WOLF GAS RANGE (p. 206)

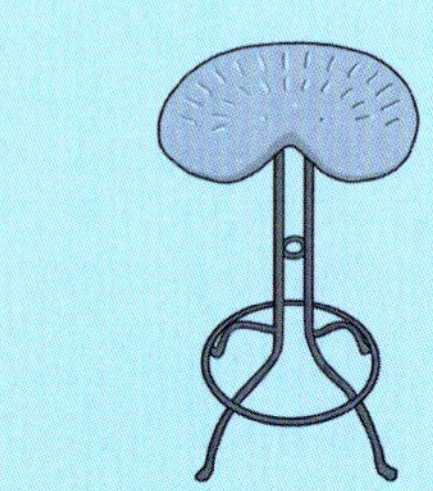

Fig. 7N TRACTOR SEAT STOOL (p. 206)

MANUFACTURER
Wolf Range Company, USA

The Wolf Gas Range's indestructible brake-formed stainless steel sheathing, conspicuous gaps between parts, kitchen-glove-scaled red knobs, and massive cast-iron grates are features found in restaurant equipment that have here been domesticated for the home cook without sacrificing their "professional" allure. Accomplished, with burners capable of 15,000 BTU, it is as capable of heating a cup of tea as boiling a cauldron of broth in quick order. With a majestic presence that confers serious kitchen credentials on the owner, this visually impressive, but difficult-to-clean appliance has muscled its way into countless otherwise refined environments.

Ubiquitous, nearly invisible in its ordinariness, but freezing cold much of the year, the original cast-iron tractor seat – called "a relic of the inquisition" – was a fixture on farm equipment until the introduction of metal-stamping machinery in the late 19th century, and with it the demise of the traditional material, to be replaced by a lightweight formed steel version that shed both heat and cold. Now a common site in bars and patios, it is no longer specified for agricultural machinery.

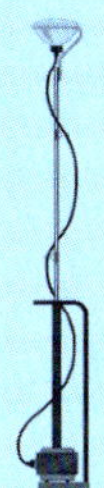
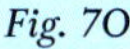
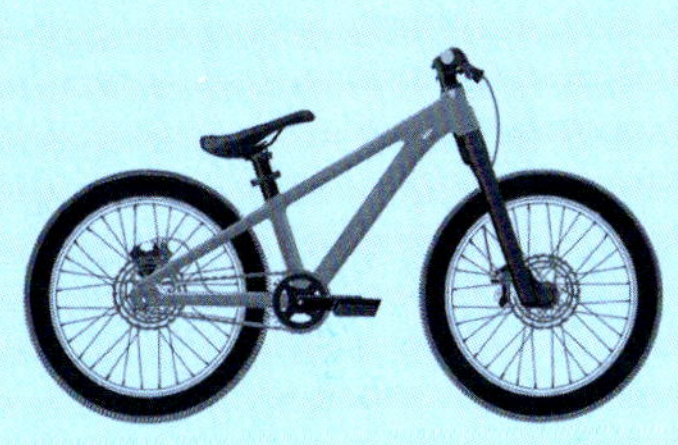

Fig. 7O TOIO FLOOR LAMP (p. 206)

YEAR 1962
DESIGNERS
Achille and Pier Giacomo Castiglioni
MANUFACTURER
Flos, Italy

Fig. 7P HEX STREET TRIALS BIKE (p. 207)

MANUFACTURER
Inspired, UK

With its combination of an automobile headlight, fishing-rod line guides, an industrial transformer for ballast and power, and common steel angles for a prosaic base, the Toio Floor Lamp successfully conveys a seemingly improvised, "off-the-shelf" functional aesthetic. By shunning common luxury design tropes and exploring concepts first expressed by Italy's provocative *Arte Povera* movement, its designers, Achille and Pier Giacomo Castiglioni, pried open the closed world of high design, setting forth a fresh new paradigm.

Bicycles, in general, and trials bikes, in particular, balance the structural logic of a rigid, unyielding frame with the visual delicacy of the *derailleur* gear-changing mechanism and its accompanying hand controller and stack of transmission cogs. All of this tech, naked and generally devoid of interpretive gloss, presents a fine-tuned utilitarian object which is venerated for its superior workmanship and no-compromises purity while simply performing a demanding job.

Utility Illustrations

Accessory Port

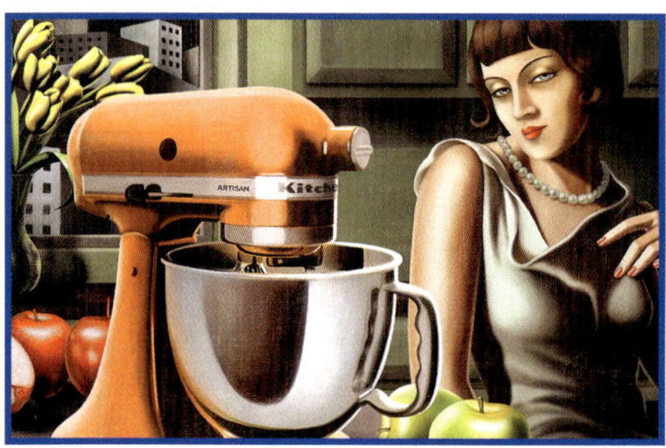

Fig. 7C

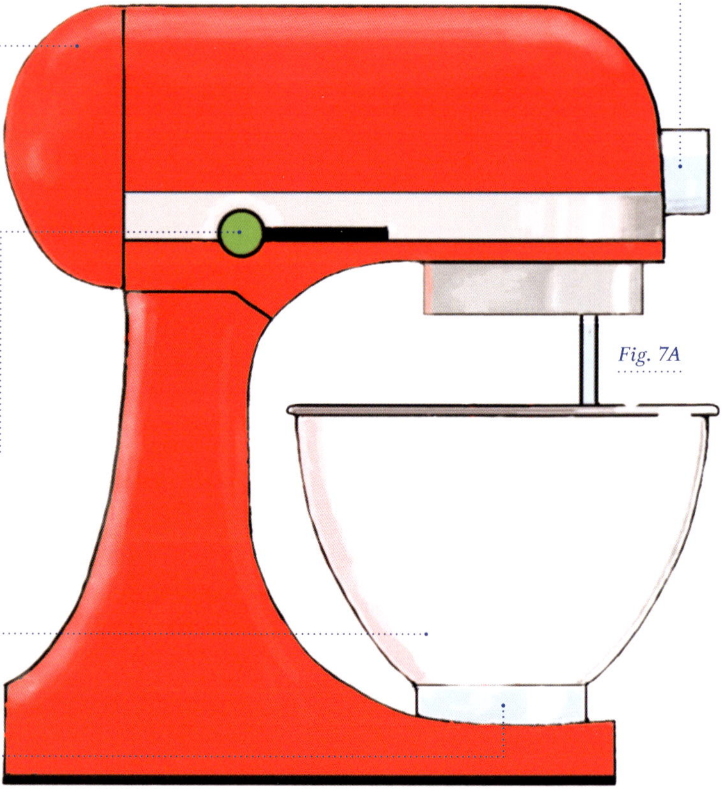

Motor housing

Head lock (R)
and speed
regulator (L)

Fig. 7A

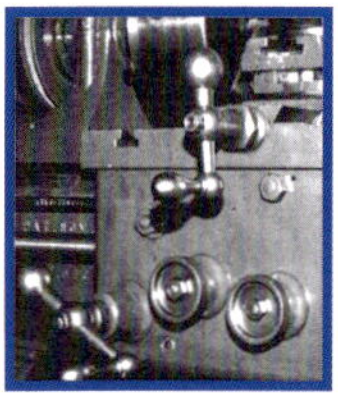

Fig. 7B

Stainless
steel bowl

Fixed bowl
mounting flange

KITCHENAID MODEL K MIXER (*Fig. 7A*), LATHE CONTROL CRANK (*Fig. 7B*), KITCHENAID BY ART DÉCO 1925 (*Fig. 7C*)

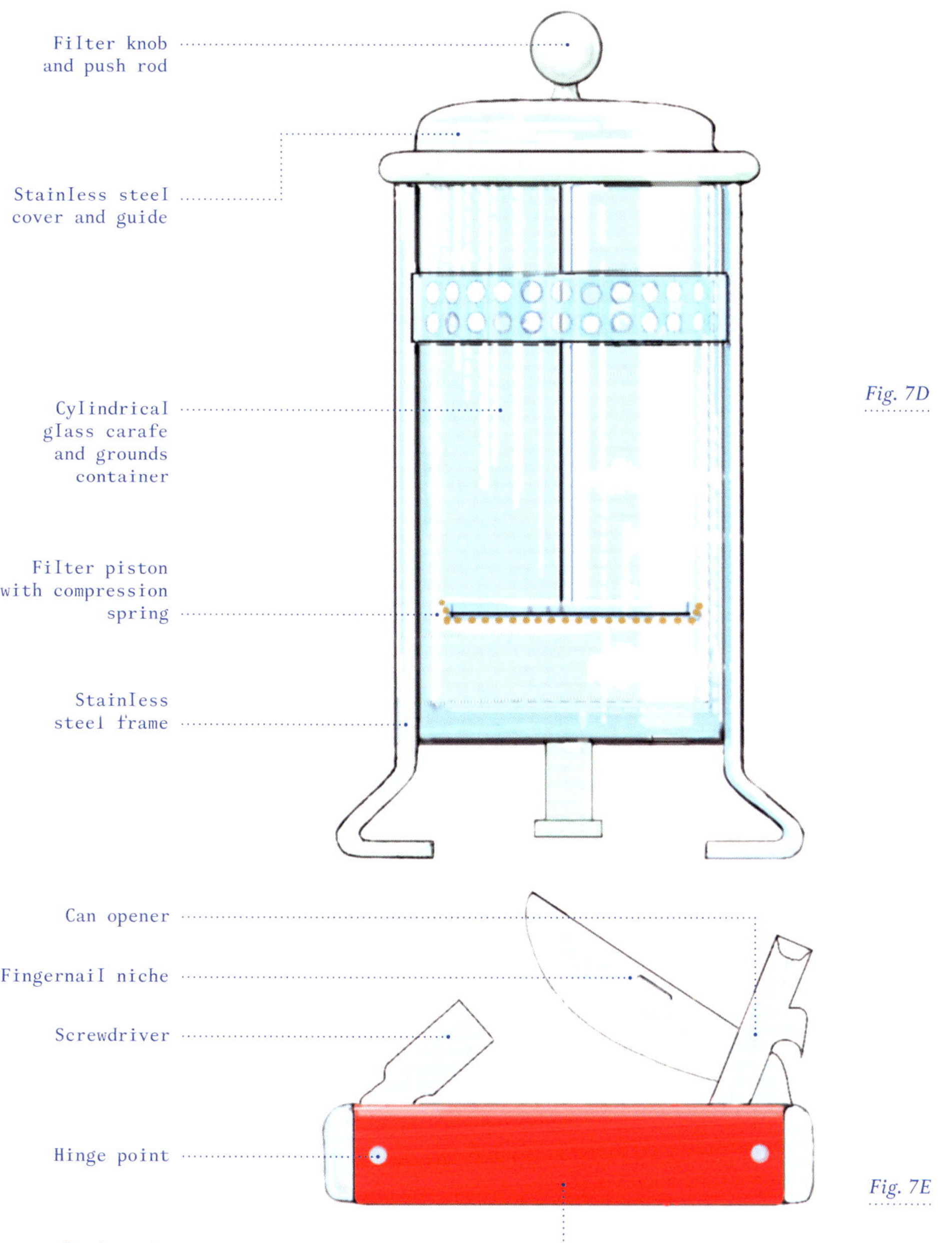

CHAMBORD FRENCH PRESS (*Fig. 7D*),
VICTORINOX SWISS OFFICER'S KNIFE CHAMPION (*Fig. 7E*)

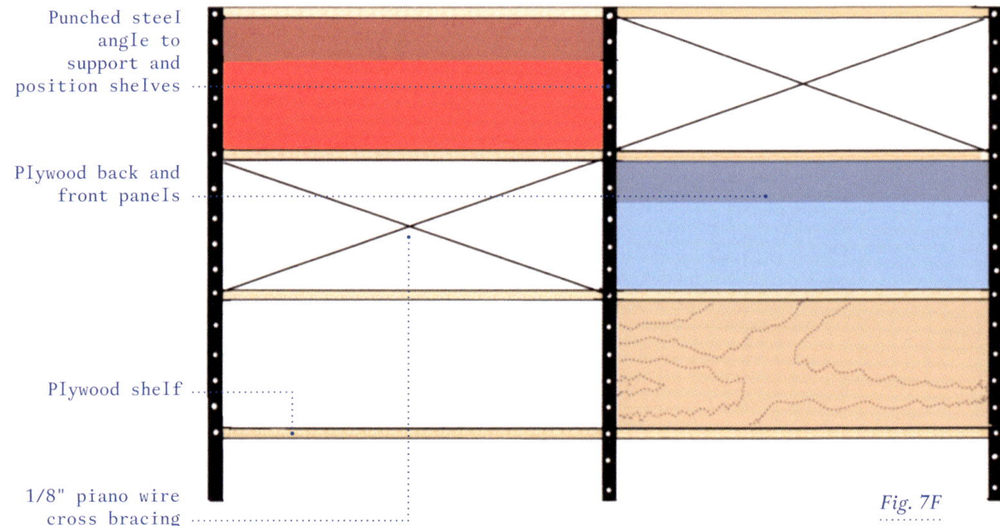

Fig. 7F

Fig. 7H.2
Externally mounted hinges and hardware facilitate replacement and repair

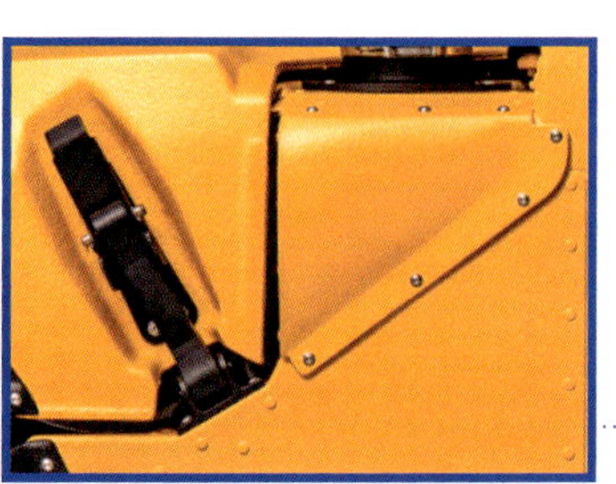

Fig. 7H.3
Molded-rubber hold-downs for access panels absorb shock and resist uncoupling

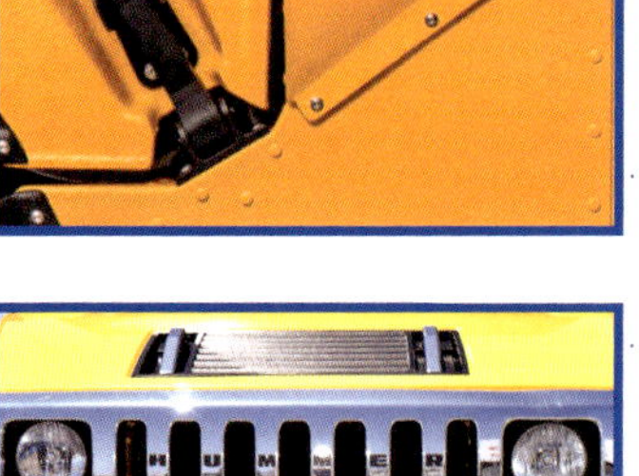

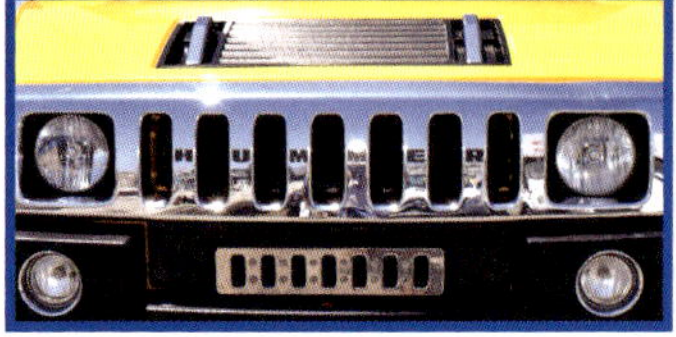

Fig. 7H.4
Robust grillage protects vulnerable components

Generous panel gaps

EAMES STORAGE UNIT (*Fig. 7F*)

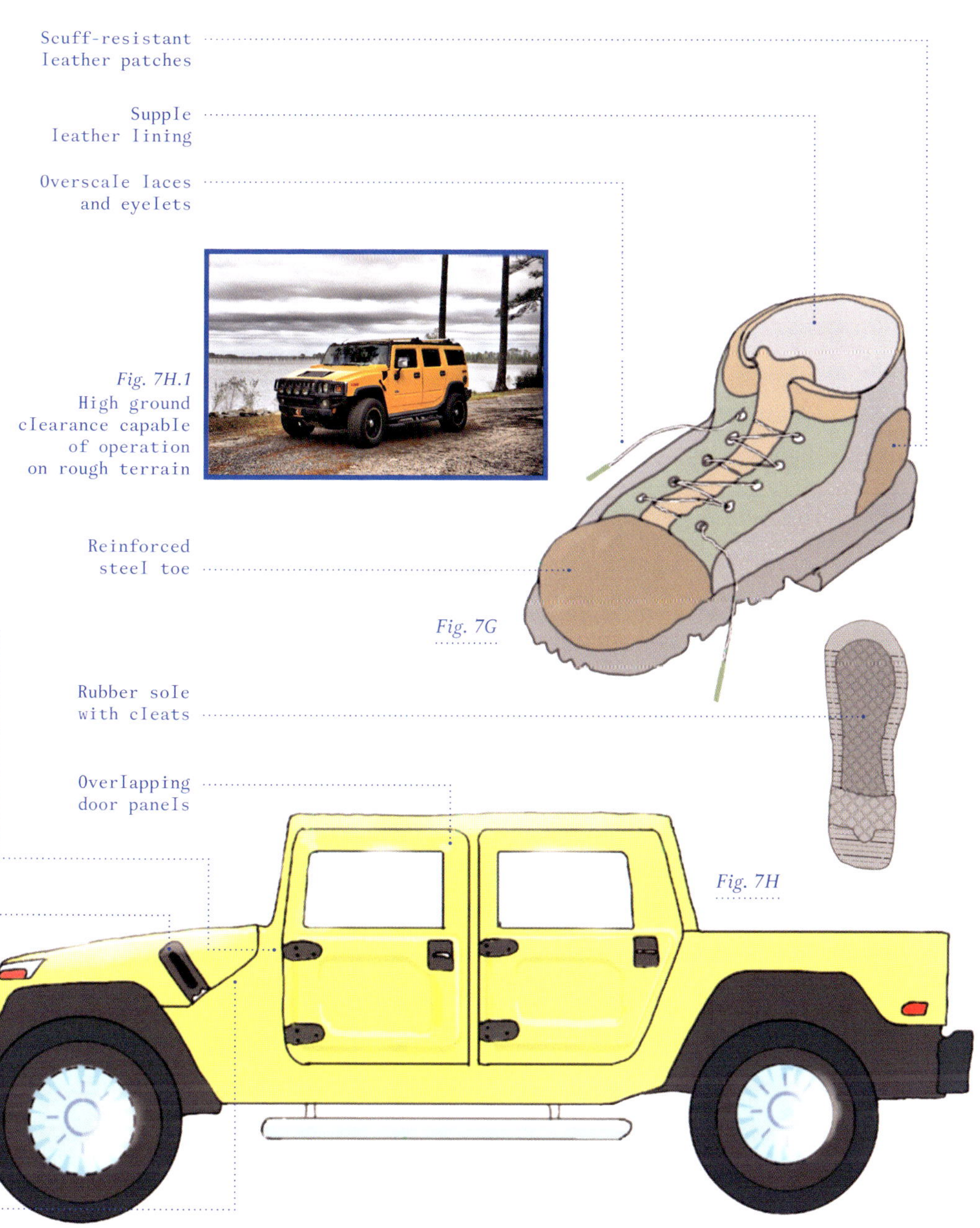

WORK BOOTS (*Fig. 7G*), HUMMER H2 (*Fig. 7H*)

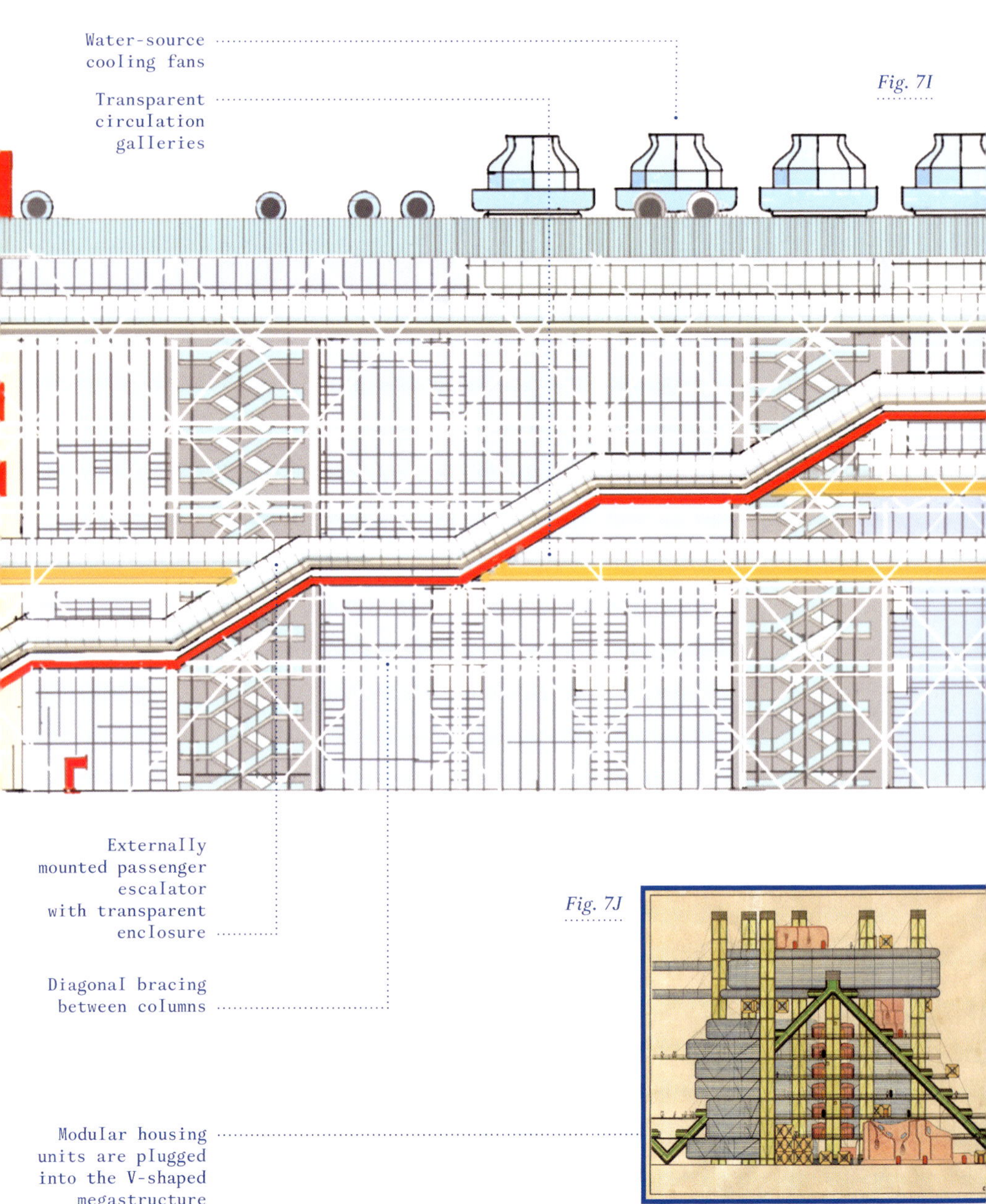

THE CENTRE POMPIDOU (*Fig. 7I*), PLUG-IN CITY DRAWING (*Fig. 7J*)

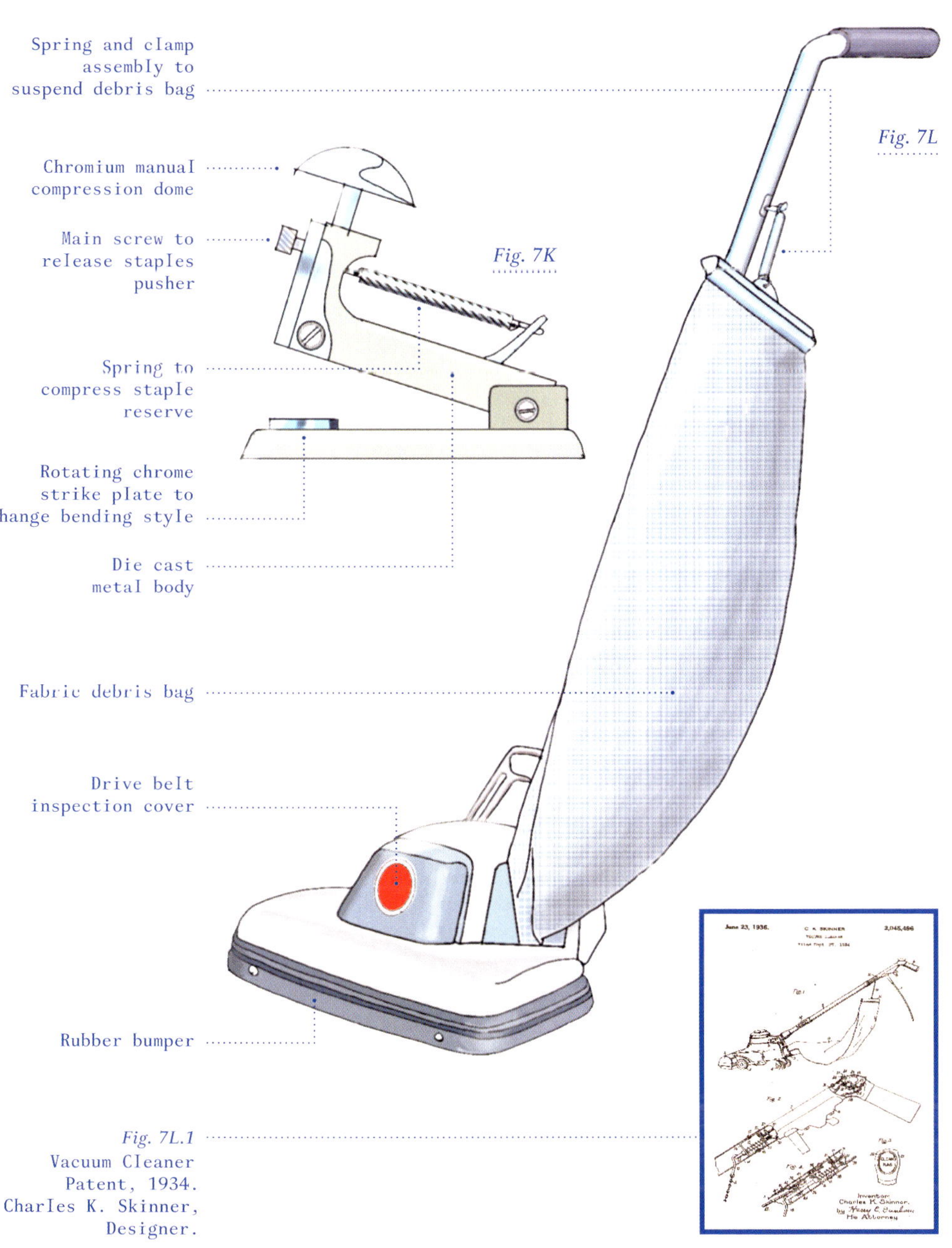

Fig. 7L.1
Vacuum Cleaner Patent, 1934.
Charles K. Skinner, Designer.

EL CASCO STAPLER M-1 (*Fig. 7K*),
HOOVER LARK UPRIGHT VACUUM (*Fig. 7L*)

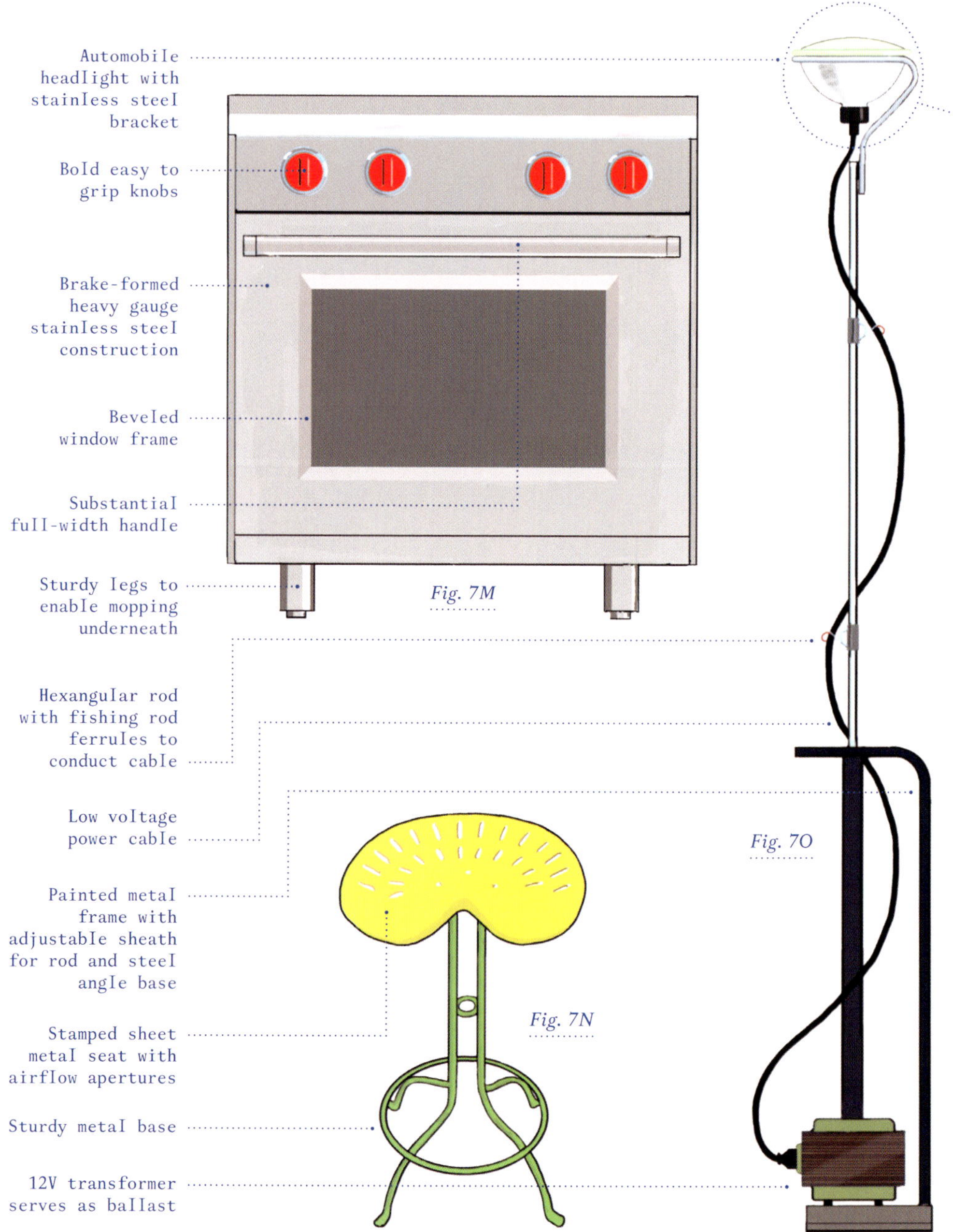

WOLF GAS RANGE (*Fig. 7M*), TRACTOR SEAT STOOL (*Fig. 7N*), TOIO FLOOR LAMP (*Fig. 7O*)

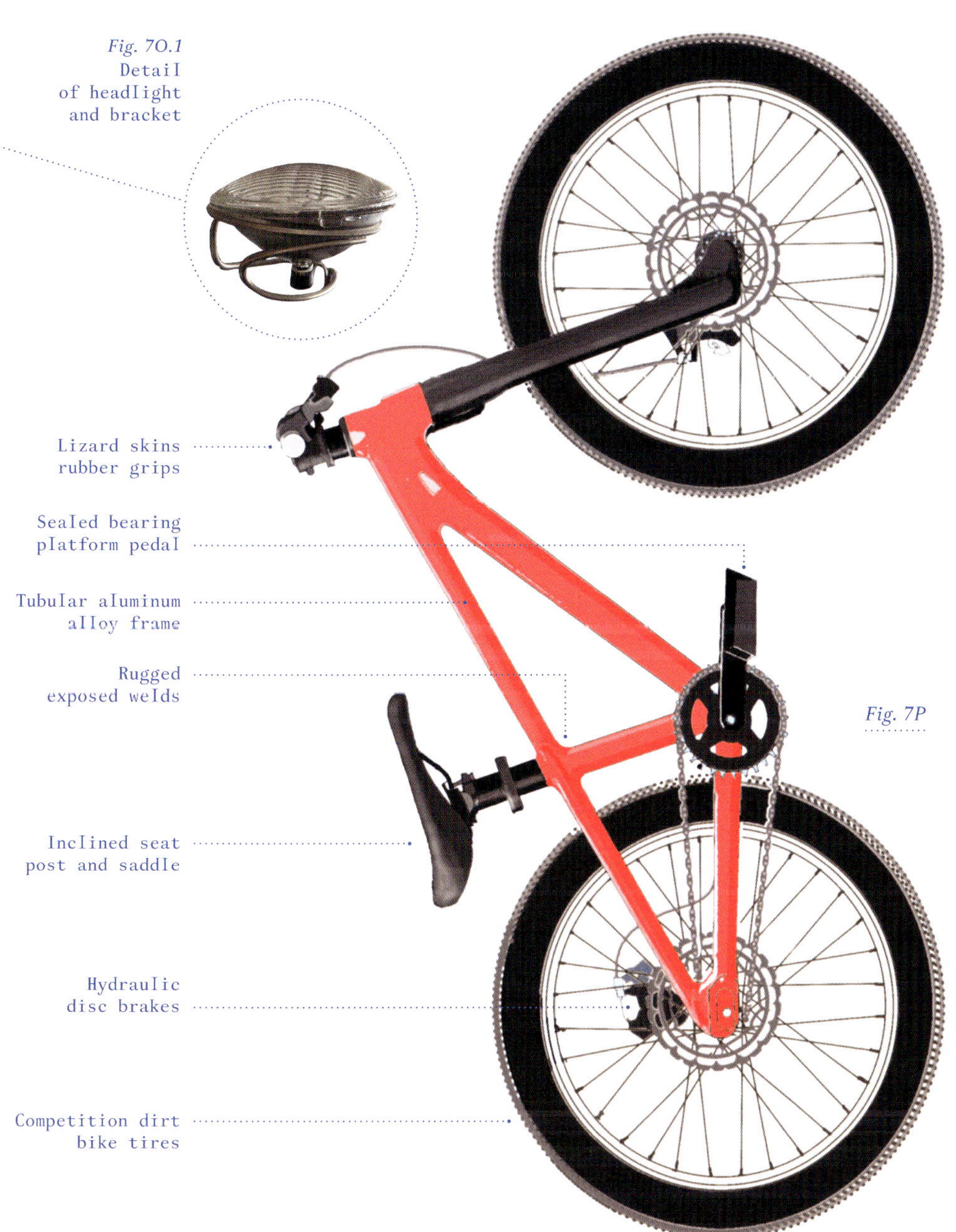

HEX STREET TRIALS BIKE (*Fig. 7P*)

MESSAGE "I do as I want to do... whatever. Use your imagination."

Funk

ATTRIBUTES Assertive, deviant attitude often bringing discordant colors, textures, or clashing forms together in a visual stew redolent of hybridized experience.

The cultural upheavals of the '70s and '80s – including the Watergate scandal, the rise of new Conservativism, and the AIDS crisis – had profound impact on goods and services, as well as the arts and politics.

New aesthetic movements in art, poetry, music, and fashion began to assert their relevance in a world turned upside down by the end of the Vietnam War (and eventually the Cold War), along with the onslaught of new technologies. Cheap recording devices challenged the supremacy of long-established music empires while a renewed interest in D.I.Y. sired a burst of hot rods, outlier house designs, and home-crafted component stereos. The reigning aesthetics of popular entertainment saw a seismic shift, dooming once-prime box-office recording artists as aggressive new rock bands and genres – notably disco, punk, and new wave – rose to top the "hit parade."

Public sensibilities in the realm of manufactured products and other consumer goods – along with the once-saccharine advertising promoting them – also saw major change. The disruption was keenly felt, for example, among automobile manufacturers, creating an opening for "off" brands from Asia and Europe and, in turn, prompting

Detroit's salvo of muscle cars to counterpunch the "anemic" overseas competition.

Postmodern design, in architecture and industrial products, and deviant Punk-influenced and ragamuffin fashion by designers including Vivienne Westwood and Betsey Johnson began to fill the vacuum, while underground clubs flourished in seedy warehouses and biker bars. By the nineties, a full-blown cultural revolution had taken over, with hardcore punk and grunge dominating clubs like CBGB's and the emergence of rebellious cultures with monikers like glam-rock and steampunk, each hellbent on defying traditional norms. Books like William Gibson's sci-fi *Mona Lisa Overdrive* (1988) rapidly became the new bibles of a hip, alienated, counterculture that ruptured long-established literary canons and slapped down boundaries. The *arrivistes* had arrived!

Suddenly, the gloves were off, and time-honored brands began to recalibrate their products to align with perceived changes in consumer taste. In the music business, hip-hop and sampling slipped into the mainstream, bringing with them a new, aggressive musical style, while a potent brew of Hell's Angels, cocaine-fueled artists, and tattooed punks emerged to define a new alternative culture: Funk.

It was a movement that celebrated abrasive non-conformity, deriding the slick, positive messages of consumerism with slogans like Hacking and D.I.Y. Anti-war sentiment morphed into anti-political, anti-corporate stances, while norms in dress were literally turned inside out, with layered outfits featuring undergarments on top, adjustable bra straps flaunted in full view as fashion accessories, and baggy pants on suspenders swinging nearly below the crotch, unabashedly exposing swaths of men's underwear. Defiance was the watchword, daring society to reign in a universal appetite for torn jeans, distressed leather, layers of excess fabric and jarring proportions.

Evidence of wear was in – spanking newness and slick conformity were out. Anything that appeared corporate was suspect, leading to a proliferation of *outré* brands that showed signs of fatigue, often featuring not just the "worn" vocabulary of ripped and threadbare fabrics, but also faded and muddled graphics. This was not nostalgia by another name. With imagery that hovered somewhere between military fatigues, clapped-out cars, and troublesome gear, the style vigorously rejected so-called "civilized" norms, in favor of a scuzzy, frayed, and wasted aesthetic.

An appreciation for wear also permeated Leonard Koren's *Wabi-sabi for Artists, Designers, Poets & Philosophers* (1994), a treatise on the poetic beauty of the imperfect and the organic effects of aging and related natural processes. Meanwhile, architect Frank Gehry emulated many of the visual qualities of degradation in the clash of corrugated metal, shingled siding, and jumbled geometries of cubes and pyramids that he employed in the evolving design of his own house (mostly emerging between 1978 and 1992). From a kindred mindset, Gaetano Pesce's furniture designs were animated by slurries of color and nonchalant rivers of bumpy plastic – carefully considered and crafted features that merely appear chaotic and accidental. Such qualities, by extension, appeared in the rusted shells of Mad Max-style "rat rods," whose misshapen bodies are propelled by polished power plants – an obvious metaphor for the undaunted soul still pulsing within the wrecked body of its host.

For aficionados, a patina, with buried references to apocalyptic events, came to infer the noble, even heroic, character of a survivor or an object that has been through it all yet, against all odds, is still among us. The scars testify to the years, decades, even centuries that it has weathered and endured. So, the funky object, often characterized by defiant posture and attitude, displays its *bona fides* with generalized disdain for polite design conventions. Instead, it tends to emphasize discordant proportions, colors, and textures, subverting convention and challenging long-held convictions. Most important, its apparent formlessness and inconclusive nature suggest a still-evolving process of becoming, an embryonic state of flux, supporting a gritty sense of shared history, rather than the clean, crisp newness of modern design. Sometimes derided in critical journals, but more often embraced by entertainment personalities and the lay public, those qualities also implicitly represent comfort and tradition. Thus, even such successful, mainstream brands as Martha Stewart and Ralph Lauren have generated product lineups designed to exploit what we know now is the strong emotional traction of incongruent goods.

Funk Observations

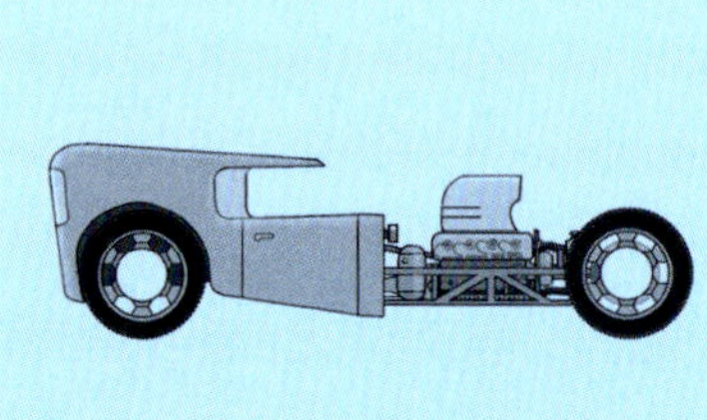

Fig. 8A 1932 FORD COUPE RAT ROD (p. 226)

ANONYMOUS
MADE IN USA

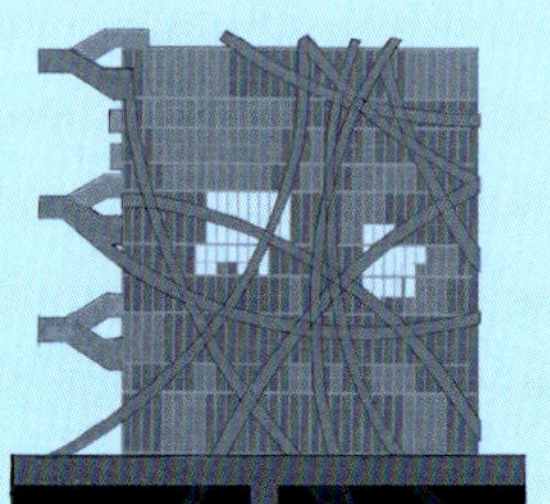

Fig. 8B (W)RAPPER (p. 226)

YEAR 2023
ARCHITECT
Eric Owen Moss
LOCATION
Culver City, California, USA

A niche group of fabricators, designers and off-roading enthusiasts proclaim their disdain for production automobiles by building vehicles that appear to be scavenged from abandoned scrap yards. With guile, technical bravura, and an aberrant sense of irony, these denizens of the desert declare their rusted shells, bloated tires, and sagging frames which have been kitted out with hungry, polished aluminum superchargers, as a certificate of independence. Flaunting their own code, the creators of these dead serious automotive mongrels have developed a *camaraderie* with its own language and unique aesthetic values.

By becoming the lead provocateur in what is known as the Hayden Tract (which is justly famous for its remarkable assortment of radical architectural interventions) the (W)rapper acts as a proof of concept, demonstrating that innovative architectural ideas, if carried out with talent and conviction, can extend architecture's reach, even in the realm of commercial real estate. With unassailable semantic logic that required innovative structural logic to achieve, the uncluttered floor plates and controversial identity represent the apogee of bold, iconoclastic architectural design.

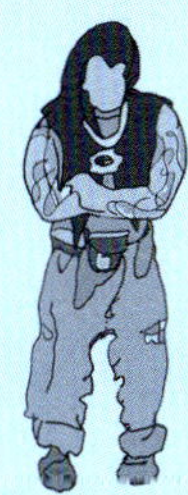

Fig. 8C HIP HOP MALE (p. 227)

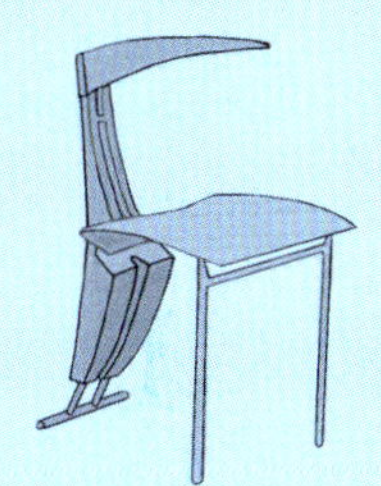

Fig. 8D NEE CHAIR #4 (p. 227)

YEAR 1988
DESIGNER
Morphosis
FABRICATOR
Farrage & Co., USA

Heavy metal jewelry, chains, and precious stones with exaggerated scale and detail reinforce the testosterone driven aesthetic embraced by hip-hop culture. Guided by the belief that "If you've got it, flaunt it," and memorialized in music videos and posters, ostentatious rap jewelry is the performer's chosen adornment. From hoodie to low-slung hips and briefs on display, the expression of ultra-alpha traits flaunts convention while projecting a careless, "gangsta" sensibility.

The asymmetrical gait of this chair suggests the wounded torso of an exhausted gladiator. With dystopian overtones and a desolate assembly of seemingly discarded parts, it offers little in the way of comfort. Yet the rudimentary perforated seat, the stumps of cast aluminum arms, and the prosthetic supports, together, create a direct challenge to the bourgeois norms of contemporary furnishing. Deeply indebted to the films of Ridley Scott, the cultural debris of the 80s, and the junk sculpture of Anthony Caro, the material palette of the chair suggests a do-it-yourself bravado in spite of its high design ethos.

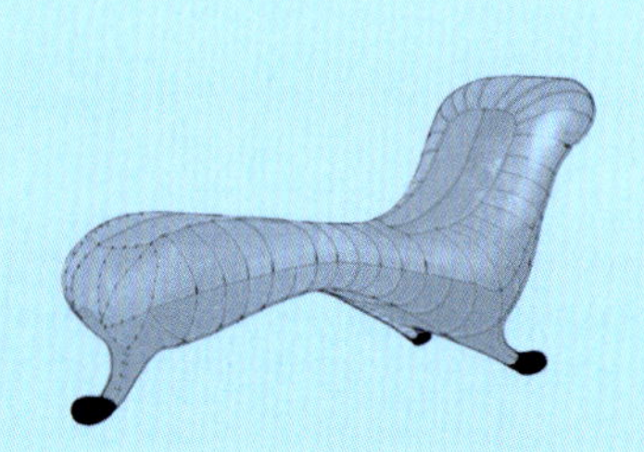

Fig. 8E LOCKHEED LOUNGE (p. 228)

YEAR 1985
DESIGNER
Marc Newson
MANUFACTURER
Basecraft for POD, Australia

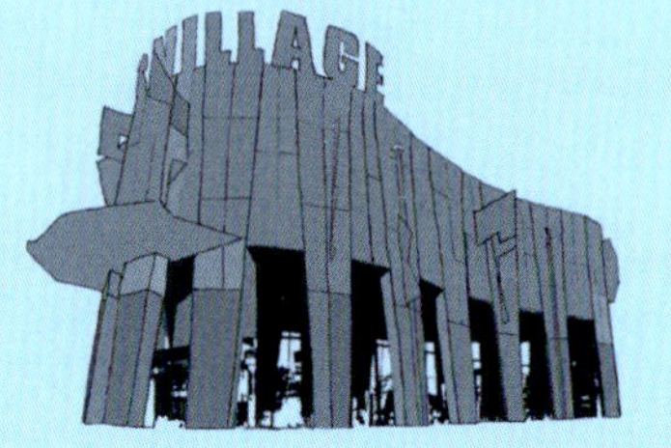

Fig. 8F PIONEER VILLAGE SUBWAY STATION (p. 228)

YEAR 2017
ARCHITECT
Will Alsop
LOCATION
Toronto, Canada

A riveted aluminum skin, paneled in the manner of an aircraft fuselage performs dual functions as a seating surface and monocoque structure. Perched on diminutive feet that tiptoe comically beneath its bulk, this chaise is as easy on the eyes as it is awkward to enjoy.

Like the platelets of an armored beast, the rusted cladding, stout red legs and elephantine proportions of this Center, while demonstrably inexpensive and functional, might well be some mythical animal. Its allusions to primitive imagery, clumsy, cartoon-like detail, and decidedly low-tech construction underscore an urban posture designed to confront the bourgeois character of its surroundings – signaling an aversion to carefully composed civic architecture.

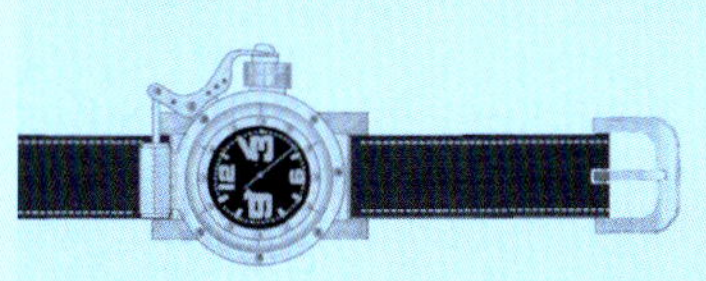

Fig. 8G PISTON DIVER WATCH (p. 229)

YEAR 2009
MANUFACTURER
Retrowerk, Germany

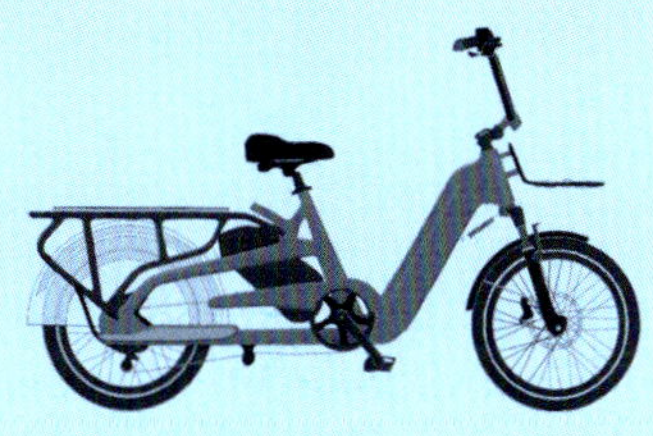

Fig. 8H FLUX ELECTRIC BIKE (p. 229)

YEAR 2016
DESIGNERS
Pete Leaviss and Robert Rast
MANUFACTURER
Revi Mobility Inc. (D.B.A. Revi Bikes), USA

If not for the outrigger regulator and the conspicuous slotted machine screws this massive wristwatch would be quite an ordinary timepiece. But it is precisely the dissonance created by its commonplace dial encased in a primordial bronzed apparatus that suggests an origin somewhere in the catalogue of prehistory – before the Swiss became the world's watchmakers.

With a form that squats as it tries to attend to every conceivable demand, a palette of functional but widely divergent materials, and a "don't give a damn" attitude about looks, this bike and others like it is an all-purpose transporter that can be found in villages and smaller communities around the world.

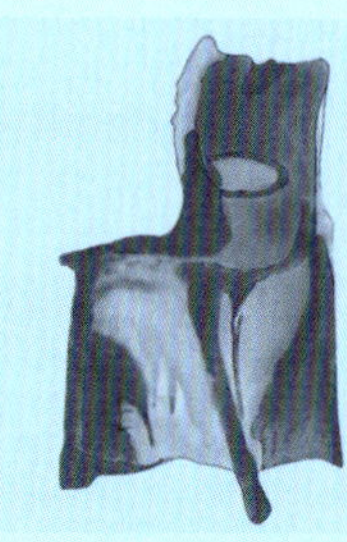

Fig. 8I PRATT CHAIR (p. 230)

YEAR 1984
DESIGNER
Gaetano Pesce
MADE IN
USA

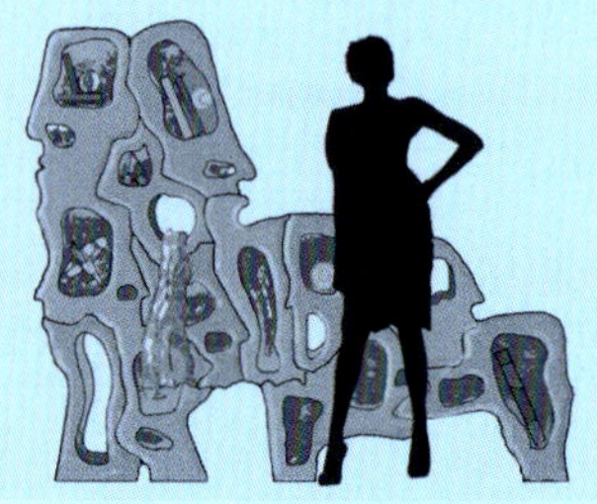

Fig. 8J BIG SPECTATOR (p. 230)

YEAR 2020
DESIGNER
Freia Achenbach
MADE IN
Germany

Is it a painting? Is it a discarded rag? Or maybe a carapace from an exotic yet-to-be named giant insect? The visual confusion surrounding this chair straddles the line between art and function to scramble definitions while asking a perfectly practical question – *where to sit?* By questioning the tenants of industrial design and production, Gaetano Pesce's chair achieves the remarkable feat of eluding classification to become the only chair in its category.

The hollowed forms of organic cavities float like islands in the sea of the irregularly shaped carved foam of the casework, which implicitly regards the well-bound book as a soon-to-be gone artifact, positing nooks for odd-ball collections as a more plausible mission. Cave-like voids and apertures animate the surface and encourage improvised storage of whatever will fit.

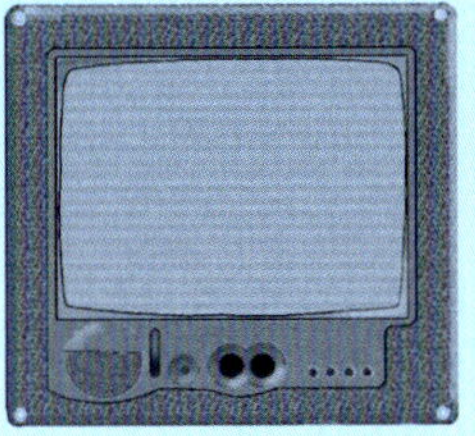

Fig. 8K

JIM NATURE PORTABLE TELEVISION
(p. 231)

YEAR 1994
DESIGNER
Philippe Starck
MANUFACTURER
Thomson-CSF for Saba, France

Introduced as a challenge to the generic black casework typical of tech components, the deft reimagining of the relationship between the "box" and the "display/control" insert in this SABA television creates a harmony of form that belies the violent juxtaposition of shapes, materials, and gesture that, like many of Starck's designs, is provocative, witty, and practical all at the same time.

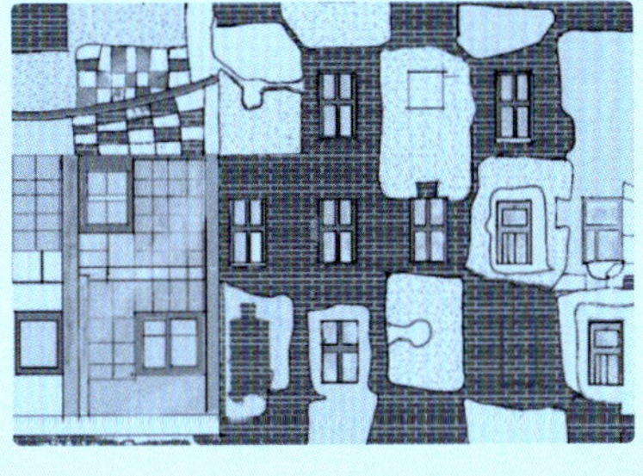

Fig. 8L

KUNSTHAUSWIEN
(p. 231)

YEAR 1986
DESIGNER
Friedensreich Hundertwasser
LOCATION
Vienna, Austria

The collection of displaced bits jostling for space on this apartment façade defy principles of architectural order and propose, instead, a fleeting, eclectic collage based on chaos and anarchy. From randomized patterns to a singular golden sphere, the design is a testament to the triumph of stubborn artistic vision over convention.

Funk Illustrations

The cobra snout of the super-charger creates an image of insolent menace

Diamond shape window announce a design DNA heavily inflected towards a Gothic identity

Fig. 8A

The radiator grill is lowered to convey a squat neanderthal posture

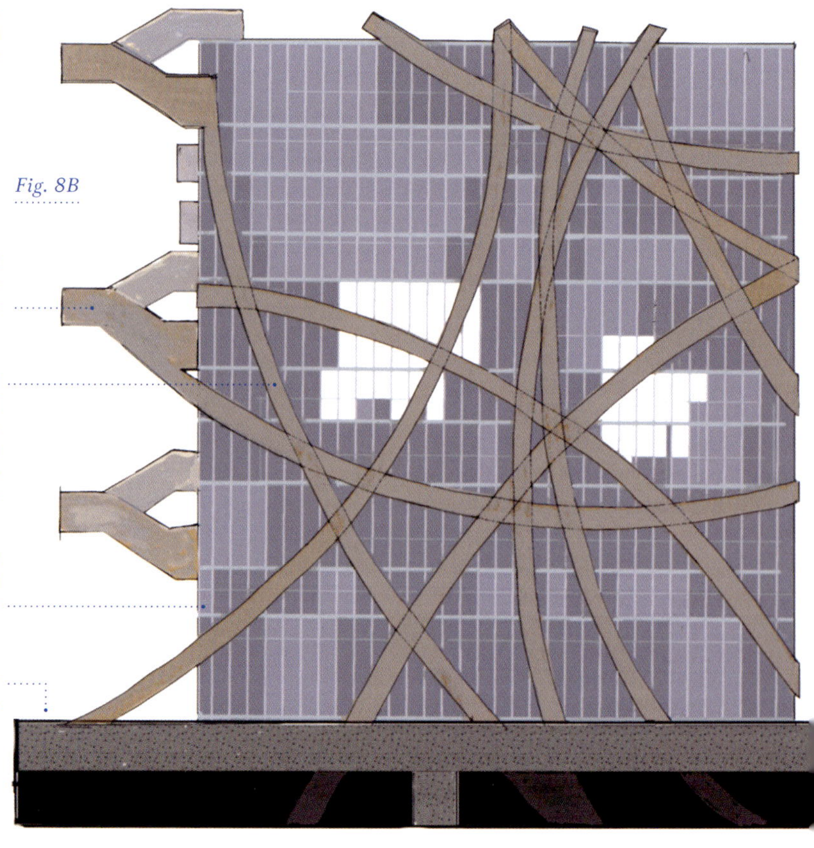

Fig. 8B

Cantilevered exterior exit stairs

Interlaced curving fabricated steel box beams form exoskeleton to support column free floors

Glass curtain wall behind fabricated box beams

Platform over parking deck

1932 FORD COUPE RAT ROD (*Fig. 8A*), (W)RAPPER (*Fig. 8B*)

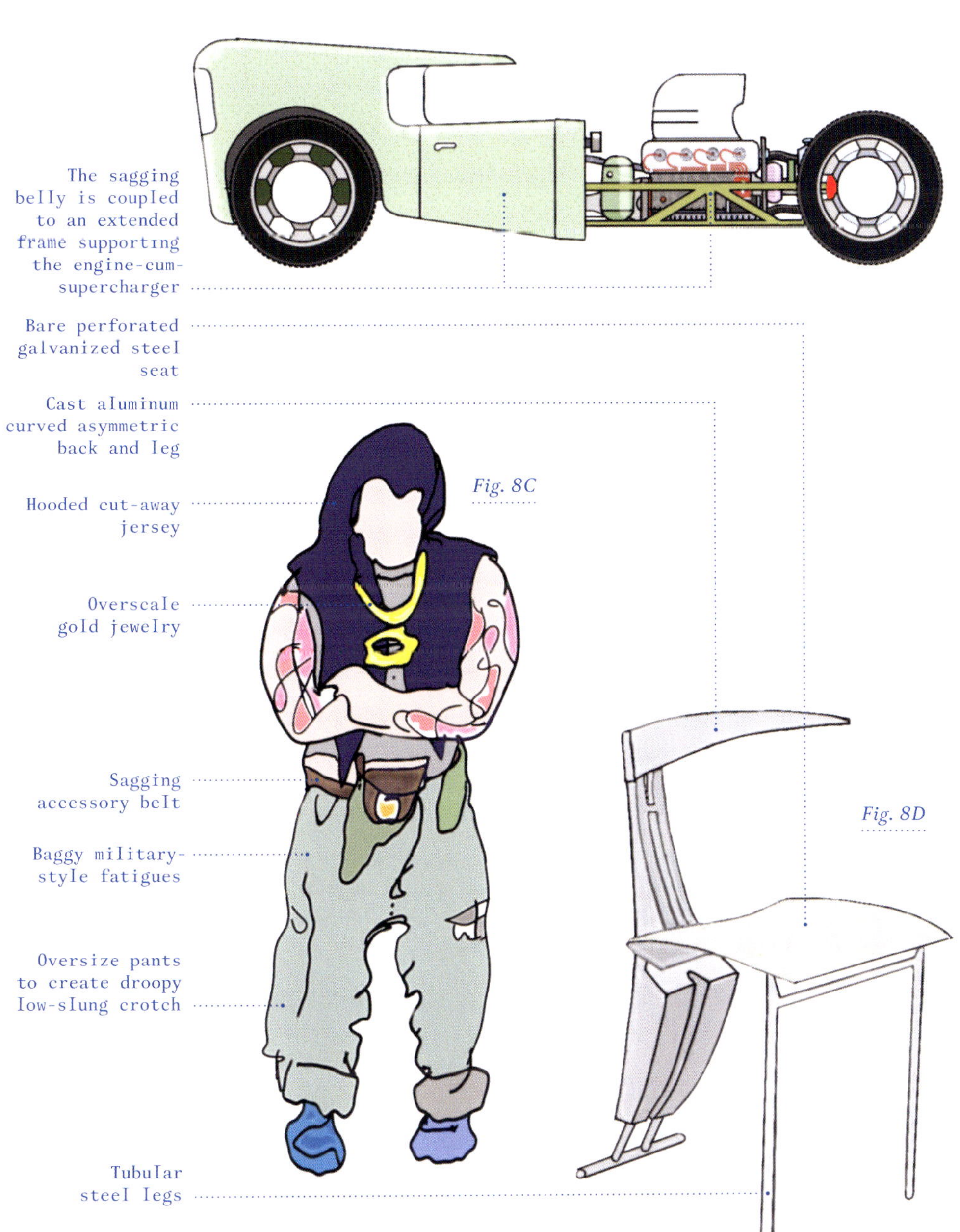

HIP HOP MALE (*Fig. 8C*), NEE CHAIR #4 (*Fig. 8D*)

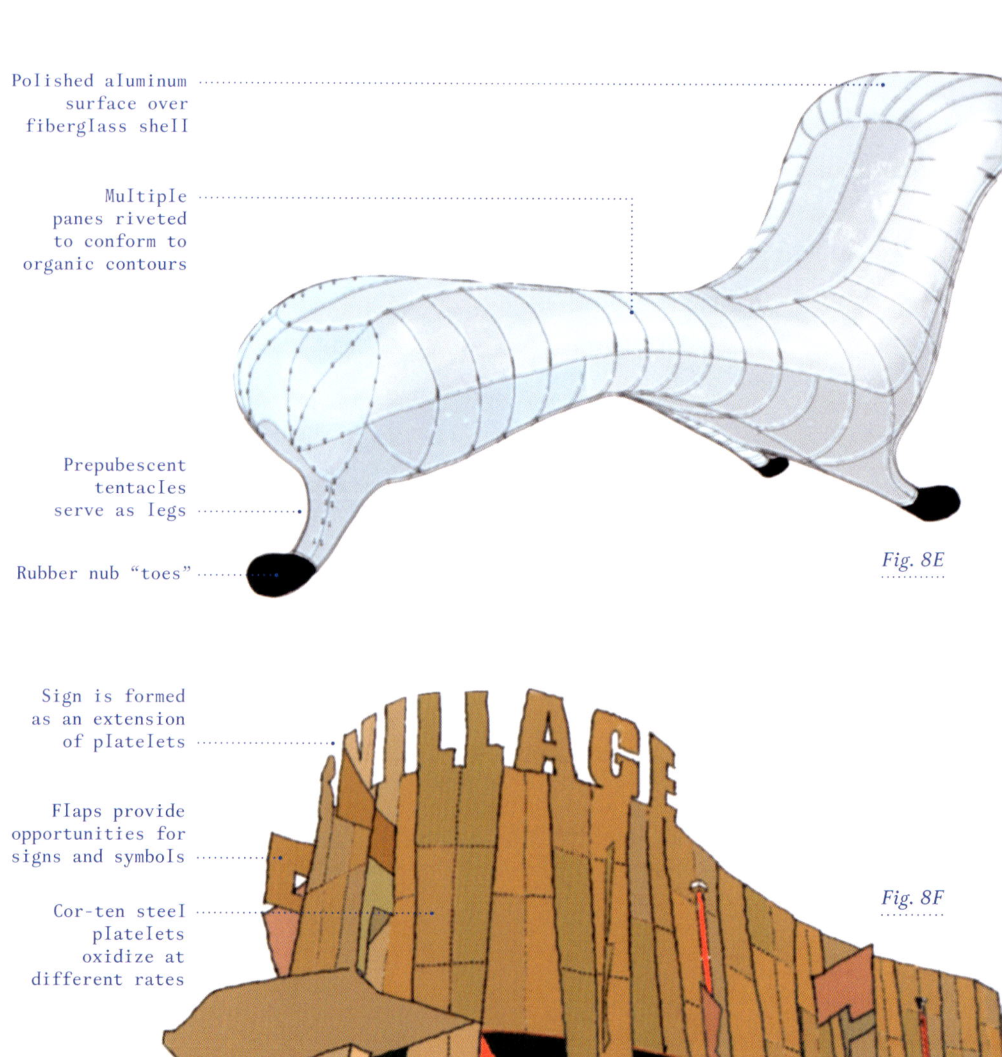

LOCKHEED LOUNGE (*Fig. 8E*), PIONEER VILLAGE SUBWAY STATION (*Fig. 8F*)

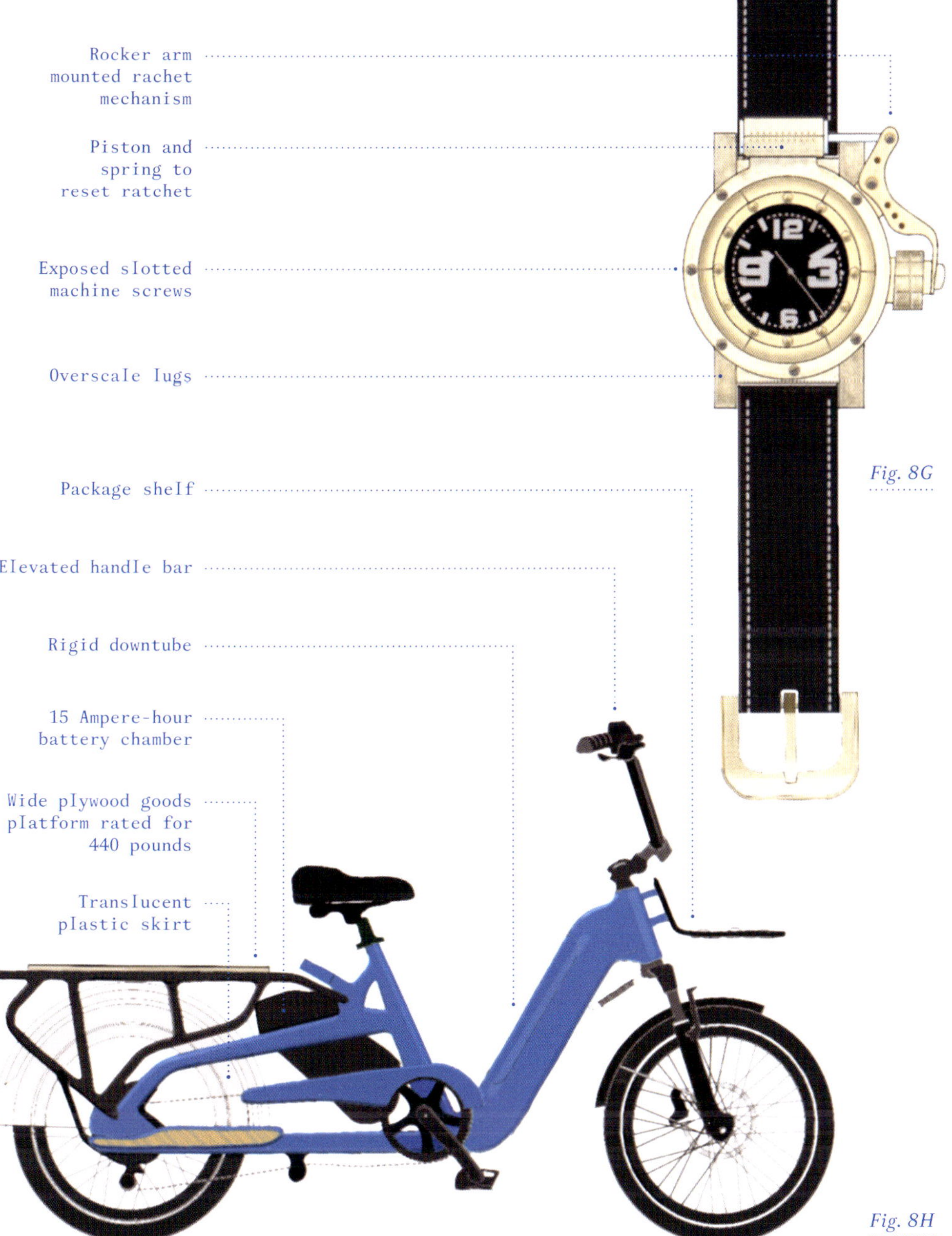

PISTON DIVER WATCH (*Fig. 8G*), FLUX ELECTRIC BIKE (*Fig. 8H*)

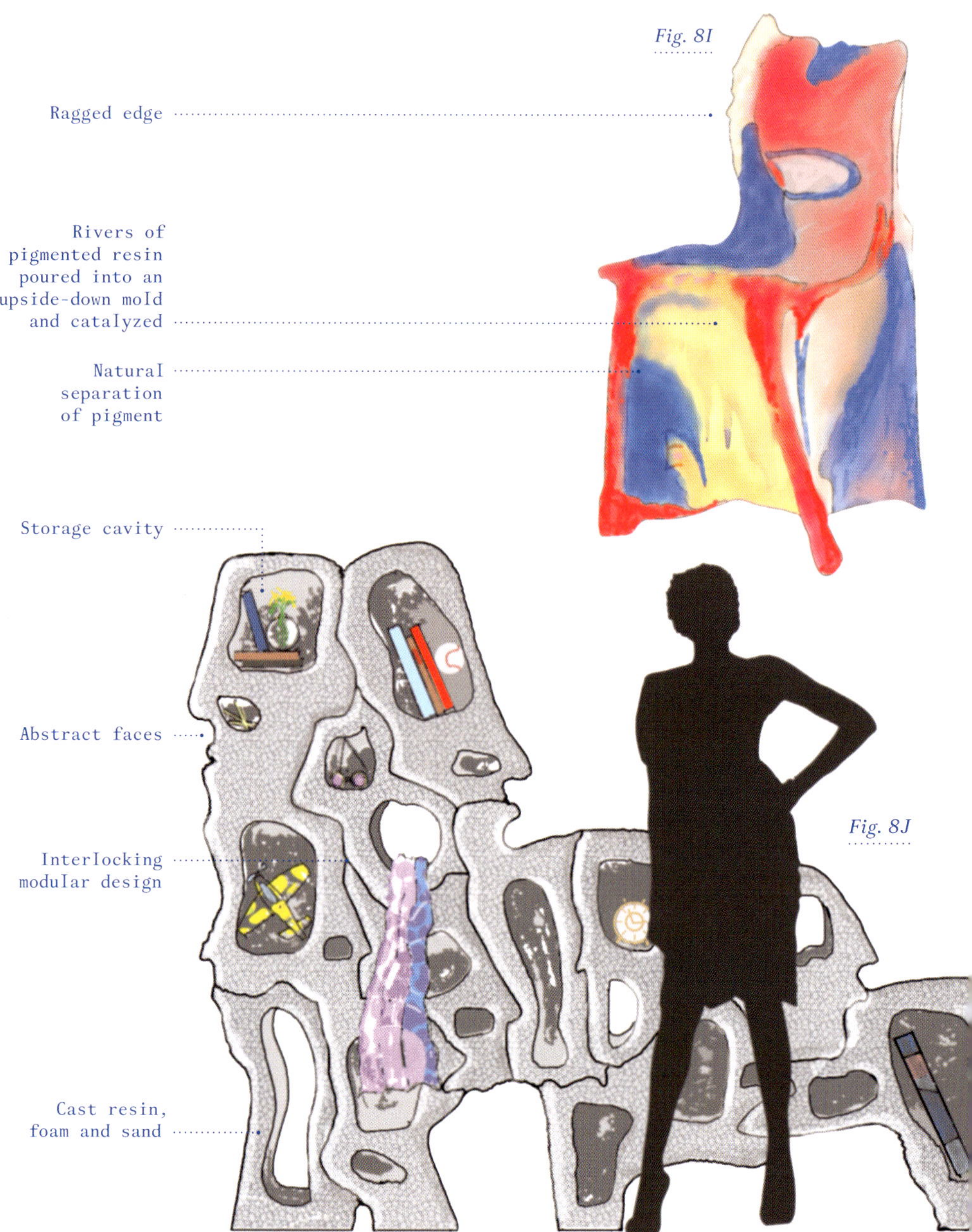

PRATT CHAIR (*Fig. 8I*), BIG SPECTATOR (*Fig. 8J*)

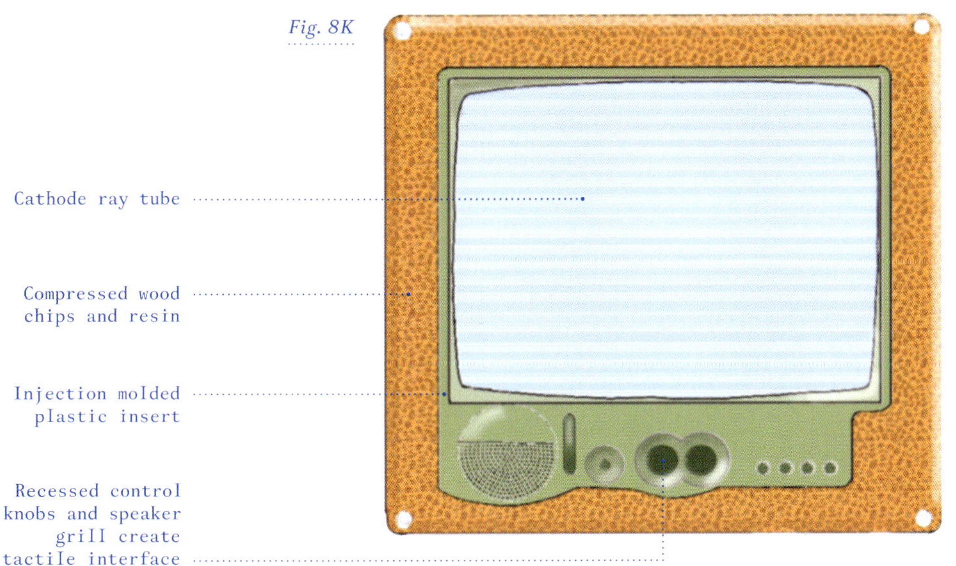

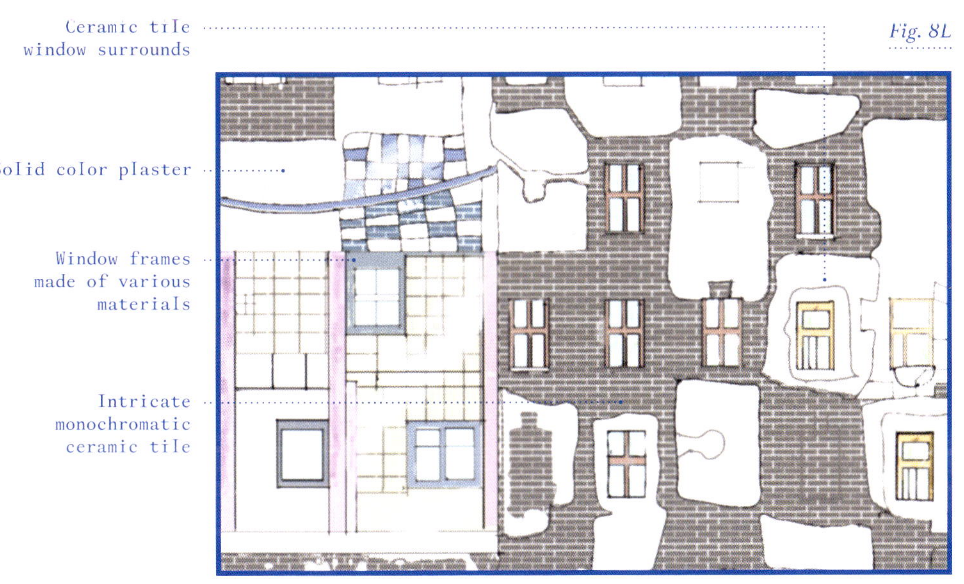

JIM NATURE PORTABLE TELEVISION (*Fig. 8K*), KUNSTHAUSWIEN (*Fig. 8L*)

ATTRIBUTES

ECCENTRIC
SHAPES
GOVERNED
BY RHYTHM,
GEOMETRY,
COLOR AND
PATTERN
IN VISUALLY
UNPREDICTABLE
RELATIONSHIPS
SUGGESTING
EVOLVING
EPHEMERAL
EXPERIMENTS

MESSAGE

"COMPOSE
A SYMPHONY
OF DISCORDANT
FORMS,
MATERIALS,
AND
FUNCTIONS."

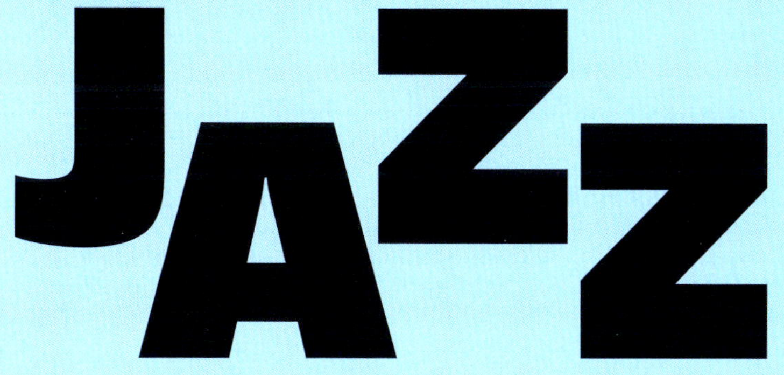

Introduction

Just as jazz's free-flowing improvisation breaks from the tightly arranged scores of classical music — injecting syncopated rhythms and fragmented riffs on recognizable and unrecognizable melodic quotations — art assemblages that integrate raw, discarded materials and objects.

As in the work of Robert Rauschenberg, it can fuse together everyday flotsam and jetsam in ways that harness dissonance and force us to look, *really* look. Creatively vaulting over, bending, warping, and otherwise distorting traditional constraints, such ostensibly improvisational work shares much with the choreography of Josephine Baker, which startled the world with its angular, animated moves – it's also related to modern architectural designs that pervert or abandon Euclidian geometries, sometimes enclosing space within complex origami-like folds.

Declaring freedom from orthogonal geometric constraints, jazz-inspired objects often favor acute angles, colliding structures, and unresolved joinery, resulting in displaced sculptural volumes, liberated from conventional structural or formal discipline. Perforated metal, random creases, and exaggerated details, thrown in just for the heck of it, like hip-hop samples, often add texture and renegade edginess. Clashing colors produce an abrasive effect, while also distinguishing among conjoined parts. For example, Peter Shire's jive-infused teapots, like many other Memphis Group designs, exploit both geometry and vivid color to deconstruct classic forms – almost perversely achieving striking rhythms in clay, a material without its own inherent, jagged beat.

Creating memorable images with limited means, certain amped-up strategies have played different scales and rhythms against one another, transforming inexpensive, straightforward forms and materials into high-impact icons. A key example is what came to be called "Supergraphics," in which oversized typography and graphic shapes, often in bold or primary colors, are superimposed on generic objects or buildings, producing disruptive patterns that alter the reading of basic forms. It was pioneered to startling effect, in the 1960s, by artist Barabara Stauffacher Solomon at Sea Ranch, a precedent-setting planned community on the Northern California coast, characterized by its simple, wood-clad, modern-saltbox buildings. Now a pervasive design trope, Supergraphics appear on everything from racing cars to stylish clothing, often providing a low-cost way to enliven (even rendering hip) otherwise ordinary apartment blocks or school buildings.

Less about improvisation and more about breaking with convention in attention-grabbing ways, the impulse to "jazz up" design also spilled into the popular culture of neon signage, with the flashing boomerang-like arrows of motel signs, the flamboyant signs of casinos, or the jittery dances of low riders, swinging their arms, putting on a show. Further animating static conditions, three 20th Century innovations have been instrumental in lending jazz's ephemeral qualities to the physical world: electric lighting, which can be turned on or off in rhythmic ways; easily programmable mechanical motion, powered by motors and solenoids; and motion sensors. In the art world, the herky-jerky movements of Jean Tinguely's motorized kinetic sculptures, which weld together precariously balanced junkyard finds, also infuse formerly static objects with captivating, syncopated rhythms. And, in a similar spirit, the plunging rooflines of Googie restaurants, the striking silhouettes of Rick Owens's runway fashions, and the visually unstable, open geometries of architect Coop Himmelblau's Musée de Confluence (2014) in Lyon, France, all teeter on the edge of imbalance, conveying the impression of improvisation – belying the extraordinary effort, craft, and structural feats that their realization actually demands.

On another, perhaps trivial front, eyeglass frames have frequently provided a canvas for jazz-inflected design. The simple basic formula of spectacles, dating from the late 13th Century – two lenses, a nose bridge, and a pair of earpieces – has inspired thousands, if not millions, of riffs over time, each catering to the whims and fashions of the period. With technological advances, particularly the early-20th Century introduction of celluloid by the pioneering French eyewear company L'Amy, came the demise of exclusively metal frames, ushering in a vast array of designs – from purely functional to outrageously idiosyncratic – facilitated by the ease with which this and later plastics could be molded, textured, and colored. Adopted by musicians and other performers, often as one-off custom designs, such glasses have become an integral part of the repertoire.

Now that contemporary technology has transcended many of the limitations of materials and processes, and popular tastes continue to break from the constraints of cultural barriers, the potential of design seems nearly infinite. Perhaps only the sway (or intransigence) of the classic design canon can hold it back.

Jazz Observations

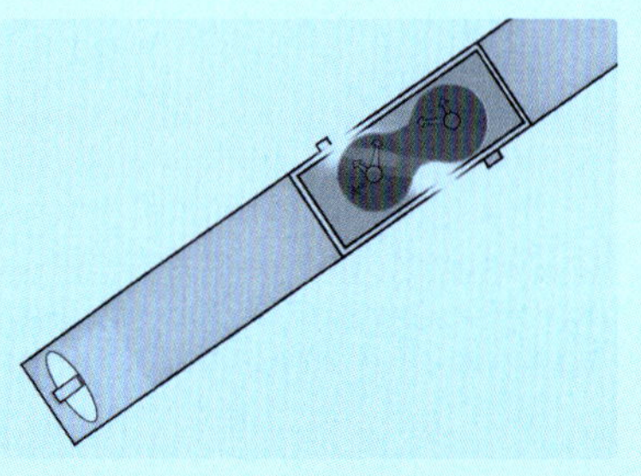

Fig. 9A BI WATCH (p. 252)

DESIGNER
Karim Rashid
MANUFACTURER
Acme Studio Inc., USA

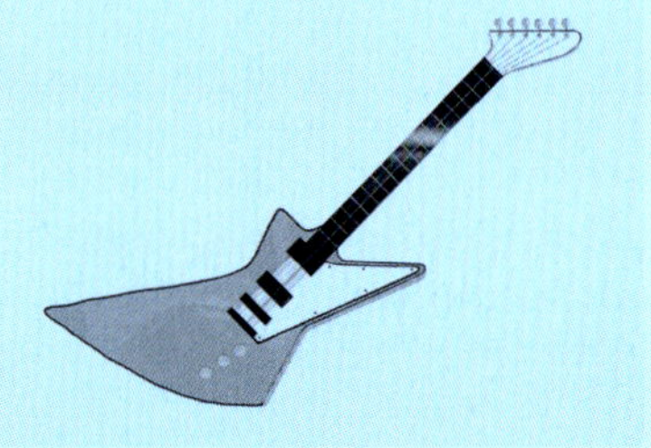

Fig. 9B EXPLORER ELECTRIC GUITAR (p. 252)

YEAR c.1970
MANUFACTURER
Gibson, USA

Like a hi-band synthesizer, this watch suppresses all references to technology and history, even traditional craftsmanship, relying instead on vivid color, reductive geometry, and space-age imagery. Legible and lightweight with a biomorphic vibe, like the coupling of amoeba, it suggests the plasticity of time.

Once shorn of its acoustic role, and the familiar form celebrated by artists from Picasso to Roy Lichtenstein, the shape of the electric guitar became an essential part of many performers' stage presence, helping to define the attitude, as well as the image of the artist by juxtaposing the form and materials of the pick guard with the akimbo posture of the instrument's solid body, to create a memorable icon.

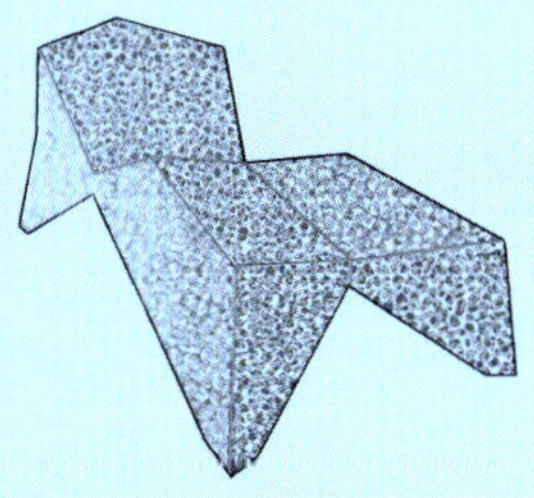

Fig. 9C ALEX CHAISE LOUNGE (p. 252)

YEAR 2010
DESIGNER
Alessandro Mendini
MANUFACTURER
Ecopixel, Italy

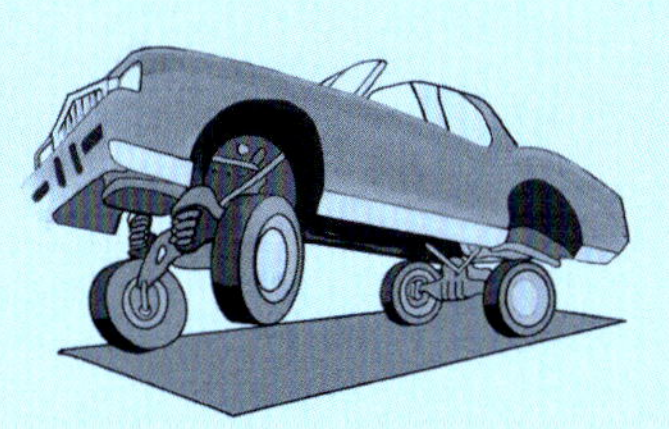

Fig. 9D CHEVY MONTE CARLO LOWRIDER (p. 253)

YEAR 2015
DESIGNER
Jason Garrett
MANUFACTURED IN USA

In departing from the classic demeanor of the typical chaise, Mendini has created an object that agitates the eye as well as the space around it, while playfully suggesting it's time to relax. Because each intermingling example is made from color-sorted polyethylene waste the surfaces display unique pointillistic color patterns.

As an alternative to the drag racing performance of the typical hot rod, the emergence of a custom car able to hop during a street parade or bounce around at a Kustom's exhibition, signaled the arrival of inexpensive controllers and hydraulic systems that could be programmed to offer entertaining performances at auto shows and country fairs, eliciting applause and chants from awed fans.

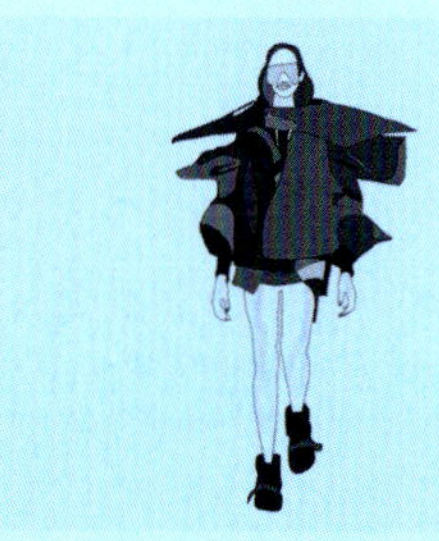

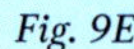

Fig. 9E

SPRING READY-TO-WEAR COLLECTION (p. 253)

YEAR 2019
DESIGNER
Rick Owens
COMPANY
Owenscorp, Italy

The image of an otherworldly Goth Amazon strutting down the street has few peers in the world of fashion, where the individuality of a designer's vision can create seismic shifts. The impact of this, and Owen's universe, is beginning to permeate the role of fashion by defining alternatives to conventional beauty and elegance.

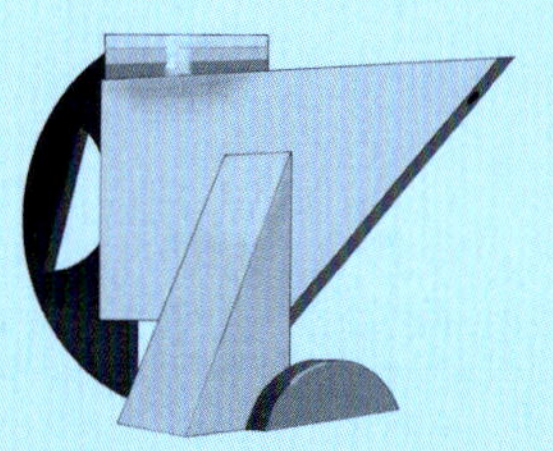

Fig. 9F

THE THIRD MAN TEAPOT (p. 254)

YEAR 1983
DESIGNER
Peter Shire
MADE IN
USA

Primary color and geometric shapes in surprising arrangements combine to create a jazzy ensemble of forms that seem to jostle, hustle, and vamp in this teapot, one of a series by sculptor Peter Shire who is one of the artists/makers who worked under the banner of "Memphis," the Italian collective.

Fig. 9G

BINOCULAR 02 SUNGLASSES (p. 254)

MANUFACTURER
Demobaza, Italy

An unbroken upper structure vaulting over the open inner corners of the lenses and the nose piece suggests an inquisitor's gaze with S&M overtones.

Fig. 9H

ELLERY FRAME (p. 254)

MANUFACTURER
Vooglam, USA

Powerful geometry and mechanistic detailing combined with unifying color provide an arresting silhouette implying a studious, introspective attitude.

Fig. 9I

ELSPETH TORTOISE FRAME (p. 254)

MANUFACTURER
Ublins, USA

Deep-set bevels surrounding the lens sculpt the frame to emphasize its mass, reversing the trend towards sleek, lightweight eyewear to counterbalance the impression of depth, and suggest an alert, imperious gaze on the part of the wearer.

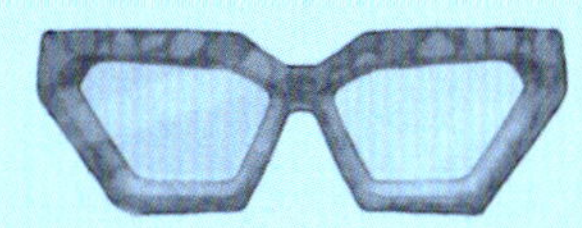

Fig. 9J

PETRIE FRAME (p. 254)

MANUFACTURER
Vooglam, USA

The rhythmic separation of black and white creates an optical interplay in which the dancing forms flicker between positive and negative to defy their function as frames suggesting the wearer's querulous persona.

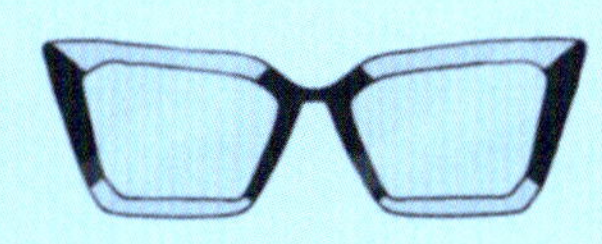

Fig. 9K

FERRARI SUNGLASSES (p. 254)

MANUFACTURER
Ferrari, Italy

By adopting the wings and foils of a Formula 1 race car's wind-cheating design strategy, the nodal points of conventional eyeglasses are redefined. Wearer's might adopt motor-sports jackets and shoes to assert their camaraderie at events and concours.

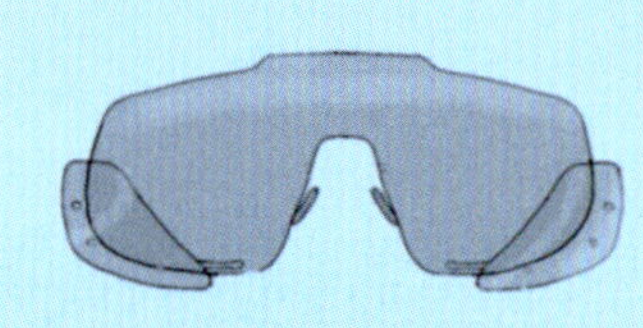

Fig. 9L

TAIGA MULTICOLOR SUNGLASSES (p. 254)

MANUFACTURER
Briko, Italy

Featuring a structured geometry and multi-hued frame, the oversized silhouette matches high-tech performance with contemporary style derived from video games and sports.

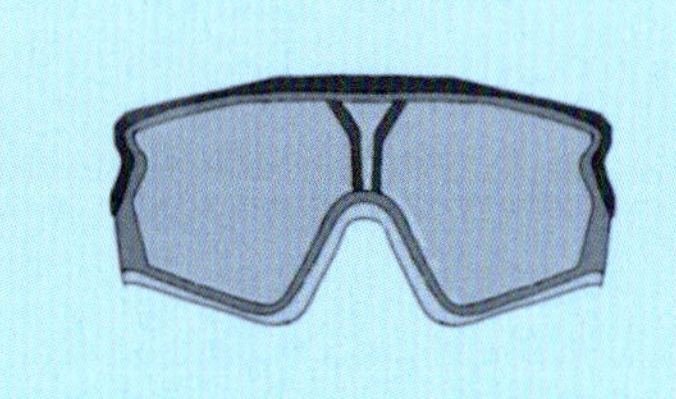

Fig. 9M

BINOCULAR GREY SUNGLASSES (p. 254)

MANUFACTURER
Demobaza, Italy

A monolithic, molded form departs from the "frame" of traditional sunglasses to assume the aesthetic principles of wearable sculpture rather than an optical device. By conferring a robotic persona to the wearer, they are able to realign both professional and personal relationships.

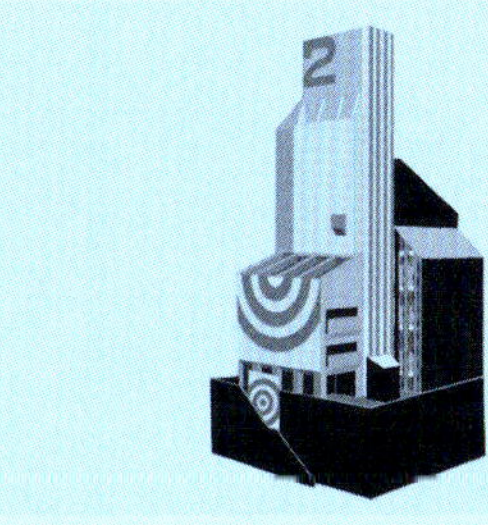

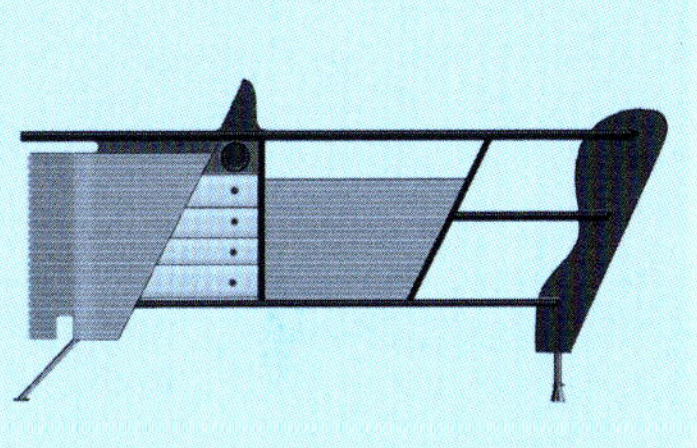

Fig. 9N NIBAN-KAN (p. 255)

YEAR 1970
ARCHITECT
Minoru Takeyama
LOCATION
Tokyo, Japan

Fig. 9O BERTRAND CABINET (p. 255)

DESIGNER
Massimo
Iosa Ghini
MANUFACTURER
Memphis
S.R.L., Italy

With applied Supergraphics and irregular, hacked-together components, the character of this Japanese tower has a comic-book-like presence in the skyline that rubs against architectural principles of unity, offering instead an ensemble of forms playing smoothly with one another.

Like a Science-Fiction movie prop that has taken a position as practical, beautifully crafted earthbound accessory, this cabinet hovers its bulk on spindly splayed legs. The canted stack of bulging doors, deep-ribbed volumes, and odd Hans Arp shaped prow give the impression of a lurching robotic object just waiting for its next task.

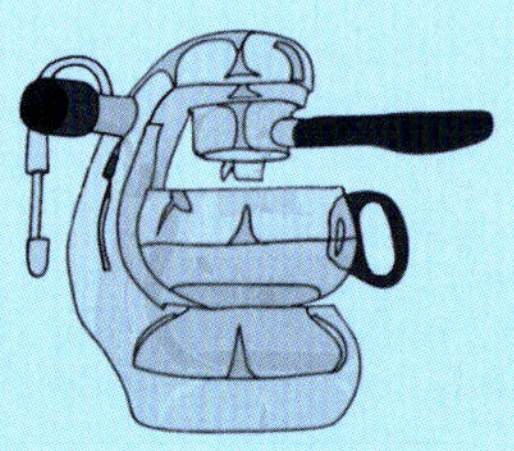

Fig. 9P ATOMIC COFFEE MAKER (p. 256)

YEAR 1946
DESIGNER
Giordano Robbiati
MANUFACTURER
Bon Trading Co., Italy

By exploiting the same casting process used to create functional automotive and aircraft manifolds, this espresso machine allows high pressure steam to flow seamlessly to the portafilter and from there to the on-board spherical carafe, while a form language reminiscent of Constantin Brancusi's polished sculpture provides an uninterrupted pathway.

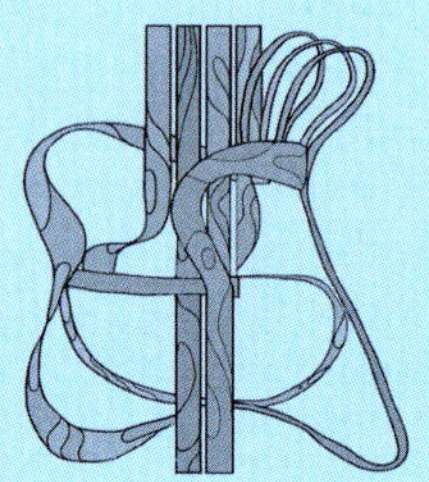

Fig. 9Q CROSS CHECK CHAIR (p. 256)

YEAR 1992
DESIGNER
Frank Gehry
MANUFACTURER
Knoll, USA

The elasticity of laminated wood and the ability to easily form it into dance-inflected curves forms the basis for the exuberant intersections of the multiple curving staves that form both structure and form of this chair. Seemingly squashable, yet sturdy and practical, the structural illusions enhance the presence of the chair in any setting.

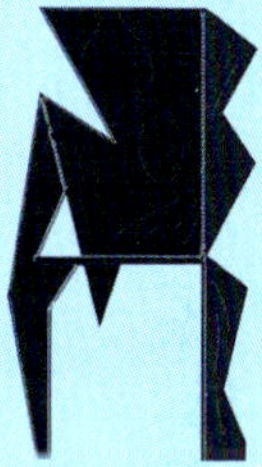

Fig. 9R ICONE CHAIR
(p. 256)

YEAR 2023
DESIGNER
Pedro Francone
MANUFACTURER
Ancestralidade
Collection,
Brazil

Allusions to primitive dance and orgiastic gestures underlie the jagged silhouette of this chair, that seems to defy the boundaries of usefulness yet provides the basics of support. Flat, welded steel plates form a rhythmic shape that takes precedence over comfort.

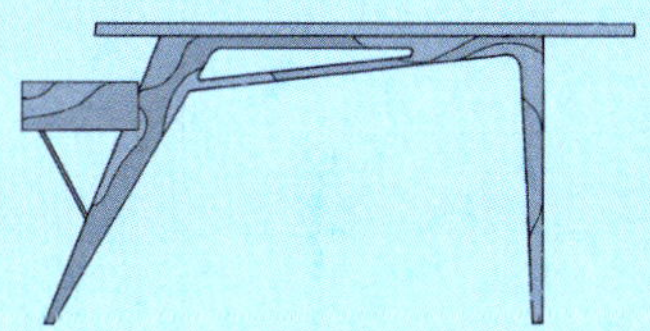

Fig. 9S PROTRACTOR DESK
(p. 257)

YEAR 1949
DESIGNER
Carlo Molino
MANUFACTURER
BD Barcelona
Design, Spain

Limber and poised cat-like, caught like a still-frame from a leap, the forward thrust of the structure is balanced neatly by the mass of the cantilevered drawers to support an utterly usable, flat, and rectilinear working surface.

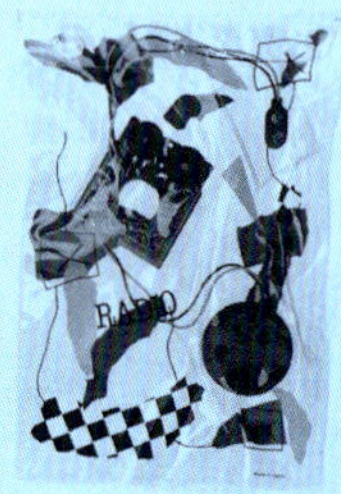

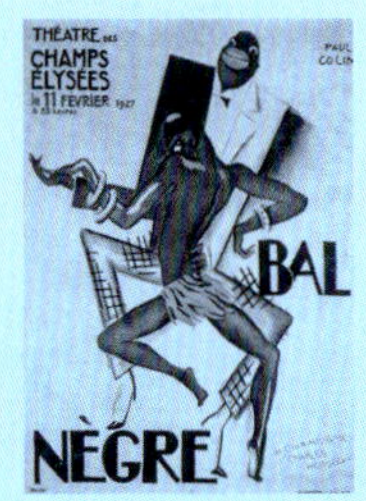

Fig. 9T "BAG" RADIO (p. 257)

YEAR 1983
DESIGNER
Daniel Weil
MANUFACTURER
Apex, Toyko

Fig. 9U BAL NÈGRE AT THE CHAMPS-ÉLYSÉES THEATRE (p. 257)

YEAR 1927
ARTIST
Paul Colin

You can shake, rattle, and roll this radio in its plastic baggie as you're listening to your favorite artist. With separate components joined with cable but otherwise free to move around, like its cousin the tambourine, this radio invites users to move around as they feed their ear buds the sounds that get them off.

The singer/entertainer Joséphine Baker that enthralled her Parisian audiences with a dance style she referred to as *hootchy-kootchy*, inspired artists and patrons alike with asymmetrical, hyperkinetic movements that perfectly mirrored the jazzy rhythms of the music of the day.

Jazz Illustrations

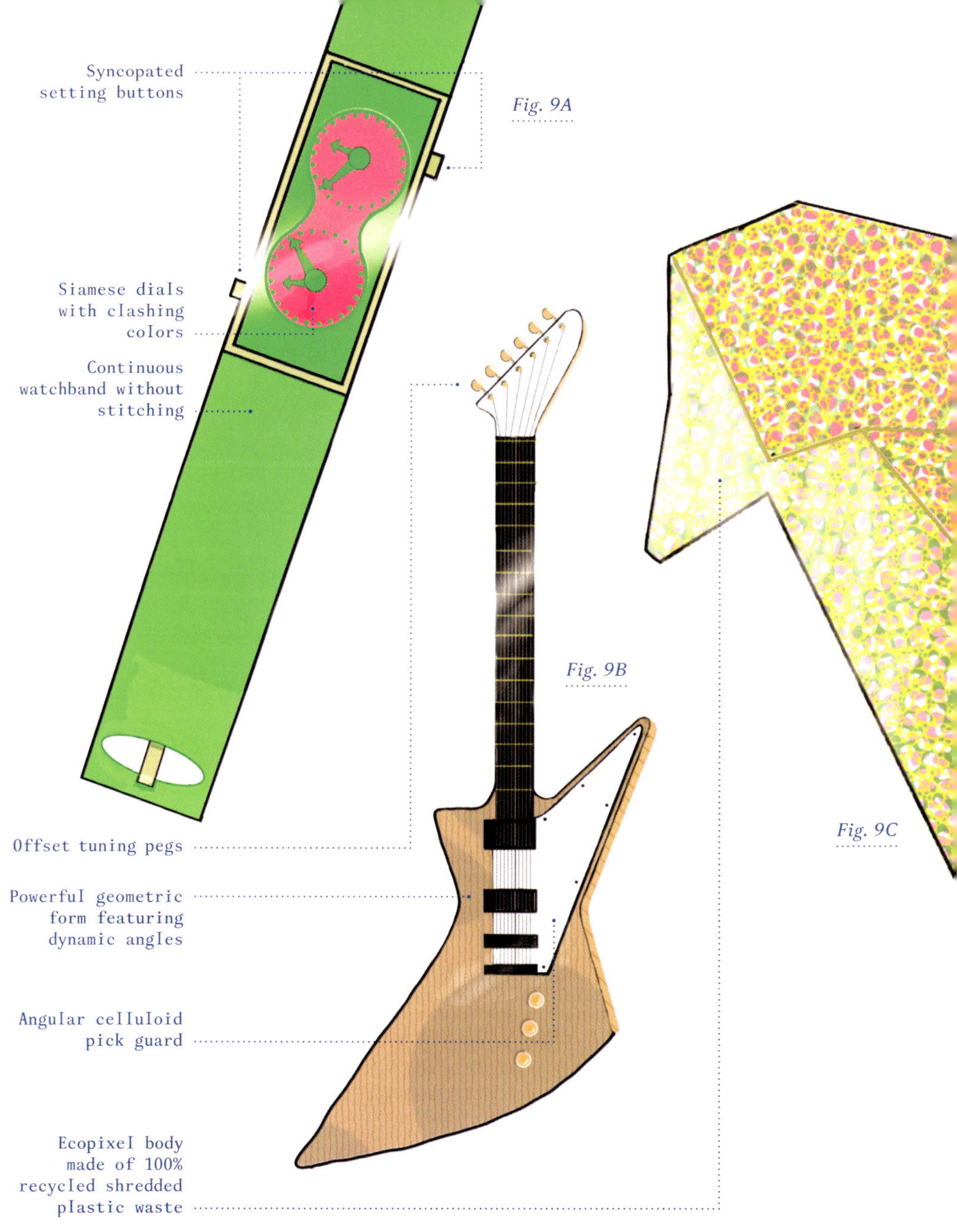

BI WATCH (*Fig. 9A*), EXPLORER ELECTRIC GUITAR (*Fig. 9B*), ALEX CHAISE LOUNGE (*Fig. 9C*)

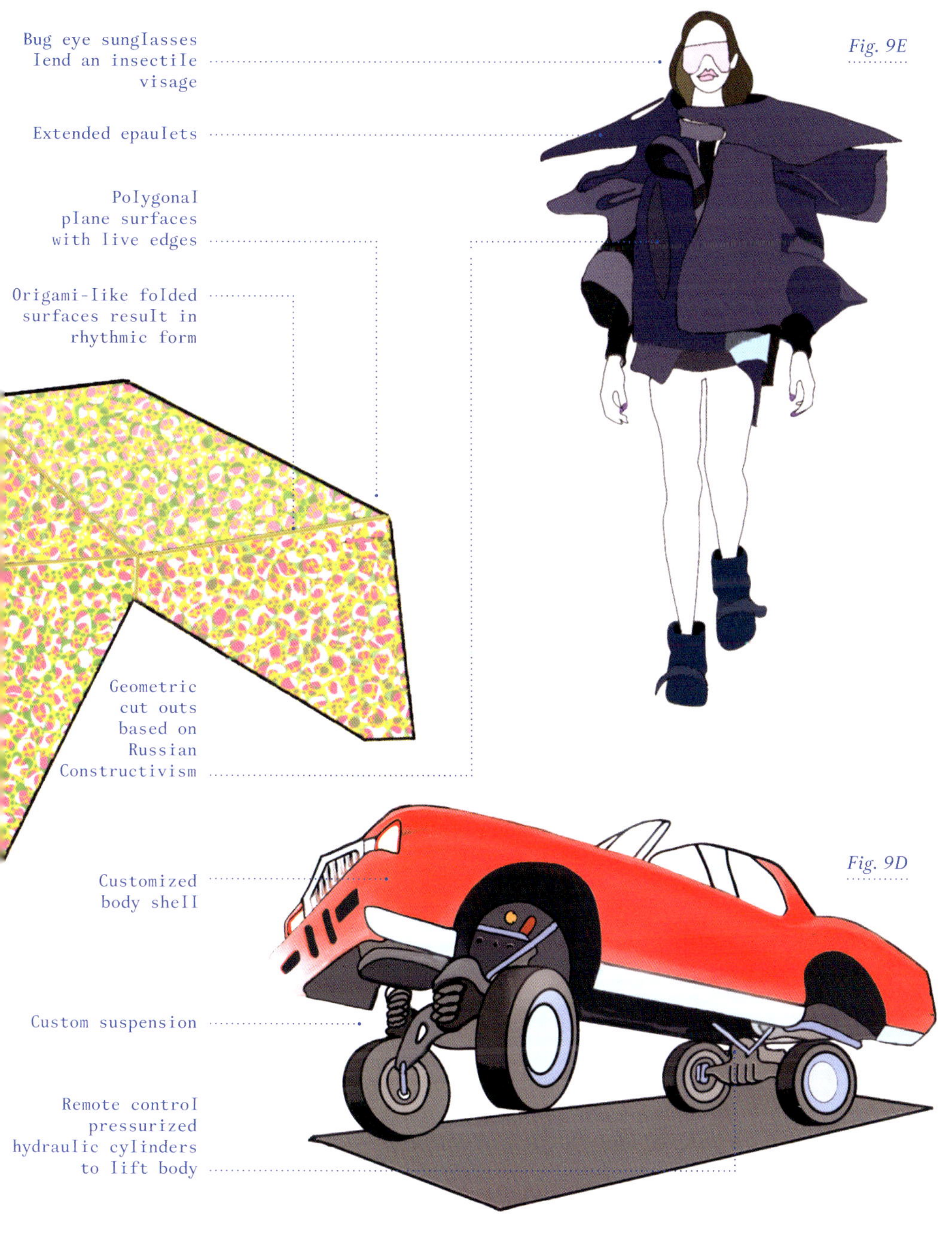

CHEVY MONTE CARLO LOWRIDER (*Fig. 9D*), SPRING READY-TO-WEAR COLLECTION (*Fig. 9E*)

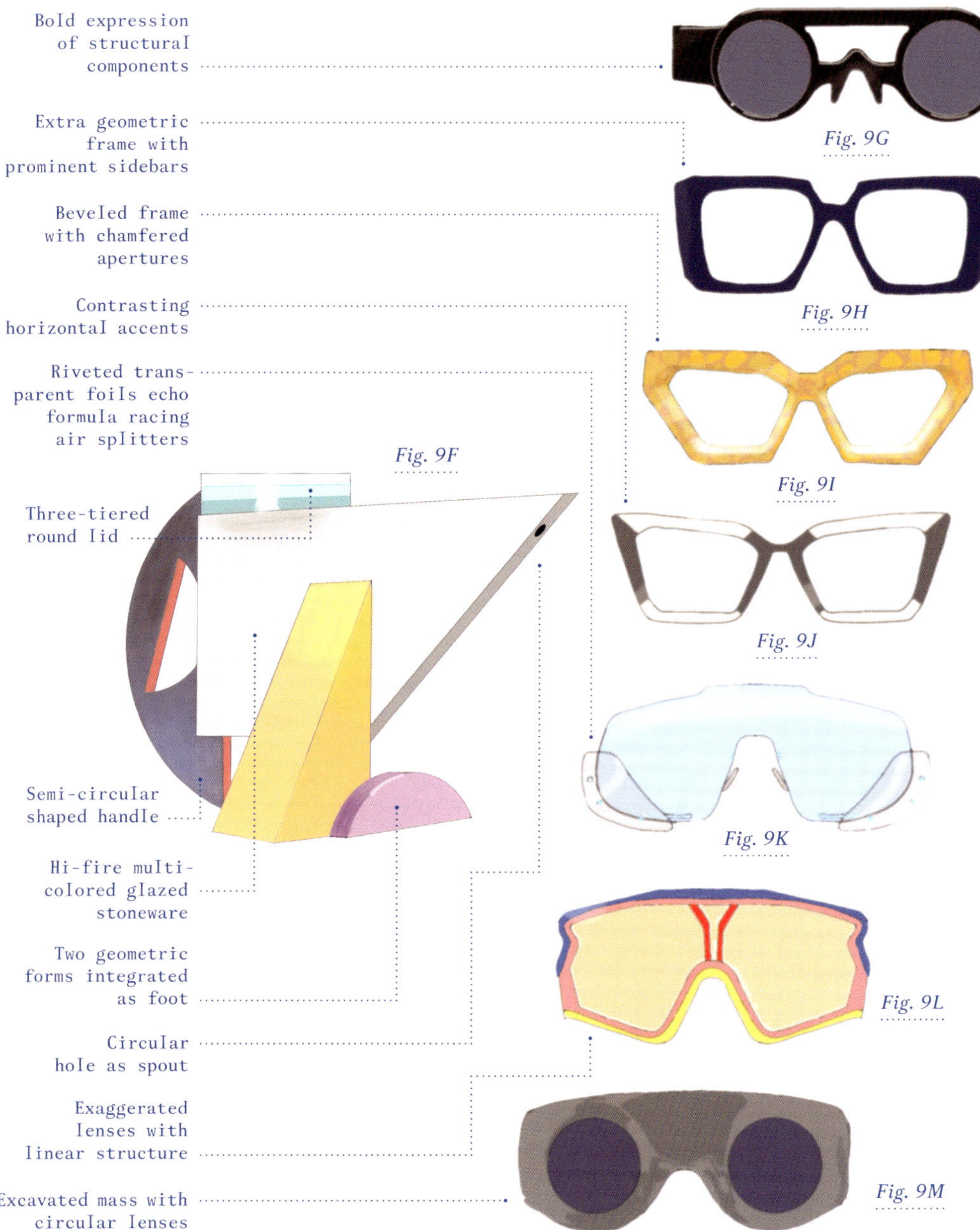

THE THIRD MAN TEAPOT (*Fig. 9F*),
BINOCULAR 02 SUNGLASSES (*Fig. 9G*), ELLERY FRAME (*Fig. 9H*),
ELSPETH TORTOISE FRAME (*Fig. 9I*), PETRIE FRAME (*Fig. 9J*),
FERRARI SUNGLASSES (*Fig. 9K*), TAIGA MULTICOLOR SUNGLASSES (*Fig. 9L*),
BINOCULAR GREY SUNGLASSES (*Fig. 9M*)

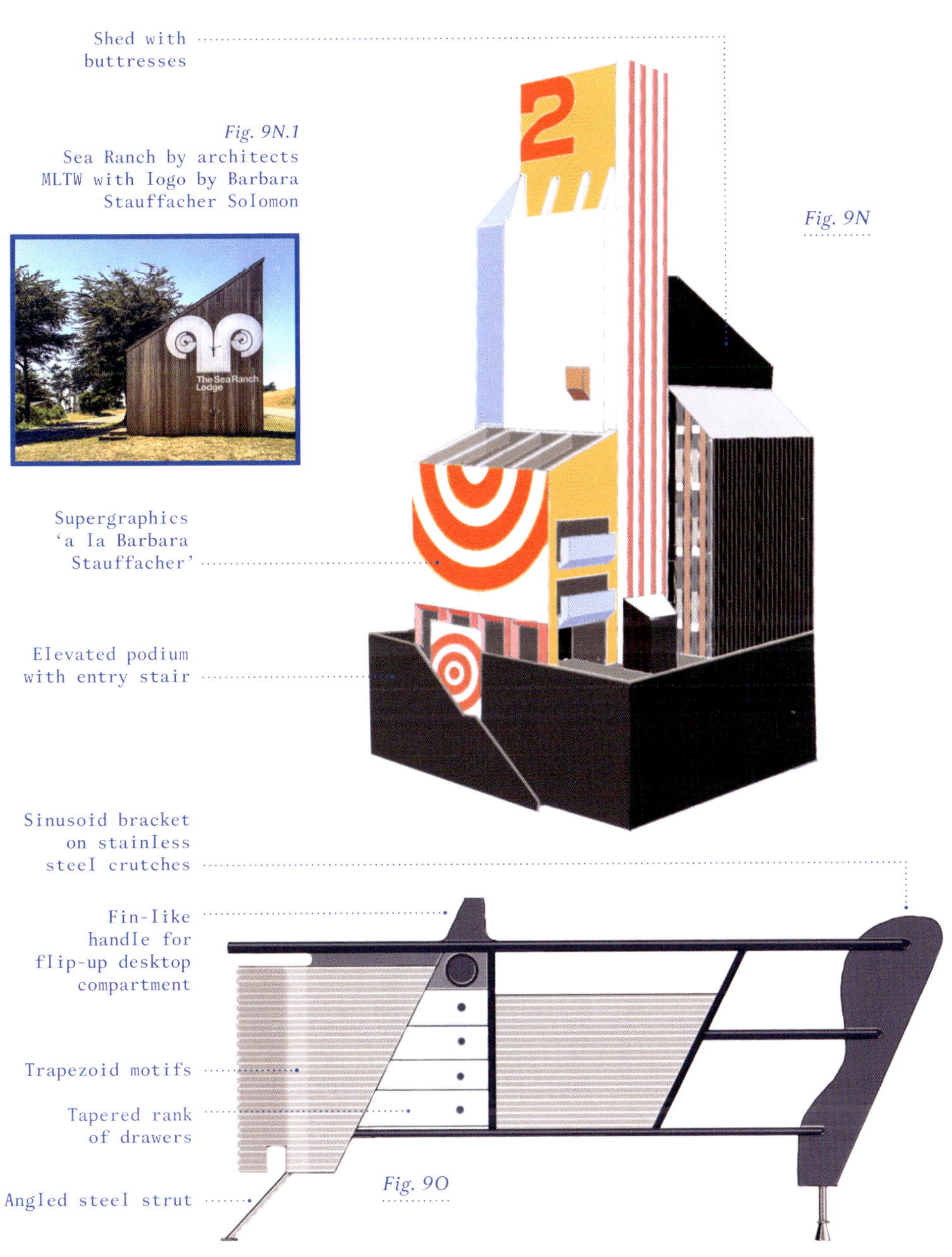

TOKYO TOWER (*Fig. 9N*), BERTRAND CABINET (*Fig. 9O*)

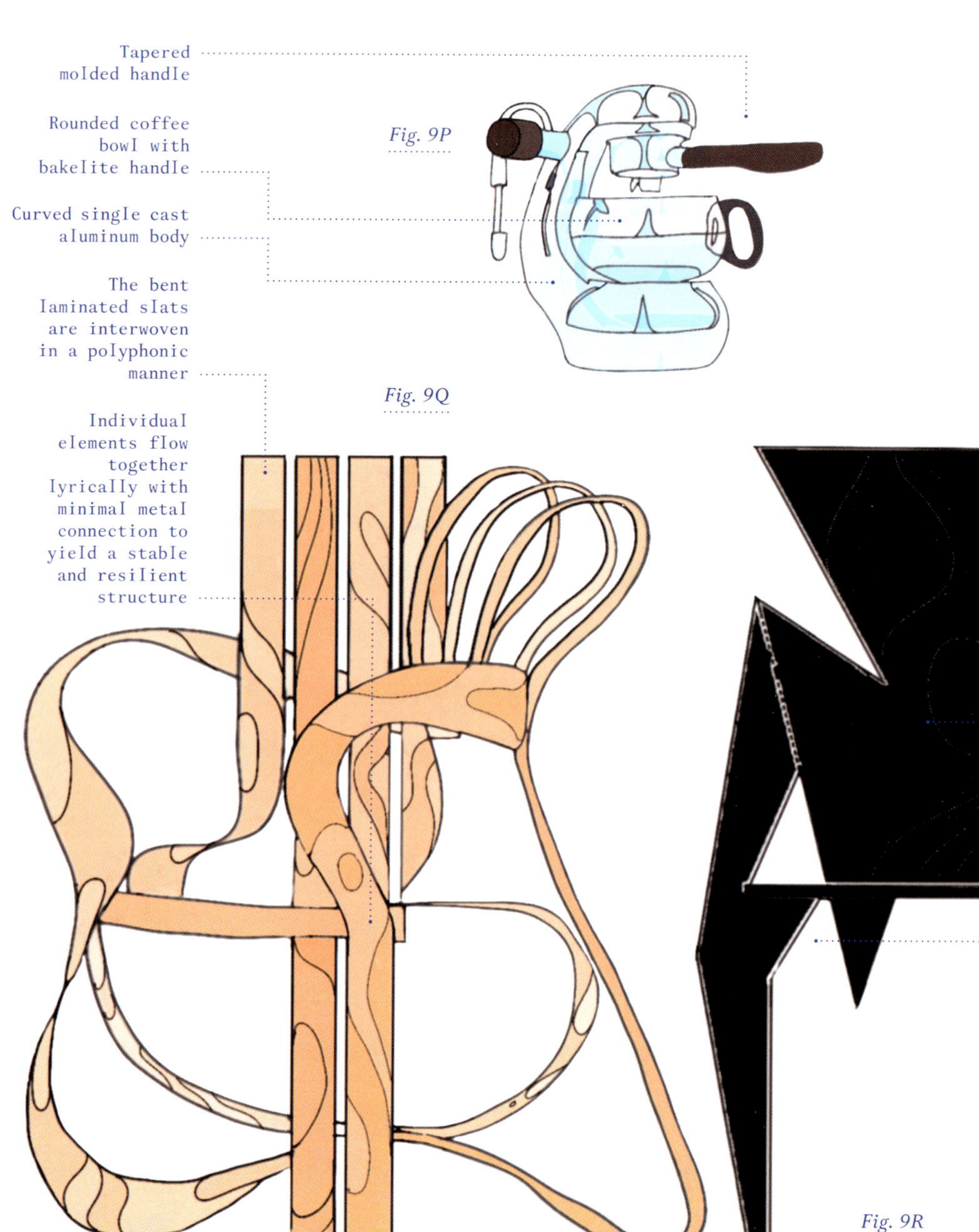

ATOMIC COFFEE MAKER (*Fig. 9P*),
CROSS CHECK CHAIR (*Fig. 9Q*), ICONE CHAIR (*Fig. 9R*)

Cantilevered drawer

Fig. 9S

Support strut

One piece frame

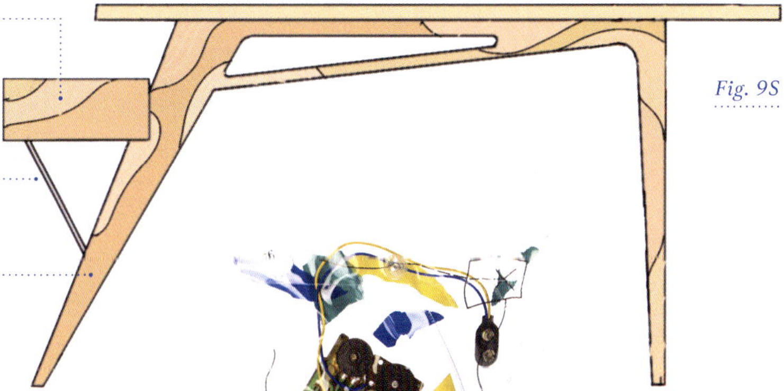

Dismantled transistor radio part

Polyvinyl chloride bag

Fig. 9T

The vertical high back welded to the flat seat conveys a dancer's posture

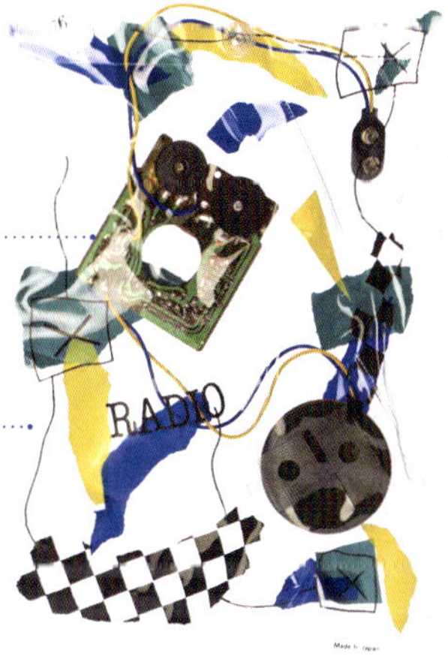

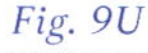

Fig. 9U

The sporadic and jagged angle cuts suggest hyper kinetic movement and clashing activity

Structural stability is achieved by a wide legged stands and origami like fold

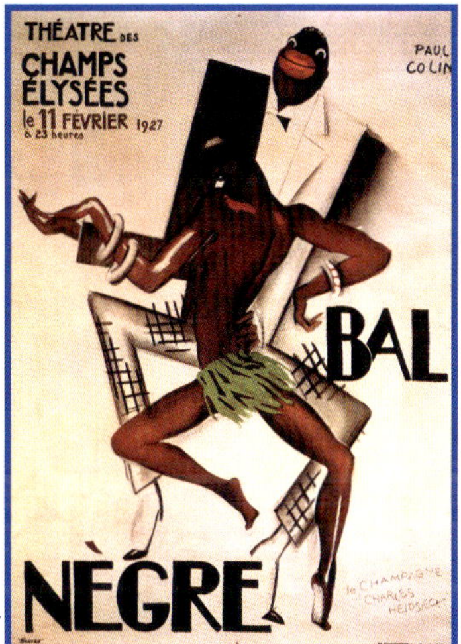

1927 lithograph

PROTRACTOR DESK (*Fig. 9S*), "BAG" RADIO (*Fig. 9T*),
BAL NÈGRE AT THE CHAMPS-ÉLYSÉES THEATRE (*Fig. 9U*)

MEANING

"Sample the good bits to give them a new identity."

®EMix

ATTRIBUTES

Insider caper using precedents to magnify, miniaturize and change scale, materials, and purpose to lift familiar imagery and create new provocative objects.

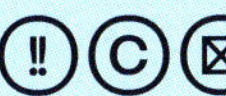

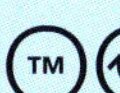

Introduction

The bravura exploitation of (SOURCE MATERIAL) has become pervasive in 21st Century art, music, and design — on (ALL SCALES), from DJ "samples" to borrowed logos, whether for nascent collages or larger assemblages. By the dawn of this century, that approach had become a (DOMINANT) strain.

Adopted today by jewelers, visual artists, musicians, and even industrial designers – featuring found objects, as well as visual references to other eclectic sources – it has been amplified by the Internet into a nearly impenetrable galaxy of appropriations, one iteration upon another into near infinity. With such copious proliferation, one might perhaps put aside the whole question of provenance and succumb instead to the joys of a multi-sourced environment, in which ideas are often seemingly free for the taking and liberated to tumble about.

In the early 1960s, artistic appropriation suddenly garnered headlines with the unveiling of Andy Warhol's *Brillo Boxes* and *Campbell's Soup Cans*. Brash, unashamed, and full of inbred undertones, those objects, transmuted by scale and materials, made their inaugural show, at the Ferus Gallery in West Hollywood, California, a must-see attraction; they also launched taxi-tycoon-turned-art-collector (and Warhol patron) Robert Scull's image into tabloid front pages for months at a time; and they helped ignite a cultural revolution that permeated everything from deadpan poets like Lou Reed to the eventual opening, in 1977, of Ian Schrager's Studio 54 nightclub in New York.

The key here was transformation. Clever reuse of existing features – whether by capitalizing on their effects or by bending inherent physical qualities to new applications – could hybridize and reframe the references. The semiotics of appropriation could take the mind on an out-of-the-ordinary journey of allusions and contradictions in scale, utility, and meaning to ultimately demand the surrender of conventional appraisal. This, in turn, could open the way to cross-fertilization, perhaps the most rewarding avenue for innovation.

Yet the very act of appropriation, with swatches or quotations shorn of their original overtones, can also indicate stagnation, creative or commercial plagiarism, or worse, violation of intellectual property. Such scenarios sometimes escalate into multi-billion-dollar disputes at the corporate level or humiliating artistic squabbles as connoisseurs and fashion brands try to squelch knockoffs. But a 1970s ad campaign for Union Carbide's textile division, featuring faux-fur coats, turned all of that on its head with advertising pioneer Jane Trahey's forthright tag line: "It's not fake anything. It's real Dynel."

In fact, recasting, transforming, quoting, or taking from other realms was nothing new. Even in the Renaissance, artists found inspiration, bordering on downright theft, by embedding into their work objects, motifs, and even compositions from elsewhere. In 1863, Edouard Manet clearly based his acclaimed painting *Le Déjeuner sur l'herbe (Luncheon on the Grass)* on a cropped corner of a much earlier, less celebrated work by Marcantonio Raimondi, an image itself based on an engraving by Raphael. And in far more recent times, instances of borrowing have included comic strip cells – that may or may not have come from actual "funnies" pages – blown up to colossal scale, with supersized Ben-Day dots, in James Rosenquist's epic canvasses or in some of Warhol's early work. The practice seems firmly embedded as acceptable artistic appropriation. Sometimes it has been a way of paying homage; sometimes it has been deliberate parody; and, in some cases, there's a pointed message, even a subversive one, embodied in the provenance and original meaning of the lifted material.

In architecture, appropriation tends to lie in the re-assignment of the roles of materials, components, and even methods. Thus, Sam Mockbee's Rural Studio used recycled automobile windshields as glittering siding for the Glass Chapel in Alabama; and Studio Works, in its South Side Settlement House (1980) in Columbus, Ohio, referred obliquely to the grandeur of Venetian architecture by deploying corrugated sewer culverts as columns that recall classical palazzi. Often with a nod to Pop culture, architect James Stirling's designs for research centers and museums made no secret of his disdain for the polite elements of corporate design by over-scaling and vividly coloring them, often lime green. Of course, they were not alone. By far, the most flagrant case of re-appropriation was by master insider Phillip Johnson, when he crowned a career full of derivative projects with the 1984 AT&T Building, a Madison Avenue tower in the guise of a giant Chippendale highboy dresser. Perfectly timed and underwritten by the then-surging popularity of the Post-Modern architectural movement, the tower none-theless faced a storm of critical ire, only to wind up as a favorite subject of local tourist postcards and souvenir baubles for its whimsiness – in other words, it succeeded as a "genuine fake imitation Chippendale."

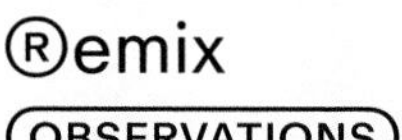

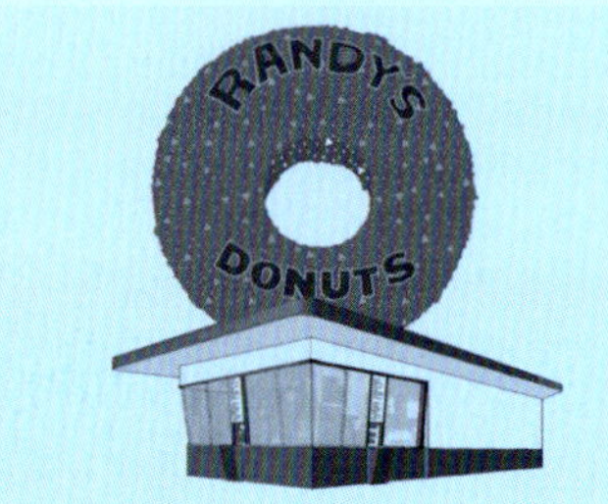

Fig. 10A RANDY'S DONUTS STAND (p. 278)

YEAR 1953
ARCHITECT
Henri Goodwin
LOCATION
Inglewood, California, USA

Randy's joins a phalanx of "Ducks" as defined by Robert Venturi and Denise Scott Brown that includes plaster Wigwams, concrete Dinosaurs, Dogs, Dirigibles and other architectural detritus which can be found scattered along highways and byways that offer a place to sleep or eat.

Fig. 10B UNION (p. 278)

YEAR 2023
ARTIST
Rita McBride
LOCATION
Los Angeles, California, USA

By repurposing a discarded free newspaper rack, and stenciling the Gothic letters spelling the word "FREE," the artist introduces a galling conundrum: what, exactly, is free? One can appreciate it for what it is – a provocative sculpture referencing the regulations and political systems for adult advertising by local entrepreneurs, and to comment on commercial exploitation and current cultural values.

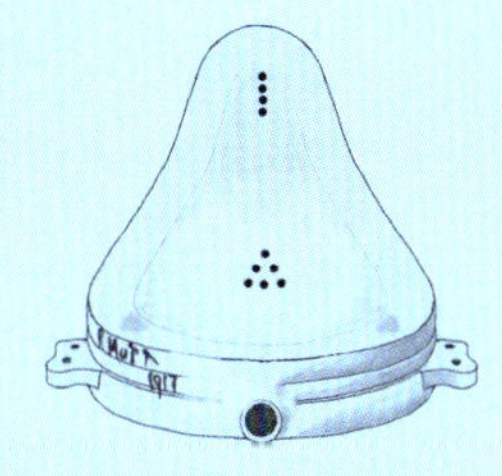

Fig. 10C FOUNTAIN
(p. 278)

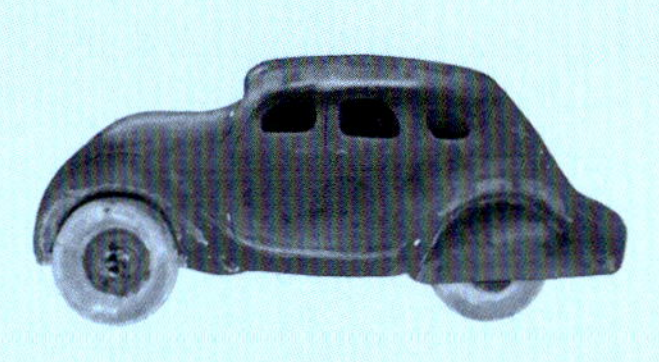

Fig. 10D VINTAGE CAST IRON TOY CAR
(p. 279)

YEAR 1917
ARTIST
Marcel Duchamp
LOCATION
New York,
New York, USA

As a disgruntled member of the Parisian Society of Independent Artists whose work was rejected, Duchamp sought to pull one on the selection committee by submitting a commercially available urinal as sculpture – signing it with the pseudonym R. Mutt. Today it is viewed as the exemplar of Duchamp's fascination with the "Readymade," and the progenitor of a form of artistic endeavor.

With headlights for eyes, and wheel wells for features, two of these toys were fused top to bottom to form the head of the mother baboon in Picasso's amusing sculpture.

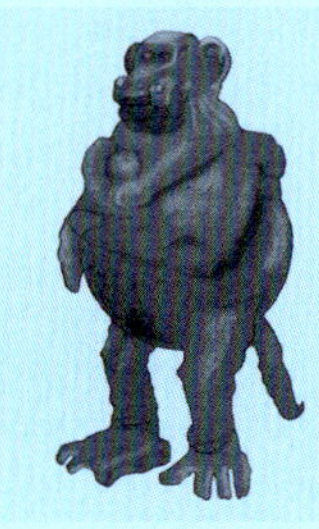

Fig. 10E BABOON AND YOUNG (p. 279)

YEAR 1951
ARTIST
Pablo Picasso
MADE IN
Vallauris, France

Bound together by improvised clay appendages, the image of a baboon-like mother and child emerges from an amalgam of found objects: a ball, an automobile leaf spring, two toy cars, and Picasso's imagination. Cast in bronze, it is a triumph of the foundry's craft as well as an entertaining glimpse into his playful nature.

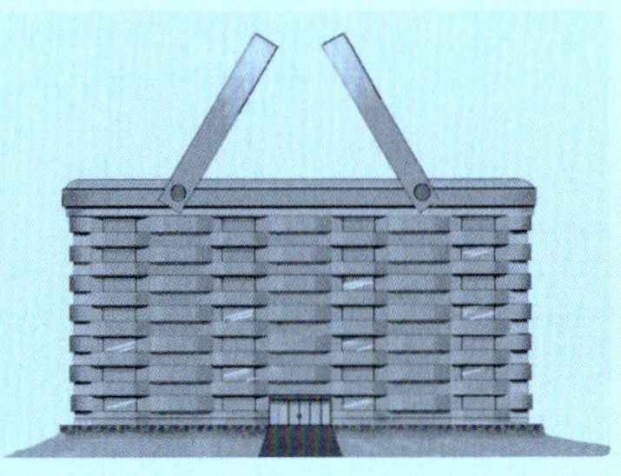

Fig. 10F LONGABERGER BASKET BUILDING (p. 280)

YEAR 1997
ARCHITECTS
NBBJ and Korda/Nemeth Engineering
LOCATION
Newark, Ohio

The history of the creation of monumental replicas of existing people and objects, which dates from Greco-Roman times, has been an effective artistic trope for artists from Jeff Koons to Claes Oldenberg, though it is unusual to create a functioning building utilizing a similar artistic premise.

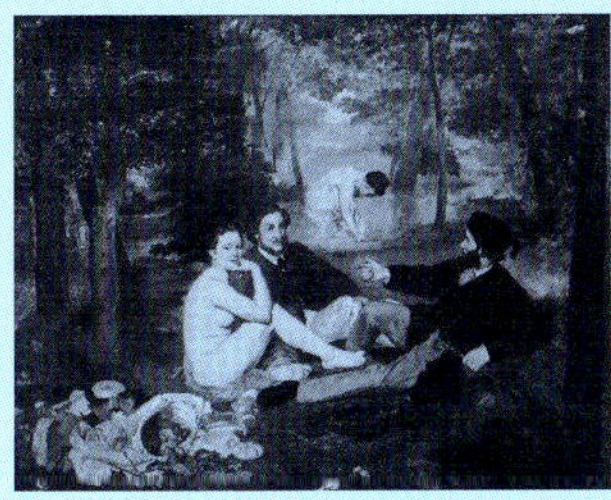

Fig. 10G LE DÉJEUNER SUR L'HERBE (p. 280)

YEAR 1863
ARTIST
Edouard Manet
LOCATION
Musée D'Orsay, France

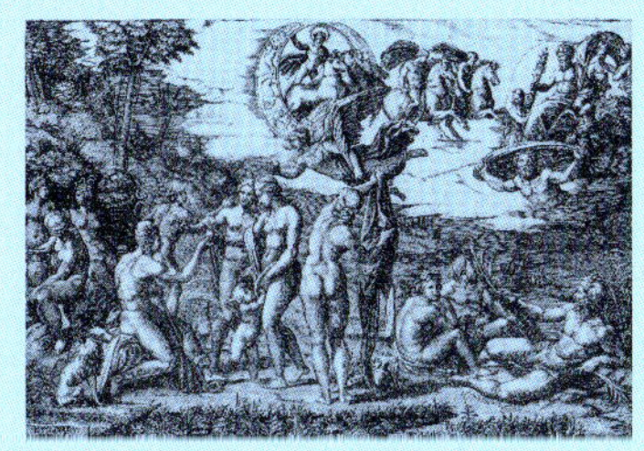

Fig. 10H THE JUDGMENT OF PARIS (p. 280)

YEAR
c.1517-1520
ARTIST
Marcantonio Raimondi, after Raphael (Raffaello Sanzio or Santi)
LOCATION
The Art Institute of Chicago, USA

The gestures and composition are the same, only the costumes and medium have been altered in this famous Manet painting that reinterprets and crops *The Judgement of Paris*, a sixteenth-century engraving by Raphael & Raimondi. That Manet's version features a nude woman in the company of fully clothed men caused a scandal when it was first exhibited in the 1863 Salon Des Refuses in Paris.

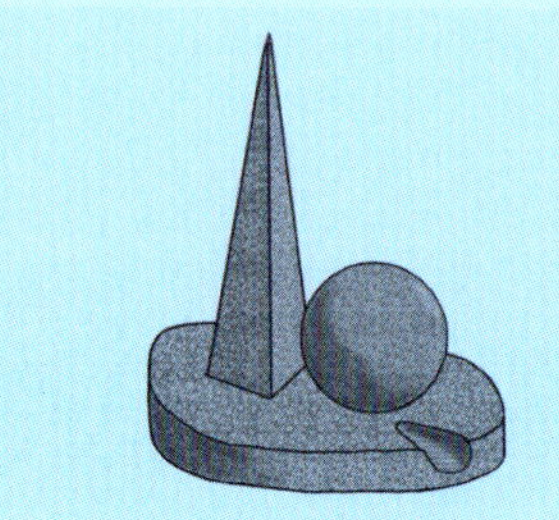

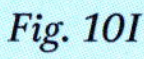

Fig. 10I

1939 NEW YORK WORLD'S FAIR TRYLON AND PERISPHERE SOUVENIR BRONZE ASHTRAY
(p. 281)

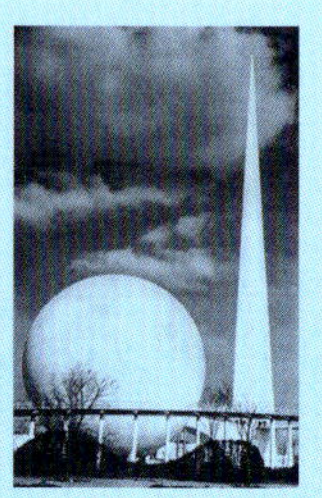

Fig. 10J

TRYLON AND PERISPHERE, NEW YORK WORLD'S FAIR
(p. 281)

YEAR 1939
DESIGNERS
Wallace Harrison and J. André Fouilhoux
LOCATION
New York, New York, USA

The pure geometry and simple forms immediately inspired a glut of tourist baubles, such as this vintage ashtray, arguably the most enduring and useful, to this day.

The 1939 World's Fair in Flushing, New York, was dedicated to the future, showcasing America's industrial might, and the innovations, from freeways to dishwashers, that would change people's lives. The towering six hundred foot tall Trylon and its accompanying Perisphere meant to symbolize the World of Tomorrow and contained a depiction of a utopian city of the future within the sphere.

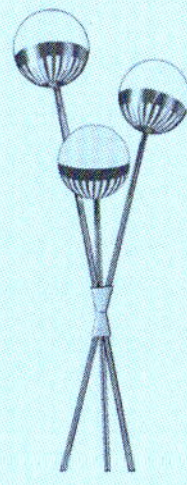

Fig. 10K CARACAS TRIPOD FLOOR LAMP (p. 281)

YEAR 2019
DESIGNER
Jonathan Adler
MANUFACTURED IN USA

Perhaps inspired by the pervasive atomic imagery of the fifties and sixties, such lamps, and their fellows, drew on popular fascination with the vocabulary of spheres, orbits, and nuclei to usher in an age of atomic imagery. Polished chromium balls were a major design trope in the fifties and sixties, inspiring disparate interpretations from domestic lighting fixtures to the giant "Atomium" at the Brussels World's Fair.

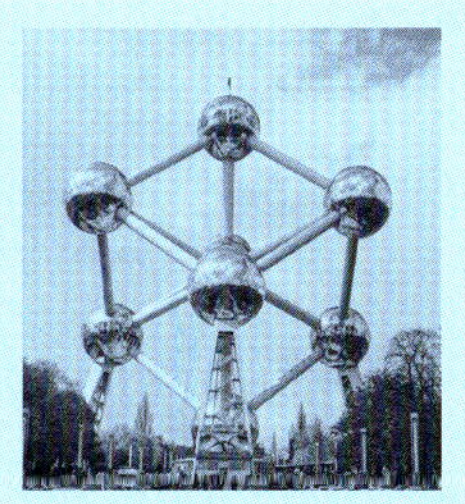

Fig. 10L ATOMIUM (p. 281)

YEAR 1956
ARCHITECTS
André and Jean Polak
ENGINEER
André Waterkeyn
LOCATION
1956 Brussels World's Fair, Belgium

Created during the height of the nuclear frenzy that contemplated both annihilation and infinite power, the Atomium gave visitors an opportunity to visit educational exhibits as they walked into giant spheres representing atomic nuclei.

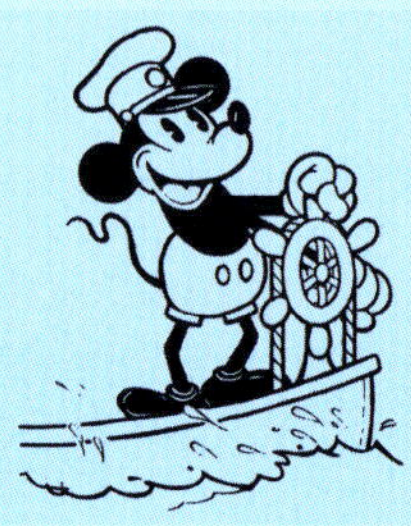

Fig. 10M STEAMBOAT WILLIE (p. 282)

YEAR 1928
ARTISTS
Ub Iwerks and Walt Disney

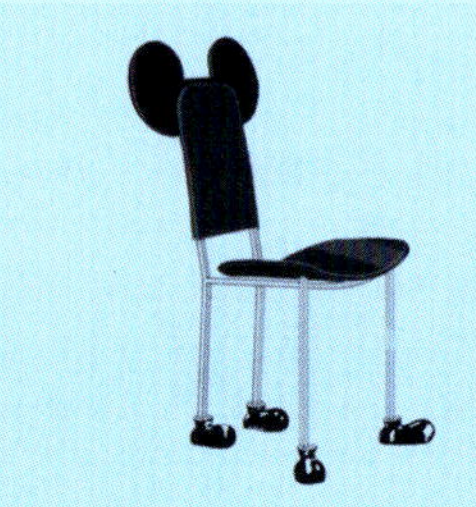

Fig. 10N GARRIRIS CHAIR (p. 282)

YEAR 1980
DESIGNERS
Javier Mariscal
MANUFACTURER
Akaba S.A., Spain

Created by Walt Disney in 1928, and arguably the most recognized image in the world, the iconic, abstract geometry that generates the face of Steamboat Willie enables multiple facial expressions without sacrificing its basic character.

Disney's genius is apparent when two circular forms positioned to the right and left of a chair's backrest instantly trigger a happy association with Steamboat Willie. The quotation is completed with the inclusion of less iconic but still relevant "Mouse Feet."

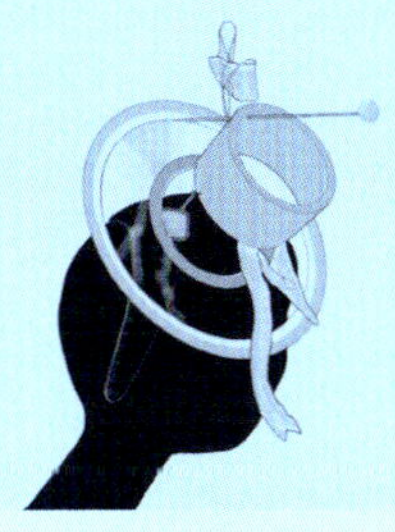

Fig. 10O CHAPEAU BANG! (p. 282)

YEAR 2010
DESIGNER
Stephen Jones
COMPANY
Stephen Jones Millinery, England

Hats at Ascot are the stuff of English legend, and Stephen Jones, most would agree, is the ultimate milliner. Seemingly able to create a compelling hat from nearly any source, here he has appropriated a cup and saucer and set them akimbo atop the head.

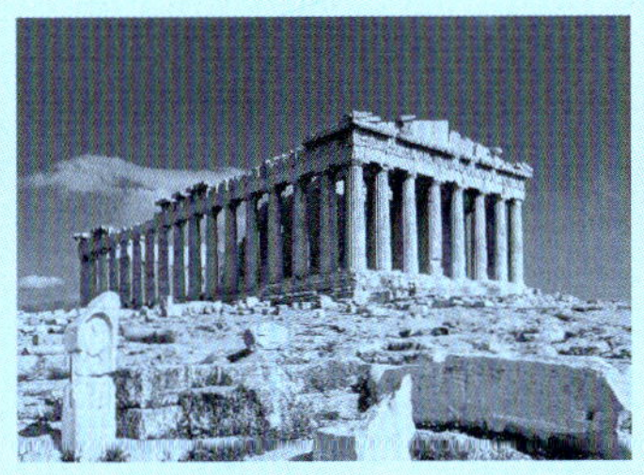

Fig. 10P PARTHENON (p. 282)

YEAR
c.447-432 BC
LOCATION
Athens, Greece

Even in its ravaged condition, the Temple to Athena reflects the system of idealized proportions that have inspired innumerable reincarnations in the guise of courthouses, government centers, and even Georgian mansions.

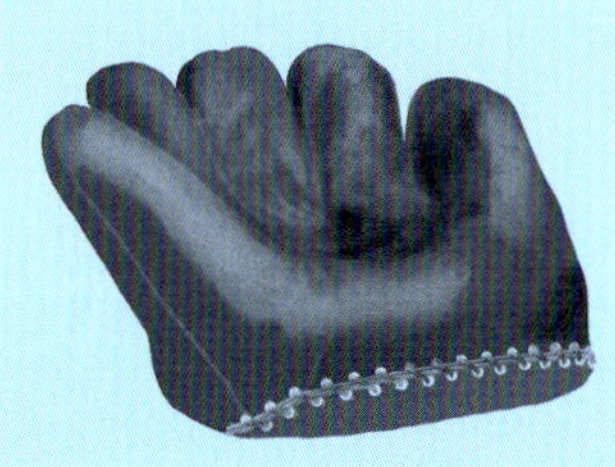

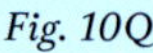

Fig. 10Q

JOE GOLD
BASEBALL
ARMCHAIR
(p. 283)

YEAR 1971
DESIGNER
DDL Studio
MANUFACTURER
Poltrovona,
Italy

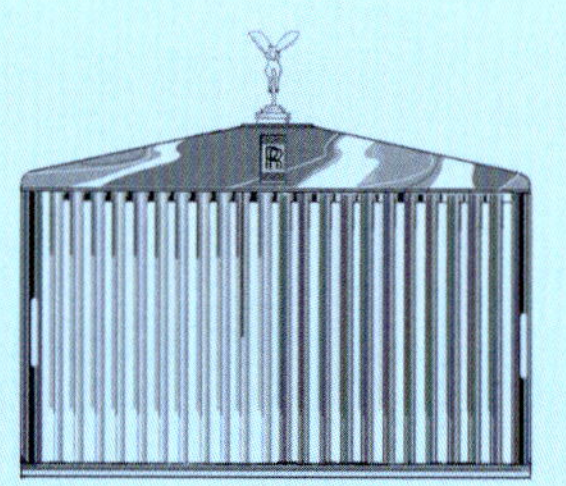

Fig. 10R

SILVER SPUR
FRONT GRILL
(p. 283)

YEAR 1986
DESIGNERS
Henry Rolls and
Charles Royce
MANUFACTURER
Rolls-Royce
plc, England

Scaled for relaxation rather than catching a baseball, the form, materials, and details of this lounger faithfully mirror those of a catcher's mitt. Created during the heyday of Pop Art as a fashionable conversation piece, its comfort and durability soon transcended its droll origins.

By hovering midway between architectural majesty and vehicular function, the Rolls radiator grill achieves an enduring clarity of purpose connoting an esteemed history and cultural relevance in a way that cannot be duplicated by other brands, no matter how distinguished. From the inception of their partnership in 1906, it was devised to reflect the character and enduring quality that they envisioned.

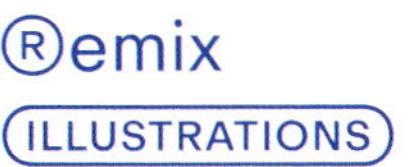
®emix
ILLUSTRATIONS

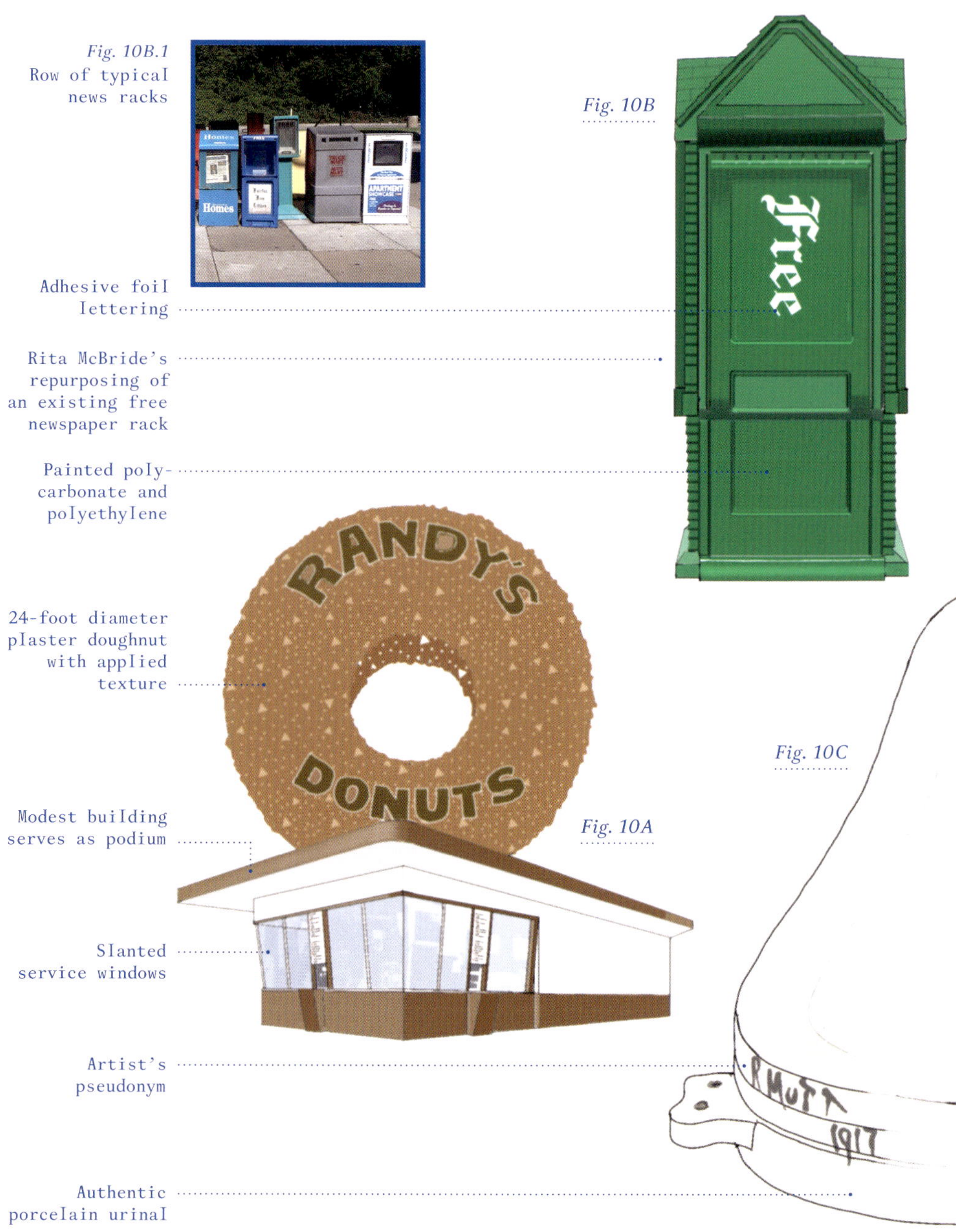

RANDY'S DONUTS STAND (*Fig. 10A*),
UNION (*Fig. 10B*), FOUNTAIN (*Fig. 10C*)

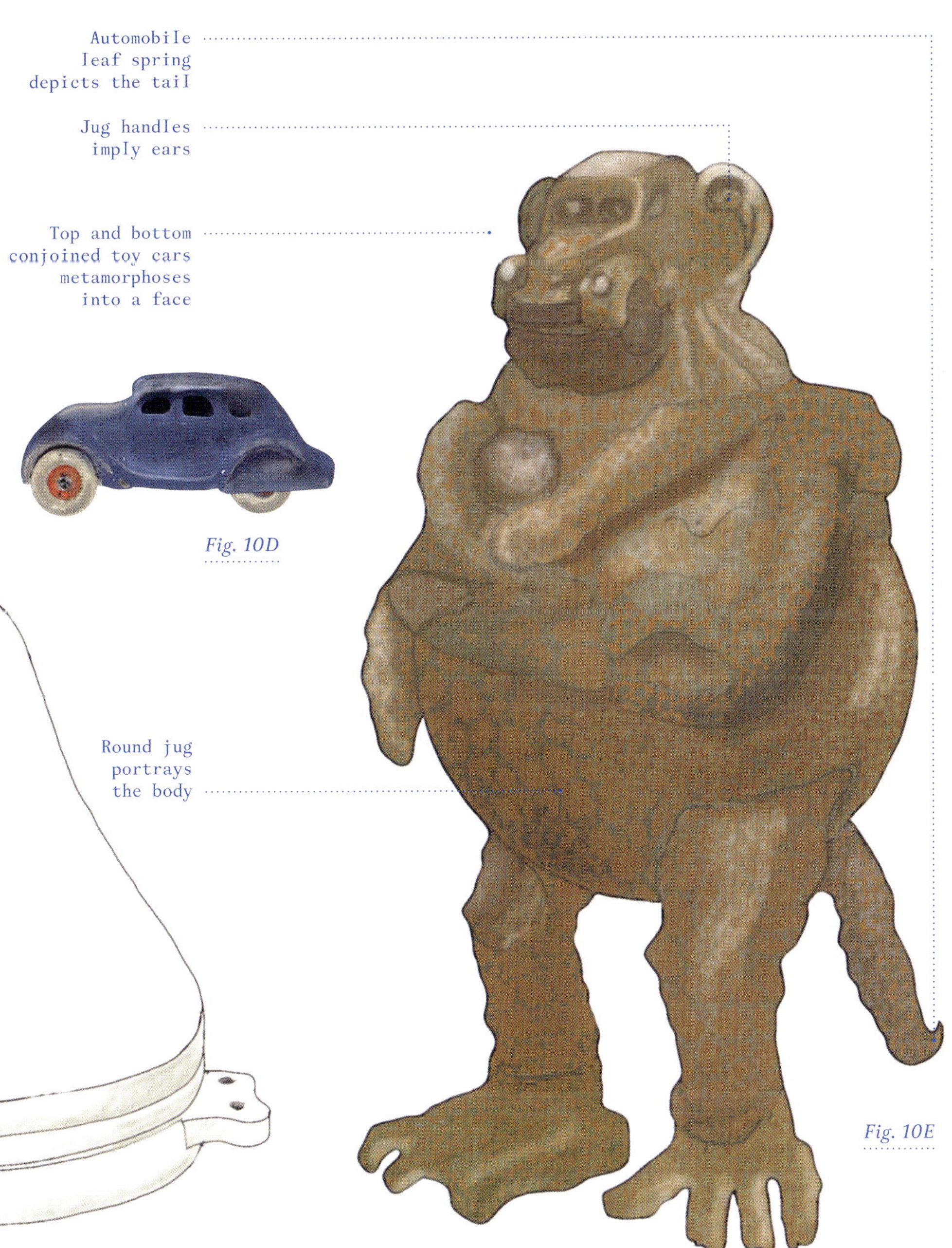

VINTAGE CAST IRON TOY CAR (*Fig. 10D*), BABOON AND YOUNG (*Fig. 10E*)

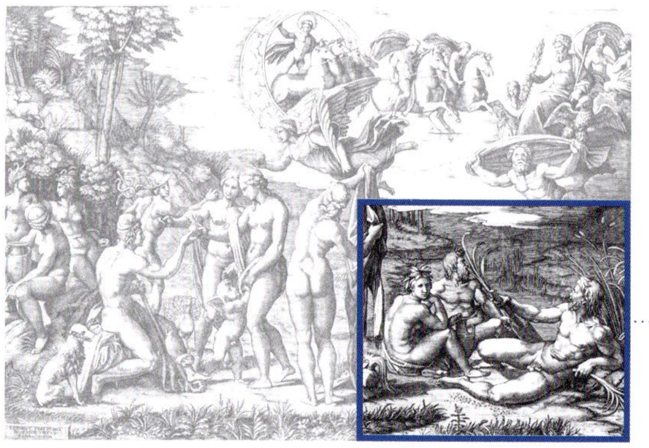

Fig. 10H

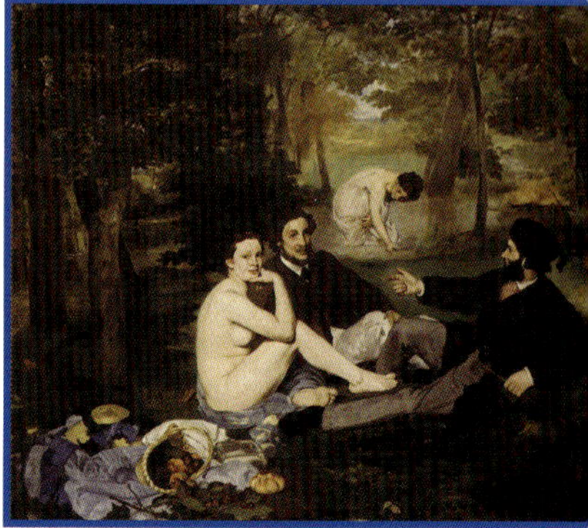

Fig. 10G

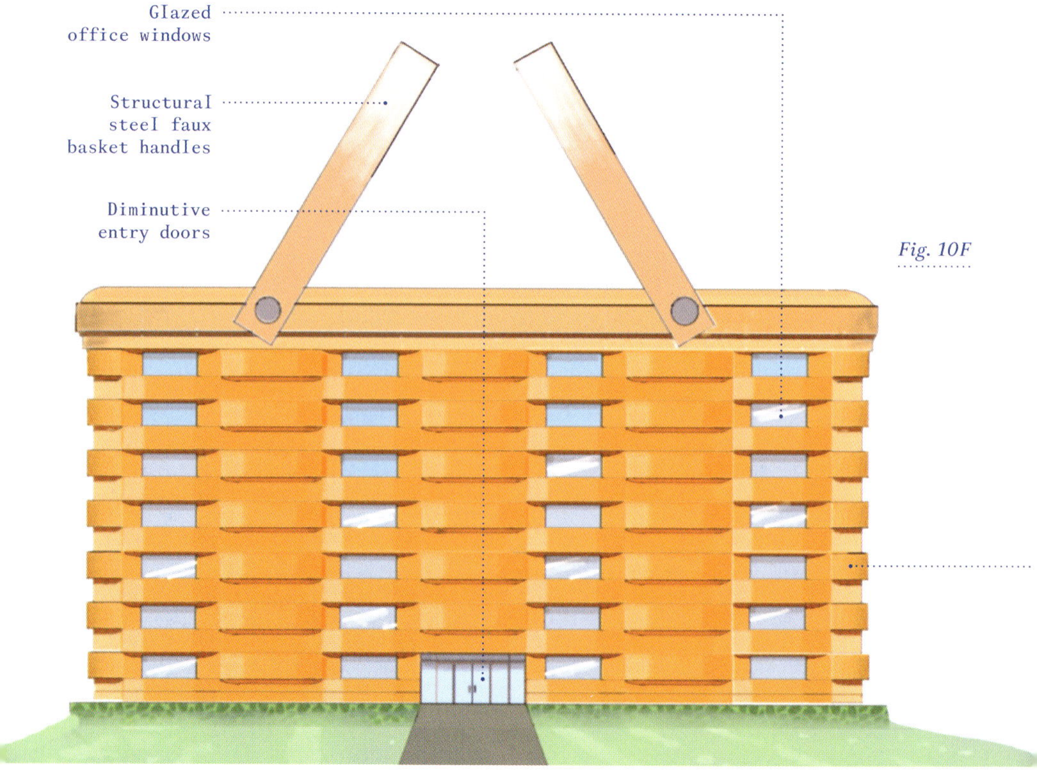

Glazed office windows

Structural steel faux basket handles

Diminutive entry doors

Fig. 10F

LONGABERGER BASKET BUILDING (*Fig. 10F*),
LE DÉJEUNER SUR L'HERBE (*Fig. 10G*), THE JUDGMENT OF PARIS (*Fig. 10H*)

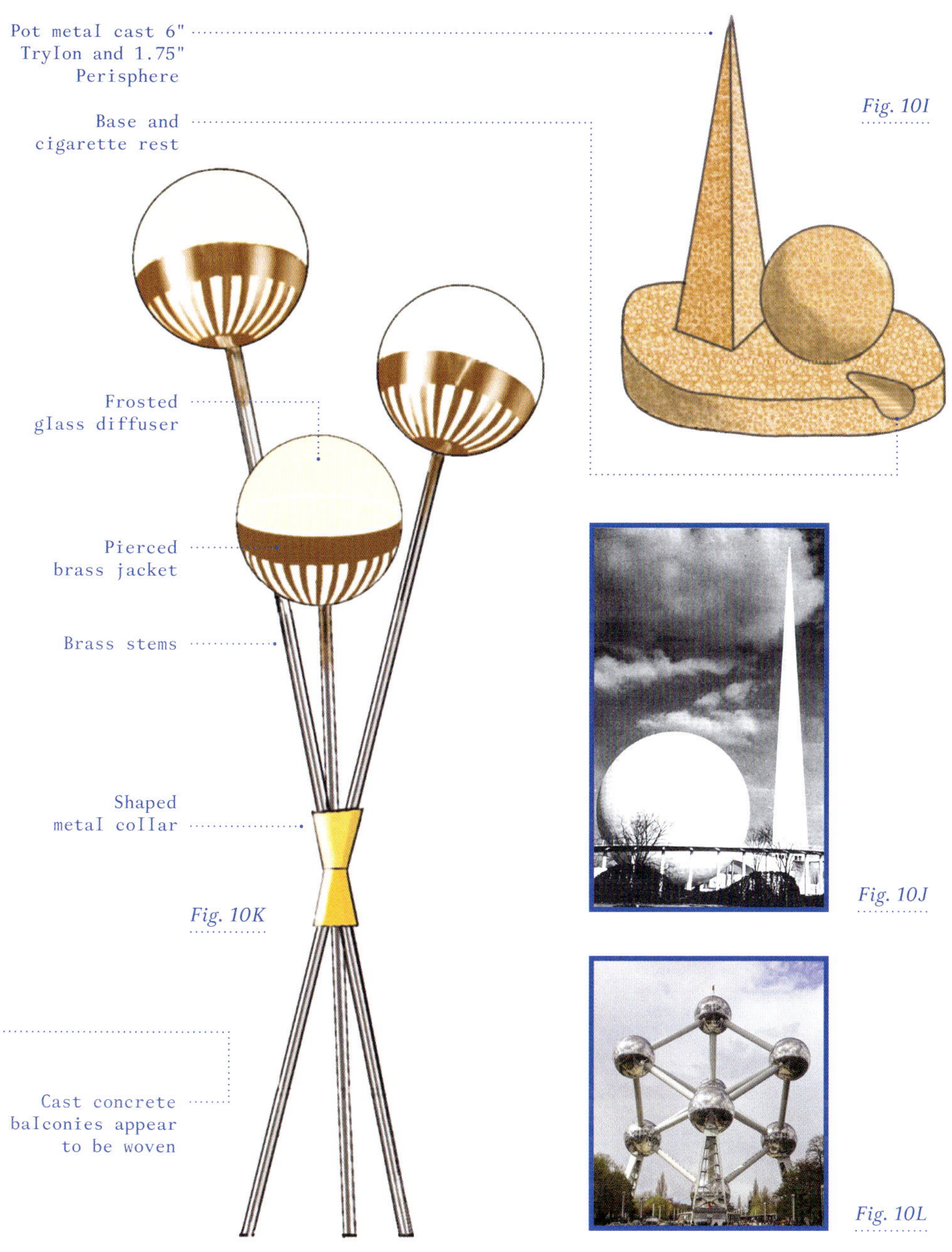

1939 NEW YORK WORLD'S FAIR TRYLON AND PERISPHERE SOUVENIR BRONZE ASHTRAY (*Fig. 10I*), TRYLON AND PERISPHERE, NEW YORK WORLD'S FAIR (*Fig. 10J*), CARACAS TRIPOD FLOOR LAMP (*Fig. 10K*), ATOMIUM (*Fig. 10L*)

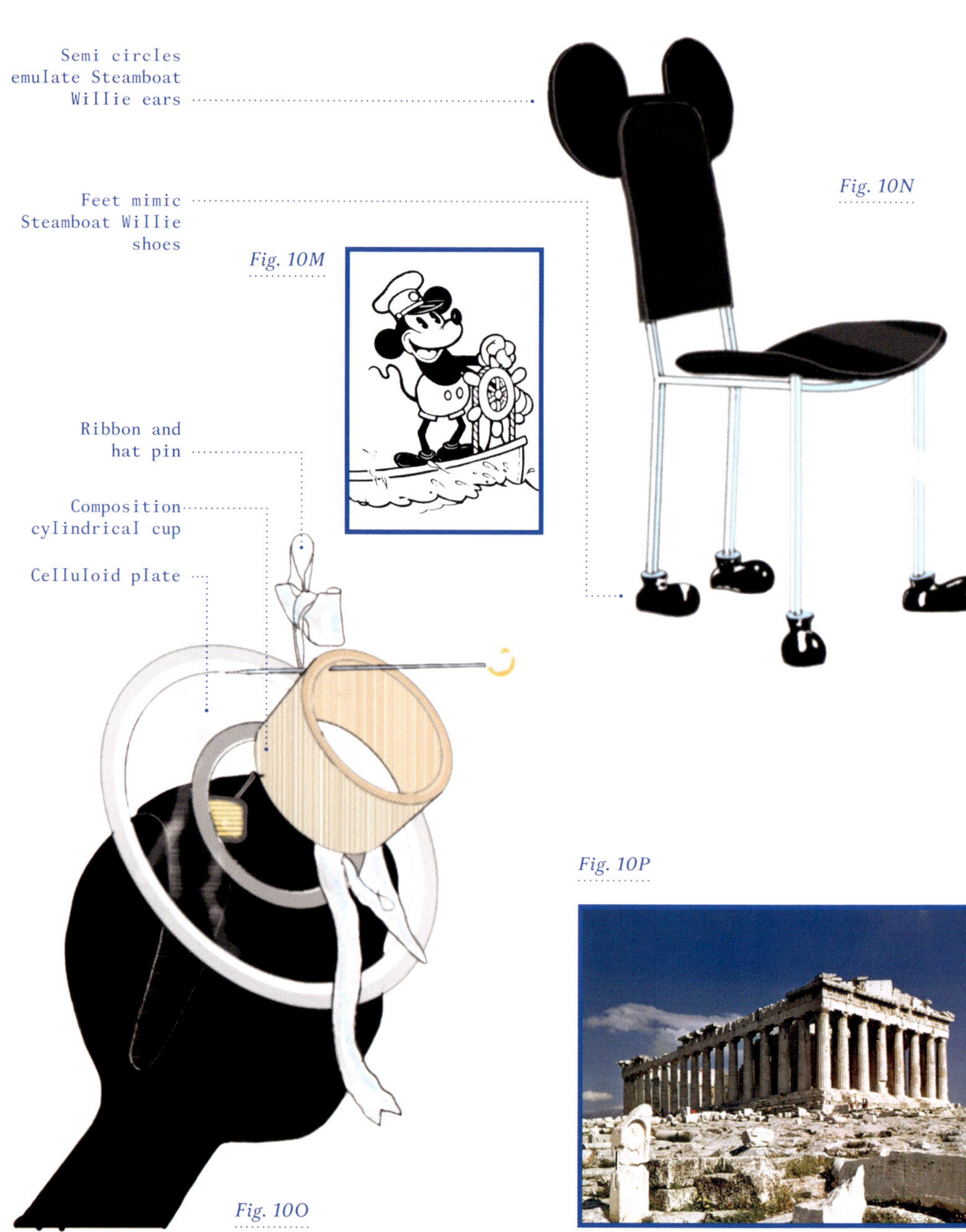

STEAMBOAT WILLIE (*Fig. 10M*), GARRIRIS CHAIR (*Fig. 10N*), CHAPEAU BANG! (*Fig. 10O*), PARTHENON (*Fig. 10P*)

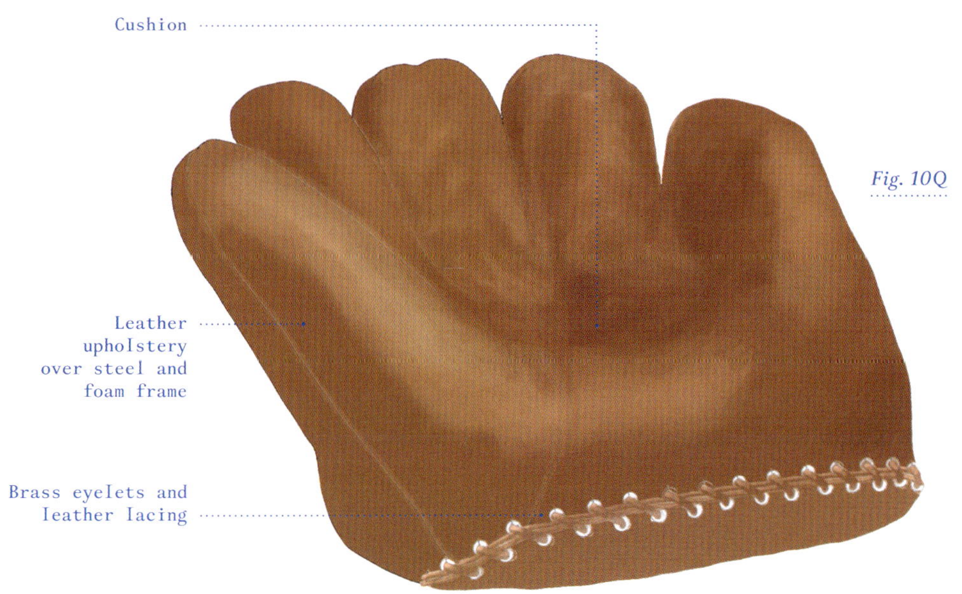

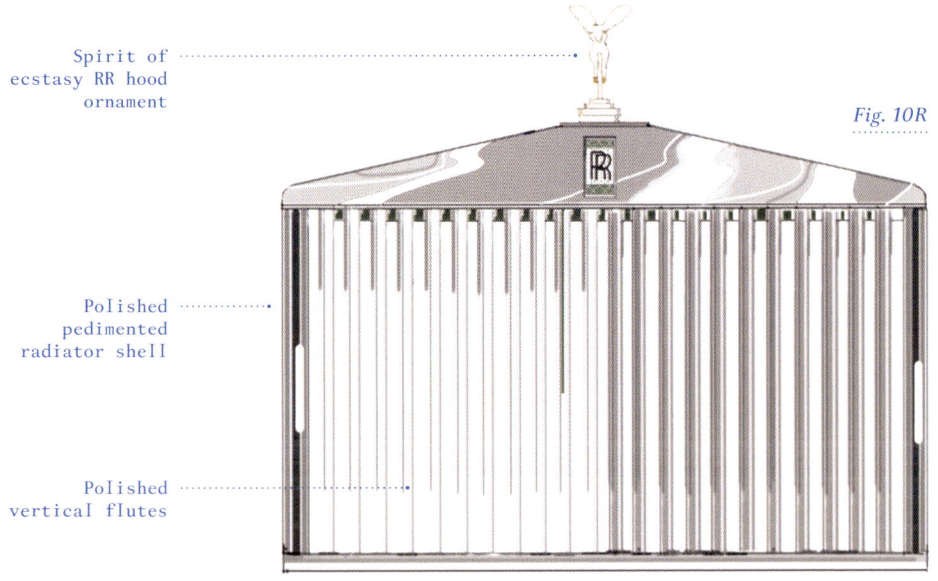

JOE GOLD BASEBALL ARMCHAIR (*Fig. 10Q*),
SILVER SPUR FRONT GRILL (*Fig. 10R*)

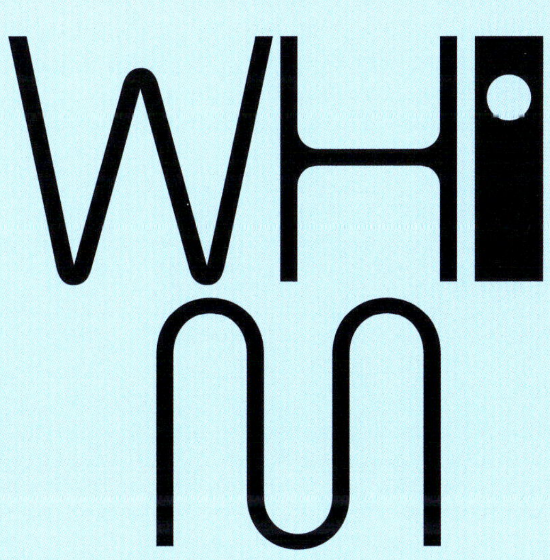

M E S S A G E
"GIVE A GENTLE NUDGE TO REPLACE HAUTEUR WITH GOOD NATURED DROLL WIT."
A T T R I B U T E S
PLAYFUL POSE, DISTORTED PROPORTIONS AND A TOUCH OF NAUGHTY EXAGGERATION APPLIED TO AN OTHERWISE EFFECTIVE DESIGN.

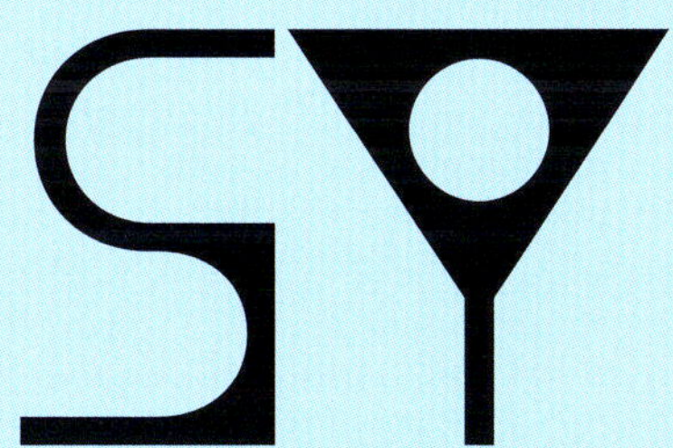

It's no secret that "play," as practiced freely and joyfully by children, tends to give way to more "adult," structured activities once puberty encroaches. In reaction, artists and designers, especially those inspired by the whimsy of Pop Art, have often taunted the inhibitions and cultural systems that support such "maturity."

Designs in that lighthearted spirit, drawing on dynamic geometries from cartoons and vivid imagery from other popular sources, have brought a reprieve from routine, primarily functional solutions for everything from furniture to airports. Notably, the later heirs to Pop design – carrying forward its bright colors and novel forms, coupled with tendencies to be budget friendly and flexible – began to infuse corporate environments and tech companies, as well as schools, libraries, and other civic places with a playful palette of shapes and patterns.

Such lyrical arrangements proclaimed freedom from conventional design principles, bucking the strict rules that govern utility, function, and even structural stability. Thus, the tilted columns supporting Will Alsop's Sharp Centre for Design (2004), in Toronto, dance between logic and fantasy, asking us to suspend reason and disbelief. This kind of semantic flair – in some cases, with mismatched table legs, seemingly frivolous colors, forms that defy gravity, and oversized, toy-like massing – asks us to delight in the design's amusing and apparently carefree attitude. Elsewhere, many of Clive Wilkinson's office environments, with their writhing conference tables and brightly colored bird's-nest cubicles, apply amusement-park tropes to inspire creative productivity while assuring that dreary rows of forlorn cubicles have met their nemesis.

Past and present practitioners of the playful genre, including Milton Glaser, George Sowden, and Nathalie du Pasquier, have reveled in applying slightly mischievous, innovative twists to staid corporate models. The 1968 Olivetti Valentine Typewriter, for example, designed by Ettore Sottsass and available only in glossy lipstick-red, is poised between a plaything and a writer's tool, famously challenging the bland options of IBM and its corporate cousins. Many such works have a cartoonish, "What, me worry?" (*Mad Magazine*) attitude. James Wines/SITE's

1977 *Ghost Parking Lot*, for instance, injected mordant humor into the big-box shopping experience, especially where the freshly poured tarmac of a mall parking lot had been invited to spread like lava, sculpturally, eerily, and amusingly entombing a row of parked cars, as part of the design. Such narratives, more explicit and idiosyncratic than those of their more strait-laced peers, were often couched in a poker-faced design language that stayed within the bounds of "good design" without straying into the sentimental or outsider status of "folk art."

The Memphis Group, operating under the wing of Ettore Sottsass from 1980 to 1987, was a fearless generator of whimsical forms, flaunting multi-hued confections, full of stripes, doodles, and clashing geometries. Eventually spawning hundreds of designs and dozens of acolytes, the Memphis moment was soon over – to be replaced by the well-crafted and disciplined corporate products of the nineties that the movement, in its idealism, had sought to replace.

Also, at the level of household accessories, Alessi and then, Target gave Michael Graves a wildly successful alternative to his critically ill-received architecture with commissions for popular teakettles, toasters, and even toilet brushes, each featuring droll, readily graspable humor with great visual flair. More designers – led by lighting guru Ingo Maurer, whose signature flying light bulbs with wings are among the world's most emotionally fraught objects – followed, injecting visual puns, acid color, and semantic puzzles, into household objects, seemingly in a search for meaning, without compromising their utility.

Providing antidotes to the canonical work of giants like Dieter Rams or Henry Dreyfuss, such playfulness – no less creatively – leavens more sober approaches with sophisticated visual quips, sexual allusions, and fairy-tale back stories. The puns underlying many of the products, from the whistling bird on the Graves teakettle to the more subliminal avian posture of the Eames DCW chair, are reminders of design's capacity to tell amusing stories without compromising primary function. They draw on our remarkable storehouses of remembered images, on the layer upon layer of collective visual wealth that animates our awareness of the spaces and objects around us. Even when veering toward whimsy, design can be a seriously powerful tool.

WHIMSY OBSERVATIONS

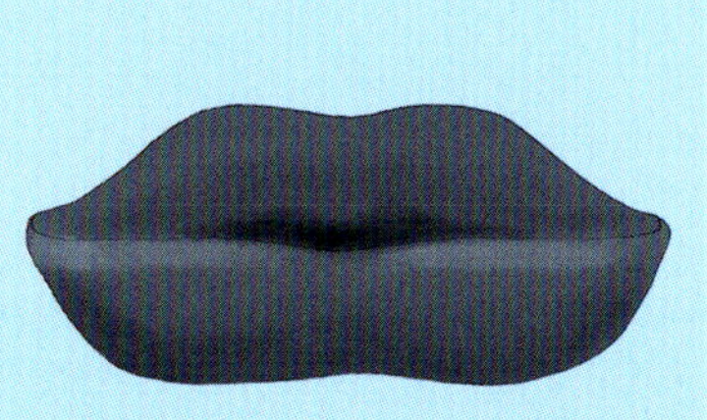

Fig. 11A BOCA SOFA (p. 304)

YEAR 1970
DESIGNER
Studio 65
MANUFACTURER
Heller, USA

With a brazen nod to artist Man Ray, the luscious curves and lipstick hue of this sofa and its pretenders offer true comfort in a stylish package that adds a surrealistic touch to any environment. Cool, hip, and beyond categorization, it is a seamless blend of comic-strip imagery and lewd, come-hither appeal.

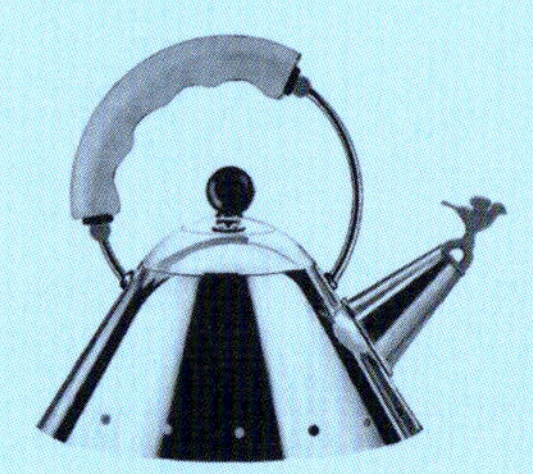

Fig. 11B WHISTLING BIRD TEAKETTLE (p. 304)

YEAR 1985
DESIGNER
Michael Graves
MANUFACTURER
Centro Studio Alessi S.p.A., Italy

By endowing this perfectly ordinary teapot with a stylish whistle in the form of a plastic bluebird, what was mundane and “invisible” became a notable kitchen accessory and an item on many bridal wish lists, that, in one brilliant stroke, had been changed forever.

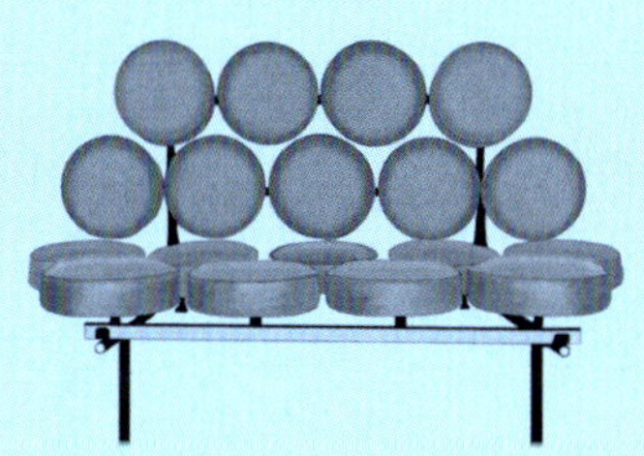

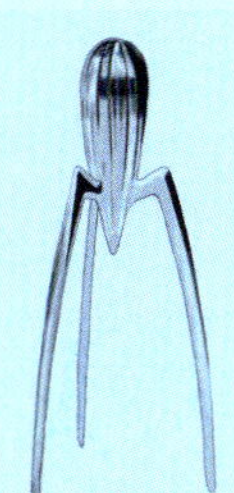

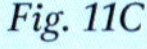

Fig. 11C MARSHMALLOW SOFA (p. 304)

YEAR 1956
DESIGNER
George Nelson
MANUFACTURER
Herman Miller, USA

Fig. 11D JUICY SALIF CITRUS SQUEEZER (p. 305)

YEAR 1990
DESIGNER
Philippe Starck
MANUFACTURER
Centro Studio Alessi S.p.A., Italy

In contriving to create a functional sofa from an amusing sketch, the designer George Nelson, whose signature work was corporate office furniture, and who was design chief at prestige furniture manufacturer Herman Miller accomplished a neat trick by creating a pop-infused icon within the domain of one of the conservative pillars of American industry.

Insectile and Surreal, and profoundly ambiguous, the sculptural form of this juicer is a witty yet fully functional rejoinder to the impersonal style of the common kitchen implement. Even though many that sit on bookshelves in living rooms have never dropped a drip of juice into a cup, the intriguing form, and the mere suggestion of utility justify its presence.

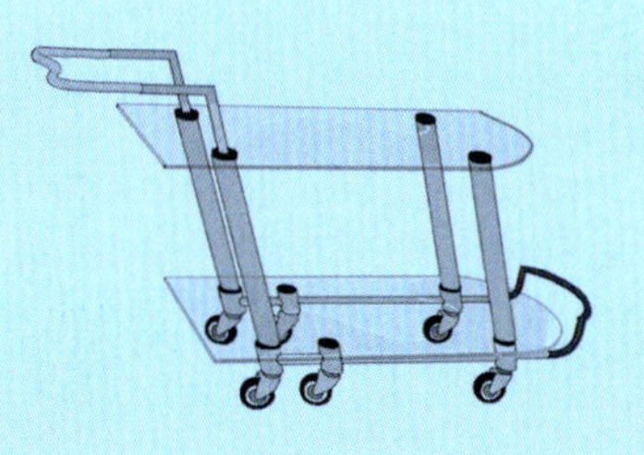

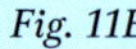

Fig. 11E

HILTON SERVING TROLLEY
(p. 306)

YEAR 1981
DESIGNER
Javier Mariscal
MANUFACTURER
Memphis S.R.L., Italy

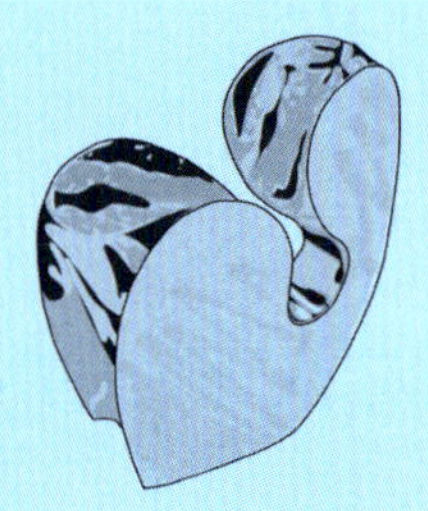

Fig. 11F

LITTLE HEAVY CHAIR
(p. 306)

YEAR 1991
DESIGNER
Ron Arad
MANUFACTURER
One Off Ltd., England

By leaning like the Tower of Pisa and adopting a "forward look" similar to Chrysler's group of automobiles in the 60's this tea cart appears to be going somewhere even when it isn't. Crafted in polished chromium and glass, its leaning posture slips unobtrusively beneath the dead-level trays it supports.

This seems to be a chair in name only as it replicates the contours of a padded, upholstered model in unyielding stainless steel. Yet the device of rendering soft with hard, texture with polish, achieves grudging admiration for its ironic contradictions.

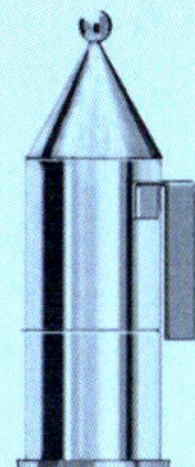

Fig. 11G LA CONICA ESPRESSO COFFEE MAKER (p. 307)

YEAR 1984
DESIGNER
Aldo Rossi
MANUFACTURER
Centro Studio Alessi S.p.A., Italy

The tall, skinny proportions of this coffee maker bring to mind the adage that one cannot be too tall, too thin, or too rich to be counted among the cultural elite. Such allusive imagery, topped by a subtle reference to a medieval castle tower resonates with dry wit and suppressed humor.

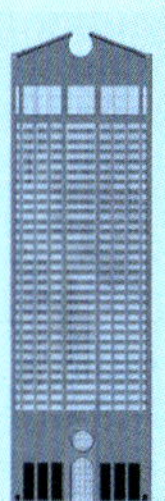

Fig. 11H AT&T BUILDING (p. 307)

YEAR 1984
ARCHITECTS
Philip Johnson and John Burgee
LOCATION
New York, New York, USA

References abound in the design of this corporate tower for AT&T. By pointing backwards in time, to Regency furniture with scrolls and a classical split pediment, the tower was a critical hornet's nest when it made its debut as the crown of Fifth Avenue. Were it not for its size, one could imagine it like a Chippendale High Chest Drawer occupying a corner niche in a traditional Georgian townhouse.

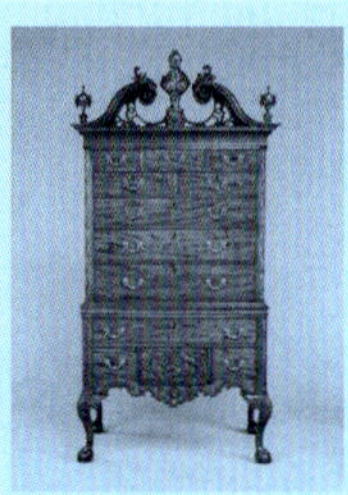

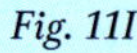

Fig. 11I HIGH CHEST DRAWER (p. 307)

YEAR c.1730-40
DESIGNER/ CRAFTSMAN Thomas Chippendale
MANUFACTURED IN Philadelphia, USA

With a characteristic "Split Pediment," this example of a work from Chippendale's workshop is one of the designs featured in his "Gentleman and Cabinet-Makers Director," a compendium of furniture designs published in 1754 which propelled him to prominence in the toney word of fashionable furniture styles of the time.

Fig. 11J XUM FLATWARE (p. 308)

YEAR 1990
DESIGNER Robert Wilhite
MANUFACTURER Bissell & Wilhite Co., Japan

Funny shapes that immediately challenge the combination of ergonomics, muscle memory, and familiarity that govern the centuries-old order of the place-setting are droll rejoinders to the sobriety of established designs. Asymmetric, off-kilter, and jaunty, without sacrificing utility and pleasure, they invite skeptical users to lighten up and enjoy the moment.

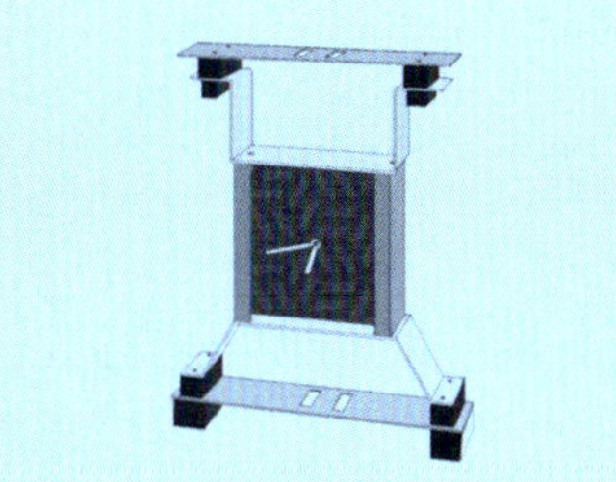

Fig. 11K 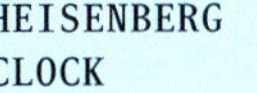

HEISENBERG CLOCK
(p. 308)

YEAR 1983
DESIGNERS
George Sowden and Nathalie du Pasquier
MANUFACTURER
ARC 74 S.A.S., Italy

Sowden's clock, with an erector-set vibe, suggests that time can be a plaything as well as an instrument that wakes and orders one's life. Animated and robotic, leavened by conspicuous fastenings and unusual colors, it has the personality of a garrulous pet, and the insouciant charm of a court jester.

Fig. 11L 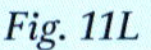

MINI TABLE FAN
(p. 309)

YEAR c.1980
DESIGNER
Kyoji Tanaka
MANUFACTURED IN Japan

Users of this fan may be forgiven for failing to recognize its frail, tentative posture. After all, it is just a fan. But the subtleties of its minimal yet assertive design, the unity conferred by its all-black palette, and the poignant reference to a child's toy are unmistakable. Composed of a fat adjustable stalk and semi-transparent blades, its pinwheel heritage and suction cup foot resonate shyly with its brawny brothers.

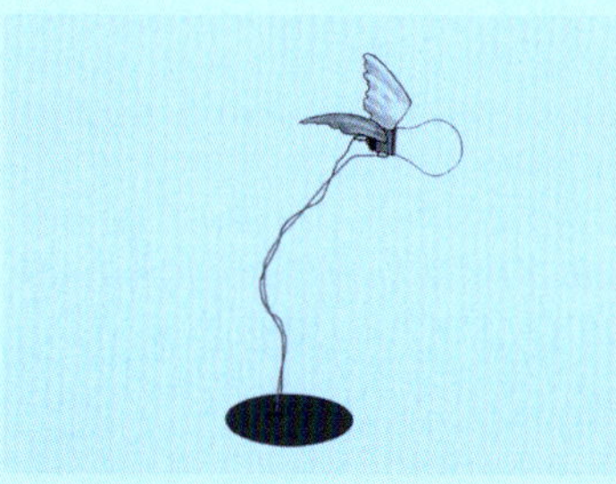

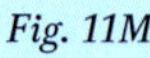

Fig. 11M LUCELLINO TABLE LAMP (p. 309)

YEAR 1992
DESIGNER
Ingo Maurer
MANUFACTURER
Ingo Maurer GmbH, Germany

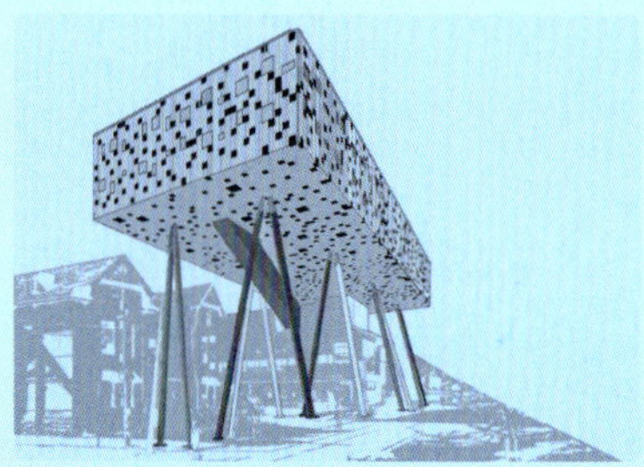

Fig. 11N THE SHARP CENTRE (p. 310)

YEAR 2004
ARCHITECT
Will Alsop
LOCATION
Toronto, Canada

The bold exposure of the brass socket coupled with the frivolity of the rudimentary wings elevates the design from merely “cute” to an exercise in semantics, i.e.: Are the bare wires that support the lamp a “structure?” Is the bare bulb a bird’s “body?” Or is the lamp “flying” as indicated by the slack/crimped wires? These and other questions make us smile every time we switch it on.

Rather than treating the feat of elevating the reading room of this library as a heroic gesture, the introduction of multiple, multi-colored toothpick-thin columns and a playful upside-down graphic not only catches the eye but inserts a playful presence into a once drab urban framework, encouraging passers-by to take a minute, relax, and enjoy life.

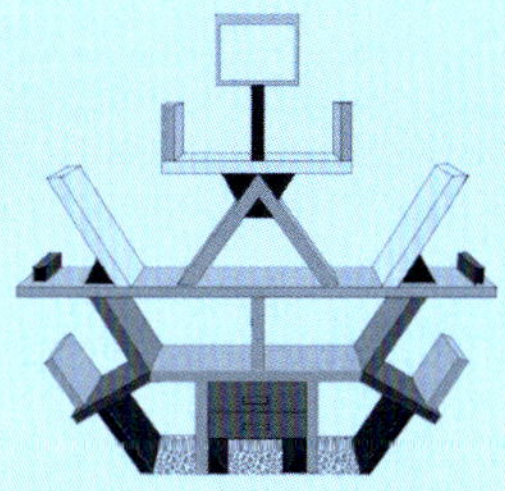

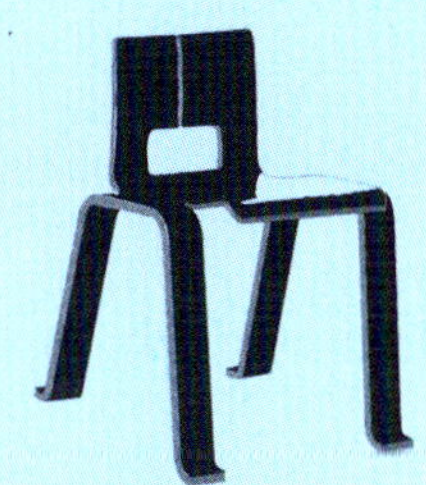

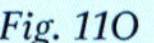

Fig. 11O CARLTON BOOKCASE (p. 310)

YEAR 1981
DESIGNER
Ettore Sottsass
MANUFACTURER
Memphis S.R.L., Italy

Fig. 11P OMBRA TOKYO CHAIR (p. 311)

YEAR 1953
DESIGNER
Charlotte Perriand
MANUFACTURER
Cassina S.p.A, Italy

Who says a bookcase needs to line up its burden like soldiers? By utilizing the force of gravity, and exploiting the resulting inclines creatively, this bookcase combines dramatic visual presence with humor, surprise, and practical functionality. Still a fashionable icon many decades later, David Bowie once devoted an entire room to its presence.

With the exaggerated posture of a stilt-walker, and the good manners of a dressing table companion, this little chair is an essay in material economy, with body and legs cut and bent from a single sheet of plywood, adding a classic to the precedent set by Aalto's Paimio Chair in 1932.

Fig. 11Q STYLO
RETRACTABLE
ROLLER BALL
PEN
(p. 311)

MANUFACTURER
Acme Studio
Inc., USA

Transposing a famous quote from surrealist Magritte that "Ceçi n'est pas une pipe" to the chubby form of the Acme pen creates an amusing cognitive dissonance, elevating the user's appreciation of the complex issues implicit in the act of drawing or writing. As a part of a series designed by invited architects and artists from around the world, it promised to fill one's pocket with a genuine work of art at an affordable price.

WHIMSY ILLUSTRATIONS

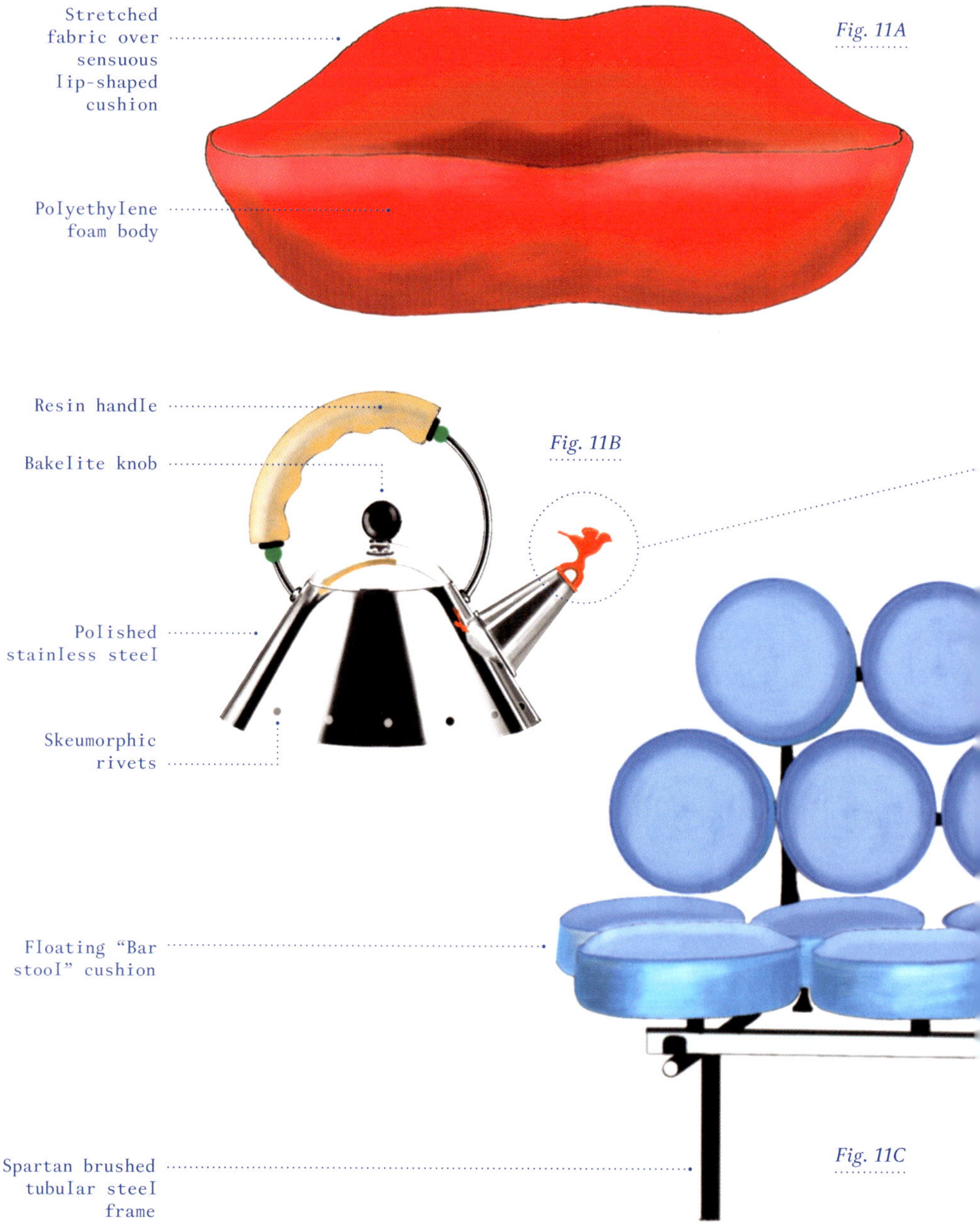

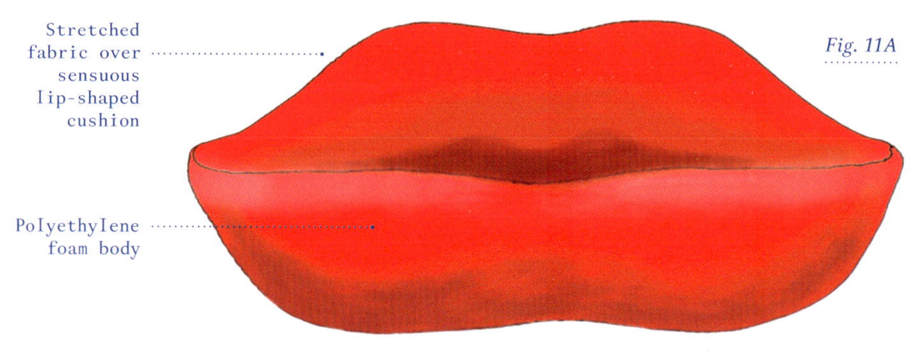

Resin handle

Bakelite knob

Fig. 11B

Polished stainless steel

Skeumorphic rivets

Floating "Bar stool" cushion

Spartan brushed tubular steel frame

Fig. 11C

BOCA SOFA (*Fig. 11A*), WHISTLING BIRD TEA KETTLE (*Fig. 11B*), MARSHMALLOW SOFA (*Fig. 11C*)

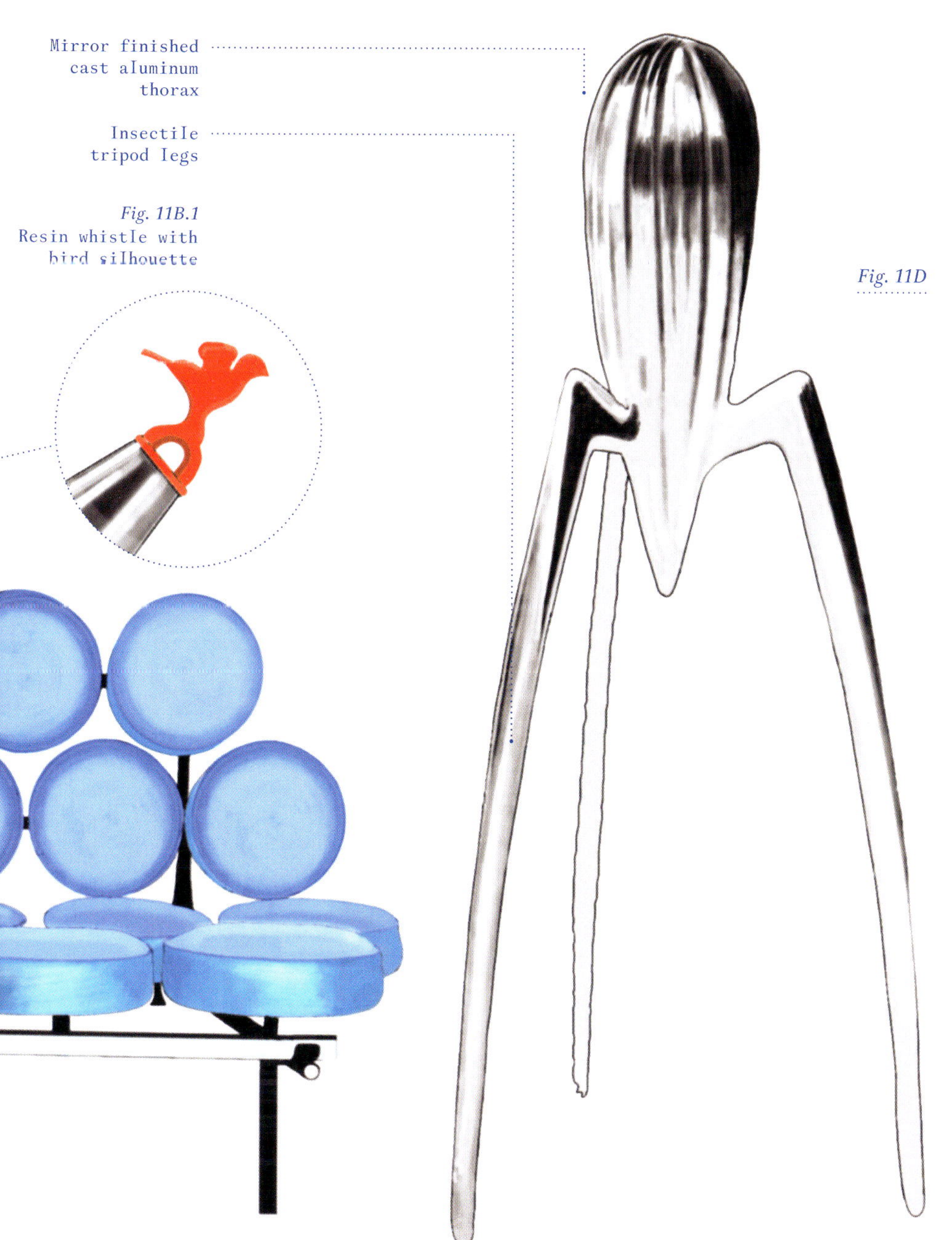

Fig. 11B.1
Resin whistle with
bird silhouette

JUICY SALIF CITRUS SQUEEZER (*Fig. 11D*)

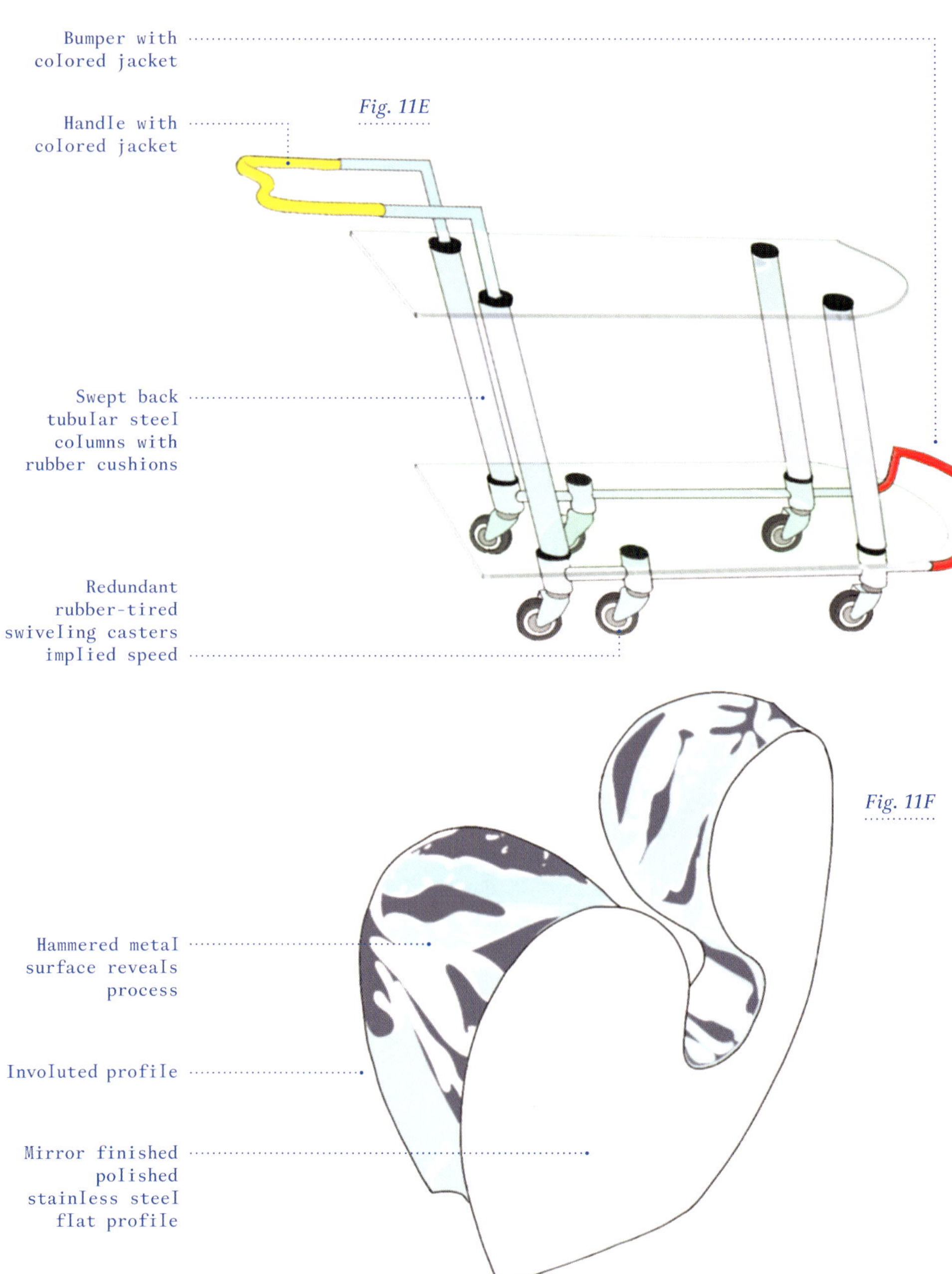

HILTON SERVING TROLLEY (*Fig. 11E*), LITTLE HEAVY CHAIR (*Fig. 11F*)

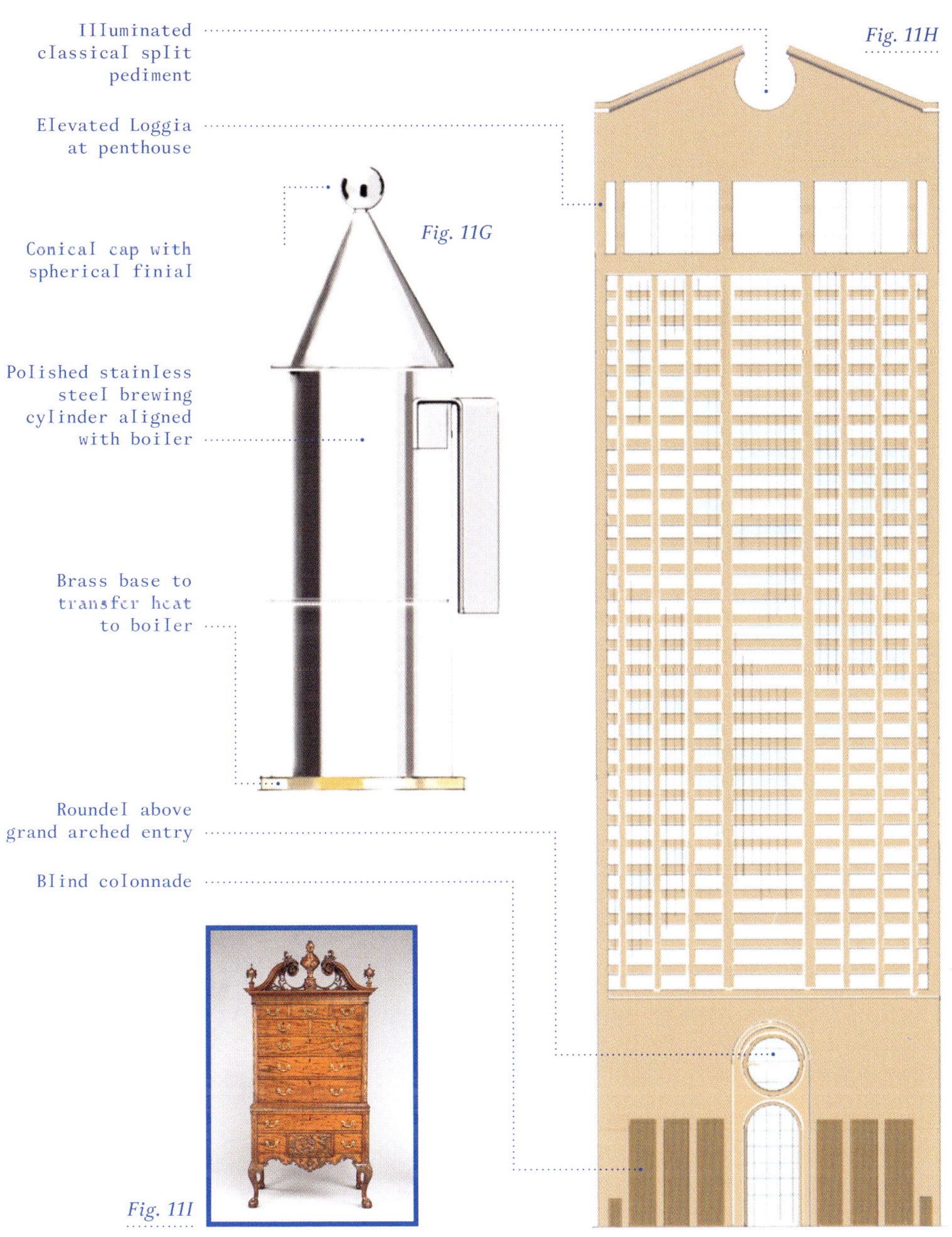

LA CONICA ESPRESSO COFFEE MAKER (*Fig. 11G*), AT&T BUILDING (*Fig. 11H*), HIGH CHEST DRAWER (*Fig. 11I*)

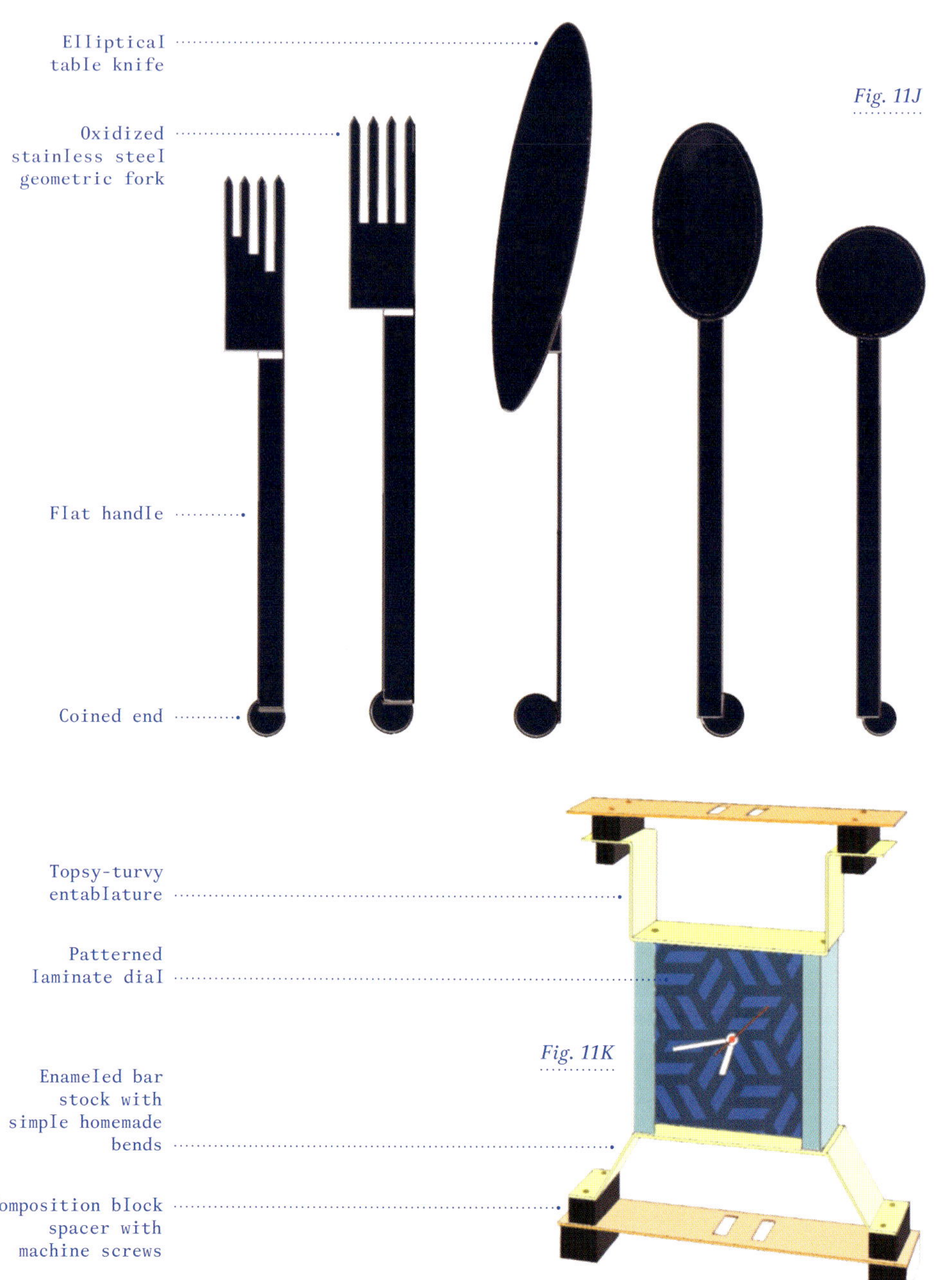

XUM FLATWARE (*Fig. 11J*), HEISENBERG CLOCK (*Fig. 11K*)

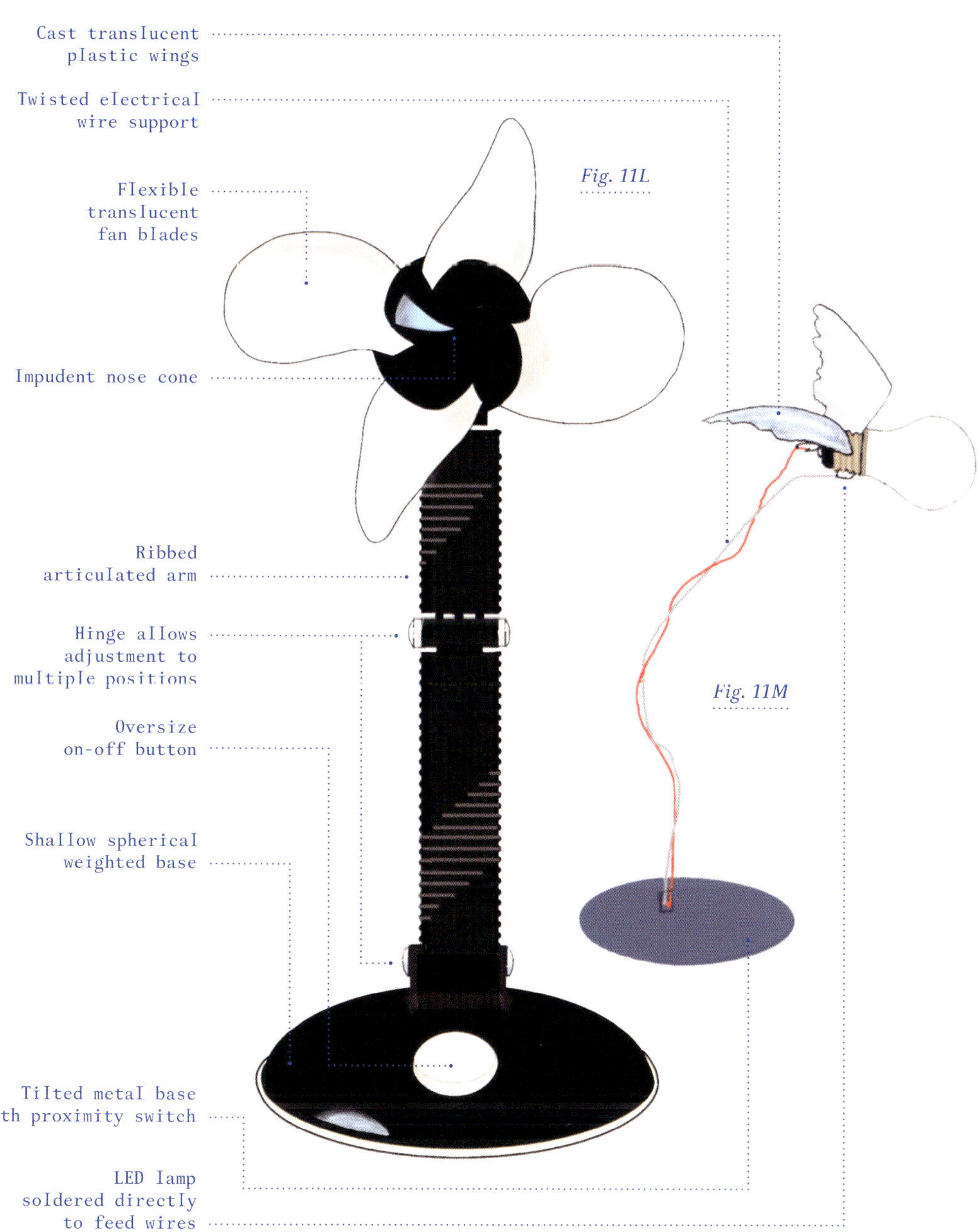

MINI TABLE FAN (*Fig. 11L*), LUCELLINO TABLE (*Fig. 11M*)

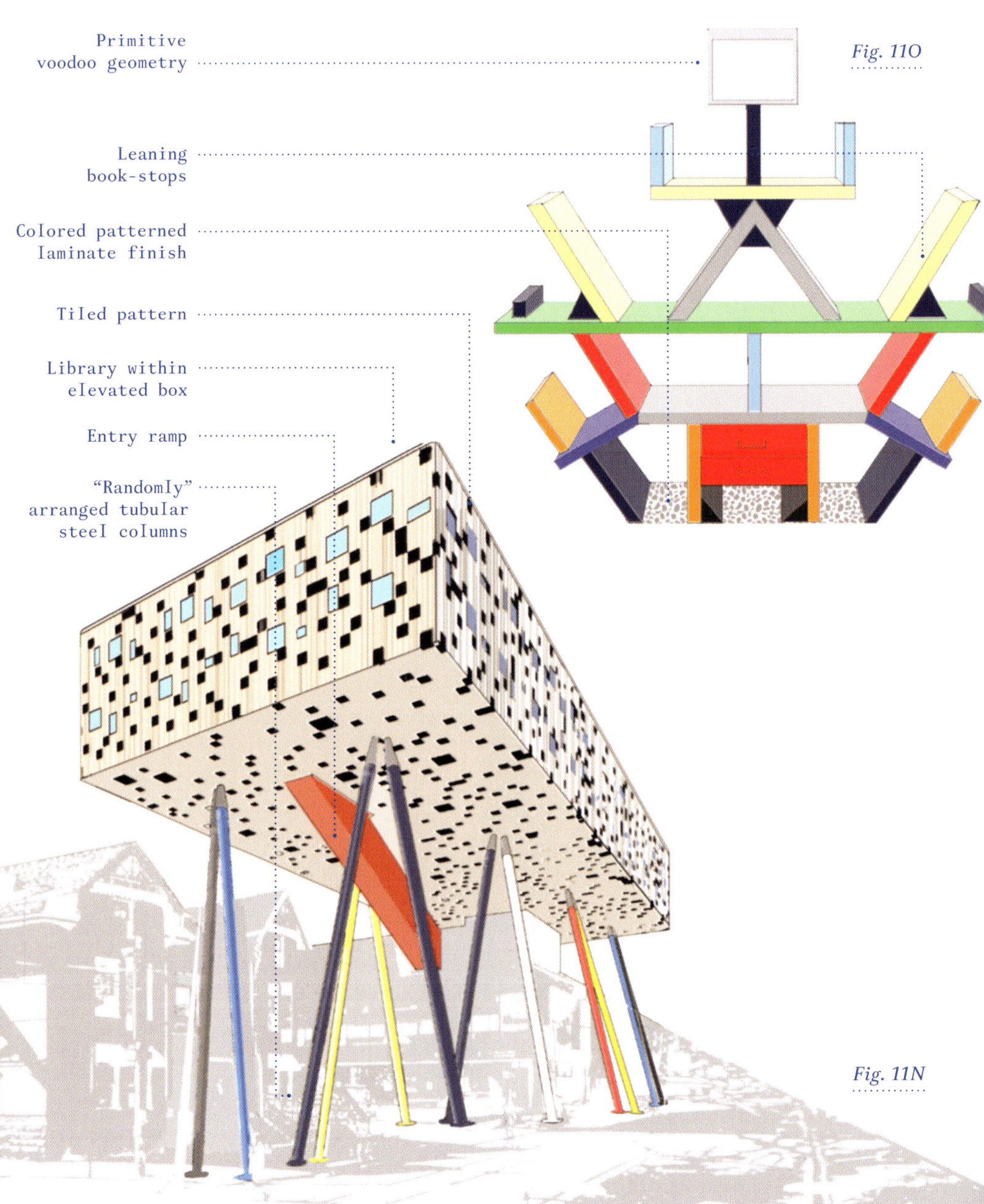

THE SHARP CENTRE (*Fig. 11N*), CARLTON BOOKCASE (*Fig. 11O*)

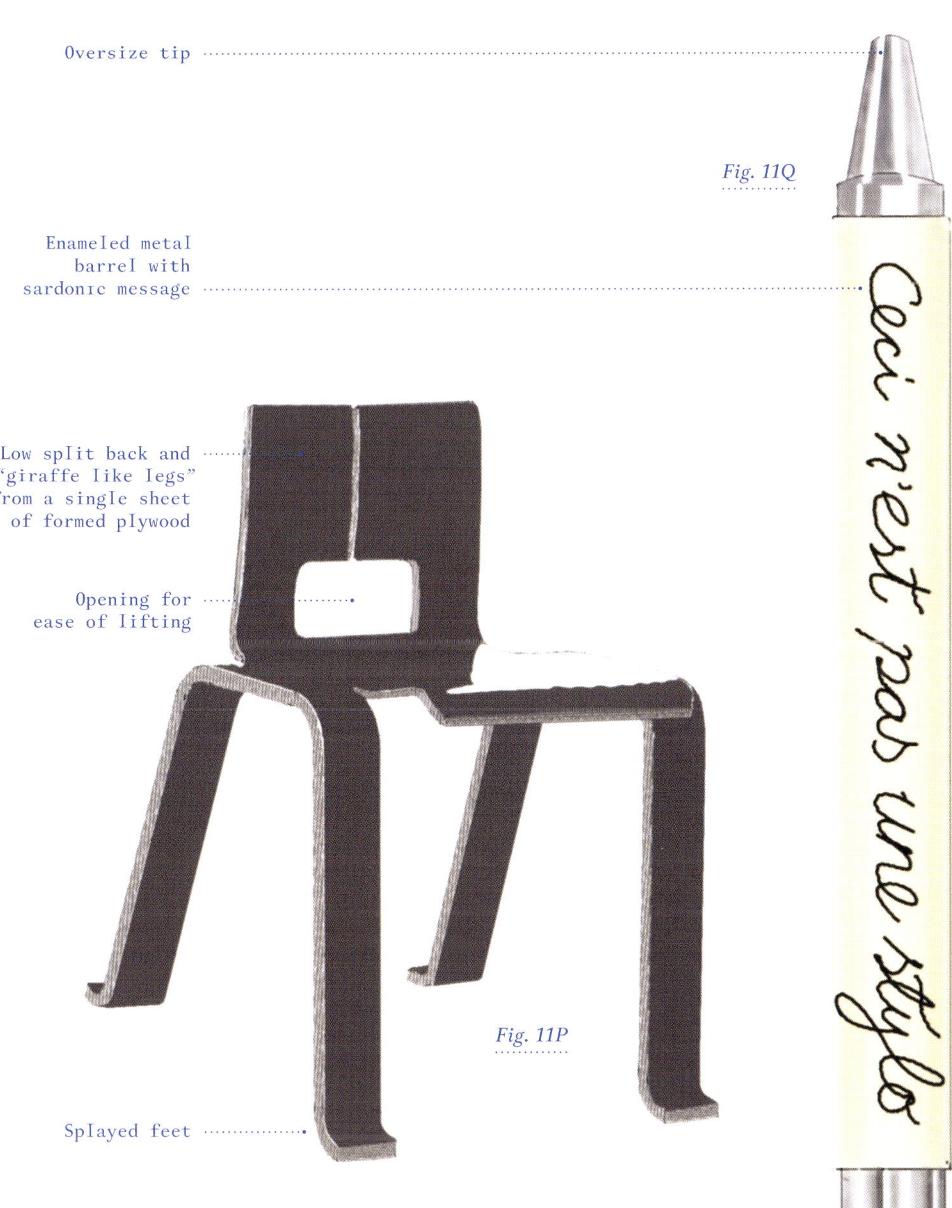

OMBRA TOKYO CHAIR (*Fig. 11P*),
STYLO RETRACTABLE ROLLER BALL PEN (*Fig. 11Q*)

Biographies, Acknowledgments and Reproduction Credits

CRAIG HODGETTS is an emeritus professor at the UCLA Graduate School of Architecture and Urban Planning and was a Founding Dean of the School of Design at the California Institute of the Arts. He is also a founding partner in the seminal Studio Works and award-winning Hodgetts+Fung Design and Architecture (HplusF).

With a background in theater arts, architecture and automotive design, Craig has created enduring designs that continue to resonate more than fifty years after their completion. Best known for the *Towell Temporary Library* at UCLA and the reborn *Hollywood Bowl*, Craig Hodgetts and his partner Hsinming Fung have been cited for the resurgence of Mid-Century design as a result of their ground-breaking exhibition *Blueprints for Modern Living* at the Museum of Contemporary Art (MOCA), Los Angeles and for the touring exhibition *The Work of Charles and Ray Eames*, for the Library of Congress, Vitra Design Museum and Los Angeles County Museum of Art.

He is the author of numerous articles on design as well as several books, including *Design Quarterly #100* dedicated to architect James Stirling, *Swimming to Suburbia*, an anthology of environmental essays and illustrations, and a signature book on science fiction icon *The Art of Syd Mead*. He and partner Fung were invited to create multiple installations at the Venice Biennale and the Milan Triennale and featured in numerous museum exhibitions including *Visionary San Francisco* at the San Francisco Museum of Modern Art in collaboration with science fiction legend William Gibson, and *Angels and Franciscans* at the Gagosian gallery.

HSINMING FUNG is a distinguished professor at the Southern Institute of Architecture (SCIArc), where she held the positions of Director of Academic Affairs (2010-2015) and Director of Graduate Programs (2002-2010). Ms. Fung serves on the board of *PLACES Journal*, and was President of the American Institute of Architects, Los Angeles (AIA/LA) as well as President of the Association of Collegiate Schools of Architecture (ACSA). She also served as a National Peer for the General Services Administration in Washington, D.C., and in 2004 served on the National Endowment of the Arts Council (NEA). She was the recipient of numerous awards and honors, including the Rome Prize Advanced Fellowship in Design Art in 1991, the American Academy of Arts and Letters Architecture Award in 1994, and the Chrysler Design Award in 1996. She was a founding partner and Design Director of Hodgetts+Fung Design and Architecture (HplusF) in 1984, and in 2006 her firm was awarded the AIA Gold Medal, and a Firm Award from the AIA/CA in 2008.

PAOLA ANTONELLI is the Senior Curator of Architecture and Design at the Museum of Modern Art (MoMA), New York. where she also serves as the founding Director of Research and Development and conducts the museum's MoMA R&D Salon. She is the author of numerous publications, including *Design Emergency, Mutant Materials, Design and Violence*, and *Talk to Me*. Named by *Time Magazine* as "one of the 25 most incisive design visionaries in the world," she was the director of the XXII Triennale di Milano (2019). Among her numerous awards, she has received the Design Mind Smithsonian Institution's National Design Award, the London Design Medal and the German Design Award.

SIR PETER COOK is a senior fellow of the Royal College of Art and Director of the Cook Haffner Architecture Platform (CHAP). He was a founder of Archigram, the visionary English architectural group in 1967, was awarded the Royal Gold Medal in 2004, and was knighted in 2007 by Elizabeth II. He is also a Royal Academician and a Commandeur de l'Ordre des Arts et Lettres of the French Republic. Cook was a director of London's Institute of Contemporary Arts (1970-1972) and chair of architecture at the Bartlett School of Architecture at University College London (1990–2006), and has been curator of the British Pavilion at the Venice Architecture Biennale.

ACKNOWLEDGEMENTS

I am grateful to Hsinming Fung, my wife and creative partner, for without her inspiration, insight, and fierce energy this book and much of our work together would not have been possible. Thanks go to Paola Antonelli whose leadership and perspective on design matters is my North Star, Sir Peter Cook whose spirited vision continues to inspire me, Sarah Amelar whose voluminous knowledge filled in the cracks, and Christina Huang who *got it* and gave the book its final shape.

I want to recognize Sylvia Lavin, who believed in me from early days and brought her scholastic chops to frame my work in a larger context, to my favorite provocateur, Aaron Betsky, for gluing the pieces of the design world into a coherent ensemble, to Greg Goldin who was always ready to share a burger at Barney's Beanery while giving sage advice on publishing, and to the students at National University of Singapore (NUS) for their enthusiastic research.

And finally, I must thank Neil Spiller who championed this project from the outset and introduced me to David Breuer, publisher of Unicorn Publishing Group who nurtured and trusted my vision, and sadly passed away during its gestation.

REPRODUCTION CREDITS

Fig. 1J Untitled
40, 49: ©2025 Stephen Flavin / Artists Rights Society, New York and DACS, London, Photo: Hsinming Fung
Fig. 1R Quaderna Table 2600
44, 53: Courtesy Zanotta S.p.A.

Fig. 2P Control knob, Château Suprême Grand Palais 180 Range
70, 79: Courtesy La Cornue

Fig. 3G.1 Gossamer Albatross
101: Photo: Donald Monroe

Fig. 7B Lathe Control Crank
190, 200: Courtesy lathes.co.uk
Fig. 7C KitchenAid by Art Déco 1925

191, 200: ©KitchenAid
Fig. 7G.1 Hummer H2
203: Photo: Karsun Designs, CC BY-ND, https://www.flickr.com/photos/karsund/8496573373/
Fig. 7J Plug-in City Drawing
194, 204: Courtesy Sir Peter Cook
Fig. 7O.1 Light Bulb, Toio Floor Lamp
207: Photo: Hsinming Fung

Fig. 9N.1 Sea Ranch Logo, 2025
255: Photo: Courtesy of the Estate of Barbara Stauffacher Solomon
Fig. 9T "Bag" Radio
250, 257: Courtesy Daniel Weil
Fig. 9U Bal Nègre at the Champs-Élysées Theatre
250, 257: ©2025 ADAGP, Paris and DACS, London

Fig. 10B.1 News Racks
278: Photo: Ser Amantio di Nicolao, licensed under CCS-A 3.0, https://es.wikipedia.org/wiki/Archivo:Huntington_newspaper_and_magazine_dispensers_-_3.jpg, cropped from original
Fig. 10H The Judgment of Paris
271, 280: The Art Institute of Chicago
Fig. 10L Atomium
273, 281: Daderot, https://commons.wikimedia.org/wiki/File:Atomium_-_Brussels,_Belgium_-_DSC07634.jpg, cropped from original
Fig. 10P Parthenon
275, 282: Steve Swayne, licensed under CCA 2.0 Generic, https://www.flickr.com/photos/68686051@N00/2416778389

Fig. 11H.1 High Chest Drawer
298, 307: The Metropolitan Museum of Art

READING DESIGN:
THE VISUAL LANGUAGE
OF COMMON OBJECTS

AUTHOR Craig Hodgetts
EDITOR Hsinming Fung
COPY EDITING Sarah Amelar
DESIGN Christina Huang
ILLUSTRATIONS Craig Hodgetts

TYPEFACES
ABC Gaisyr, ABC Maxi Round, ABC Repro, Antique Olive Compact, Arial Rounded MT, Cooper Nouveau, Dala Floda Roman, Didot LT Pro, Helvetica Neue, ITC Kabel, Le Corbusier Condensed, Windsor Pro.

PRINTER
FineTone, Türkiye

Published in 2025 by Unicorn, an imprint of Unicorn Publishing Group, Charleston Studio, Meadow Business Centre, Lewes, East Sussex BN8 5RW.

www.unicornpublishing.org

ISBN 978-1-917458-48-1